THE HOUSEHOLD
ECONOMY

Books by Scott Burns

SQUEEZE IT TILL THE EAGLE GRINS

THE HOUSEHOLD ECONOMY
(originally published as
Home, Inc.)

THE HOUSEHOLD ECONOMY

Its Shape, Origins, and Future

Originally Published as *Home, Inc.*

SCOTT BURNS

BEACON PRESS BOSTON

Copyright © 1975 by Robert M. C. Burns

The Household Economy was originally published
in a hardcover edition under the title *Home, Inc.:
The Hidden Wealth and Power of the American Household.*

First published as a Beacon Paperback in 1977
by arrangement with Doubleday & Company, Inc.

Beacon Press books are published under the auspices
of the Unitarian Universalist Association

Printed in the United States of America

(paperback) 9 8 7 6 5 4 3 2 1

Library of Congress Cataloging in Publication Data
Burns, Scott.
    Reprint of the 1975 ed. published by Doubleday,
Garden City, N.Y., under title: Home, inc.
        Bibliography: p.
        1. United States—Economic conditions—1971–
2. Home economics.   3. Cost and standard of living—
United States.   I. Title.
HC106.7.B87   1977   338.4'7'640973   76-7738
ISBN 0-8070-4789-9 (pbk.)

To Jasper and Ollie

Contents

hold economy as a vital buffer between the individual and
powerful institutions.

Part Three   WHY THE MARKET ECONOMY MUST
DECLINE

Acknowledgments

As ONE WHO HAS SPENT MUCH TIME in libraries or otherwise surrounded by books, I have often felt quite overwhelmed at the depth of my ignorance. Alas, it grows deeper by the year, in spite of my heroic efforts to have it otherwise, and even on those few occasions on which I feel I know something, I must admit to myself that the ledgers seem to reveal my intellectual assets are more than balanced by my intellectual debts. It would require another book to acknowledge them all.

Much of the background material in the book is derived from the work of five people I have never met: Victor Fuchs and F. Thomas Juster, of the National Bureau of Economic Research and the Survey Research Center in Michigan, respectively; Staffan Burenstam Linder, formerly on the staff at Columbia; Ismail Sirageldin, at the University of Michigan; and Kathryn Walker, at the New York State College of Human Ecology.

I also am grateful for the enormous help and advice I received from my friend Norm Colb; to Marie Johnson, who helped excise and otherwise refine; to Mary Gileece, friend, who had the patience to type some of the manuscript; to Kathy Haas, who finished it in spite of being eight months pregnant and about to withdraw happily from the market economy; to Pearl Robinson, who typed it once more; to my wife, Wendy, who said we were going to finish the book; and to John Ware, my editor at Doubleday, who finally rescued the book from near oblivion.

Nor should I forget the indulgence of the Boston Athenaeum library for its long loans of books; or my happiness that Boston and Brookline both support public libraries that ease the writer's job; or Bill Banks, at the Market Bookstore in Falmouth, who got books I needed even when it was necessary to borrow them from strangers.

Part One

The Invisible Economy

The size, form, and growth of the household economy

1

The Revolution
in Middle America

AMERICA is not going to be transformed by greening, blueing, drugs, magic, pure love, or a more equal distribution of orgasms; nor will it be restored to wholesome goodness by the resurgence of all that is virtuous and clean, by more cops, blacklists, or the benevolent power of General Motors. America is going to be transformed by nothing more or less than the inevitable maturation and decline of the market economy. The instrument for this positive change will be the household—the family—revitalized as a powerful and relatively autonomous productive unit.

The household is the hero and subject of this book. It is an unlikely candidate for admiration. Radical psychologists condemn it. Conventional psychologists tolerate it for lack of anything better. Sociologists worry about its survival and speculate on its ultimate demise. And economists hardly recognize that it exists, caring little beyond that it consume an adequate number of dishwashers and continue to save at the appropriate rate.

The household is the hero of this book *because it is an economy* and, unlike the market economy, which has caused so much anxiety of late, it is healthy, stable, and growing. It is, in fact, probably our strongest and most important economic institution. But, more important, it is an institution and economy whose growth and strength hold the promise of a democratic, egalitarian society in a stable world.

The household economy is the harbinger of revolution—the nexus of future culture and experience. We are not going to be led to this revolution, nor will we find it violent. It will have no leader, no single spokesman, and no conscious ideology that will stir great loyalty and excitement. It will not separate the young and old or the idealistic and cynical; nor will it hang, burdened with transcendental meaning, over the heads of a few prophets. We will simply stumble into it, pressed on by the mute forces of economics and the natural course of development. Demography cannot be made a martyr; neither can the blunt forces of economic life long be held hostage by any idea.

We are creatures of the moment, without knowledge of the future and blind to the past. We see and know only that for which we have a vocabulary; we admit to experience only those events which fit the constraints of our ideas, and our ideas, sadly, are largely defined by the market economy, the economy of money and exchange. Even the most vocal critics of corporate America and industrial society—those offering revolution and radical change—have described their particular vision by no more than a change of "attitudes" or "consciousness." *The society of the future is most often described by what it is not rather than what it is.* It is "post-industrial," no longer alienative, co-operative rather than competitive, and graciously devoid of exploitation. It is everything that our present society is not.

The instrument for change, unfortunately, usually remains vague, undescribed, mysterious. Hence, prophets are seldom credible and suffer their ambivalent but obligatory fate because it is their role to have knowledge that cannot be shared with others.

But the instrument—the bald, obdurate hardware—for that change is here, now, and has always been with us. The family household has been a central fact of human culture since the beginning of history; it has also been the only economic institution shared by virtually all human societies over all of human history. Now it exists in the shadow of the market economy. It has been rendered largely invisible by the ideas and habits of thought that have dominated Western culture for more than two centuries. But, irrespective of its lack of visibility, it is there—nascent, growing, and revolutionary.

The idea that the household is a productive economic institution is probably a novel one to most readers. We are educated to consider the household as a *consuming* institution, dedicated to absorbing that which is produced by the marketplace. At best, we are likely to think of the family as a means for transferring traditions, values, and habits from one generation to the next; at worst, we are inclined to think of it as a vestigial institution whose continued existence is painful and embarrassing.

But the household *is* a productive economic institution. It produces goods and services with a tangible economic value. Like the market economy, the household economy employs labor and capital and strives to increase the benefits that accrue to its owners and managers. The main reason that we have failed to perceive the household as a productive institution is that it was, until recently, relatively less important than the marketplace. This, as we shall see, is no longer the case.

Another reason we have failed to perceive the household accurately is that it is peculiarly handicapped. It has no means of exchange; thus it employs labor but pays no cash wages, and it invests in capital goods but issues no cash dividends. It uses no money to measure its production of goods and services. Its economic product is accounted for by transfers *in kind*, within the family proper. It has, quite simply, been defined out of existence by the conventions of economic accounting and is assured of remaining officially invisible for some time to come. In the market economy, only cold cash counts, and the market economy, for the moment, directs and defines conventional perceptions.

What *is* the household economy? It is the sum of all the goods and services produced within all the households in the United States. This includes, among other things, the value of shelter, home-cooked meals, all the weekend-built patios and barbecues in suburban America, painting and wallpapering, home sewing, laundry, child care, home repairs, volunteer services to community and to friends, the produce of the home garden, and the transportation services of the private automobile.

There were, according to the 1970 Census, more than fifty-one million family households in the United States. More than one million new families are created every year. Each employs labor. Although the vast bulk of the labor employed is provided by housewives, significant contributions are also made by husbands and children. Some research surveys have indicated that the total amount of time devoted to household labor is increasing rather than decreasing. Similarly, each household invests in, and accumulates, a stock of capital goods that are distinct and separate from the market economy. These goods include the house, car, household appliances, and TV set, as well as the lawn mower, storm windows, power drill, and portable saw. The return on these investments is measured by the services rendered rather than in dollars; thus, it fails to appear in conventional statistics of national product or in orthodox economic teaching. While all these goods are usually considered the useless paraphernalia of a passive consumer society or the concrete burden of a bourgeois life, they are, in fact, the productive capital of a vital and very private economy.

While it is difficult to imagine surviving, let alone sustaining, most of what we now consider to be the good life, without the organization and output of the market economy, the household economy is, in fact, quite capable of producing many of the goods and services now produced by the market. The household economy of the future, like the household economy of the past, will be a central and creative force, rather than an inconvenient institution organized to perform the tasks not yet taken on by the marketplace.

Knowledge of the household economy is a prerequisite for an understanding of both the present and the future; the chapters that follow are devoted to showing not only the size, shape, and development of the household economy but also the reasons for its increasing importance and why it must ultimately supplant the market economy. Necessarily, we must also deal with the decline of the market economy and the corporations that dominate its activity.

For the moment, we will consider only the size and social implications of the household economy. How large would this invisible economy be if it could be measured in dollars? *Very* large. According to one study, the total value of all the goods and services produced by the household economy in 1965 was about $300 *billion.*[1] This was about equal to the gross national product of the Soviet Union at that time. If all the work done within the household by men and women were monetized, the total would be equal to the entire amount paid out in wages and salaries by every corporation in the United States. Similarly, the assets commanded by households, *worth more than a trillion dollars*, produce an annual return in goods and services almost equal to the net profits of every corporation in the United States. Very, very little of this appears in conventional accountings for the gross national product.[2]

This neglect is rather like assuming, say, that the entire European Free Trade Association (Austria, Denmark, Norway, Portugal, Sweden, Switzerland, and the United Kingdom) has no economic product. It is also like assuming that somewhere between a quarter and a third of our total economic product does not exist—a large lump to hide under any rug.

The invisible household economy might also be called the matriarchal economy, because it is dominated by women. They perform most of the labor, make most of the household decisions, and are employed as managers for the labor and assets of the household.[3] More than a few observers have noted that the household economy is invisible precisely *because* it is controlled by women and that present accounting conventions have the effect of demeaning the work and value of women. The economist or sociologist who allows his perception of the world to be circumscribed by the measures of the market economy—as most do —allows his ideas, observations, and theories to be dictated by the limits of the marketplace, thereby excluding a legitimate third of our economic activity and most of the activity of women. His habit of thought is repeated in the larger world.

Women have responded to this injustice not by insisting on a proper social valuation of their work in the household but by leaving the household for paid employment. While there is much (justified) noise about the unequal pay received by women, relatively little has been said about the fact that women have won more than two of every three new jobs created since 1940, a statistic that suggests that low wages reflect a bargaining wedge as well as discrimination—and the price women have reluctantly paid to enter the visible economy, where self-esteem is possible.

All this would deserve little more than discussion in obscure journals of accounting and social policy if the household economy were shrinking and becoming less significant. It would, after all, represent no more than a temporary and self-correcting flaw in our social and economic vision, and the flight of women from the household would serve to mark the final attrition of that institution.

But the household economy is not shrinking; it is growing. Its rising relative importance has radical and positive implications for how we perceive both the present and the future.

A major implication of this book is that *women are abandoning the household at precisely the wrong time;* they are, in effect, transferring from lifeboat to sinking ship. This new pleasure of rising above steerage is likely to be short-lived. The painful irony is that various studies have shown that the average woman at home is worth as much as (or even more than) she is in the paid, market economy.

Rather than fighting for position in a declining institution, women should be learning to extend the household economy; fortunately, this seems to be occurring, because the household arts are thriving even as women throng to the job market.

Another major implication of the household economy is that *money is no longer an adequate measure of our economic experience. Time,* not money, is the fulcrum and measure of our experience. Although time and money have been regarded as interchangeable since Ben Franklin, they are not. Time is absolute; money is relative. There are about four hundred thousand healthy waking hours in a lifetime. Only eighty thousand of these hours are devoted to demonstrating the identity of time and money. When we take into account all those who do not work for money, or do so intermittently or for short periods, we find that, on the average, *only one hour in eight* is devoted to working for money. The future holds even less time so employed. Few sane men would suggest that these hours are the only productive work we ever do. The hours of work done *outside* the money economy rival those done inside and will soon surpass them. Time is the ultimate unit of exchange. Money is an aberration, an artifact of the market economy, *an institution whose logical fulfillment and destiny is to occupy less and less of our time and attention.* Yet we continue to measure our experience by its units of exchange. This will change as the household economy rises in importance and recognition.

Another implication of the household economy is that *the sociology and economics of corporate America are largely mythical* and represent circumstances that reached their alarming peak in the late 1950s. Sadly, the rhetoric of corporate oppression continues while the facts of earnings, corporate returns on capital, and employment opportunities tell a different story. We are reminded frequently, for instance, that corporate wealth is increasingly concentrated, that where the largest one hundred industrial corporations controlled 39.7 per cent of all corporate assets in 1950, they now control 48.5 per cent. We never read that the corporate share of *total* national wealth has *decreased* since 1929 and continues to decrease as this is written.

The accepted socioeconomic liturgy informs us that it is our fate to live in corporate America: the land of the big. Nasty Big exists to exploit poor Small. We will, the liturgy tells us, be subject to subtle and coercive demands from gargantuan corporations. Worse, we are to see a mounting complicity between business and government. We are to enter the age of organization men and technocracy, an age of mobility and status, marked by boredom sometimes, and by fear always. The future is to be like the present, only more so.

The alternative to this stolid vision of bureaucratic orthodoxy is the world of fey visionaries and transcendental alternatives. Thus we are trapped between unbelievable orthodoxy and incredible radicalism.

In fact, both these perspectives—the orthodox and the transcendental—are the product of conditions and a consciousness that will soon cease to exist. When we substitute a measure of economic activity larger than money and the market economy— when we explore our true economic life more carefully, as this book attempts—we find that the age of corporate America reached its zenith shortly before corporations became either the handy butt of all social criticism or the source of transcendental technology.

The hegemony of corporate America had been broken years before the rise of the counterculture and the insistent drubbing of criticism presently directed at the commercial heart of industry. But these are only *symptoms* that the hegemony has been broken; they occur because the influence and power of corporate America are receding. The reasons for this are simple, though largely unexplored, and revolve around the maturation of the goods-producing industrial economy and the concurrent rise in the importance of the household economy. Both mean that *money no longer measures the human effort called upon to complete a productive act.*

The largest impediment to developing a new understanding of our economic life is not the difficulty of the ideas involved but the enormous burden of conditioning most of us carry. Sadly, we associate money and the market with realism, a quality of mind widely admired and abundantly rewarded. All beyond it is suspect and flighty to some, or merely criminally subversive to others. Just as the medieval rulers could not envision the development and power of the market economy, our sociologists and economists, products of the market economy, have no vocabulary for imagining the development and future of the household economy. Yet it is there, and the balance of this book is devoted to exploring its size, development, and future.

Part One explores the dimensions of the household economy. Only a comparison within the measures of the market economy will suffice. I show the amount of labor employed and the wages imputed to that labor. I show the accumulation of household capital and the returns, again imputed, earned by that capital. They are highly competitive with returns available in the market economy. Finally, I show that the accumulation of household capital has outstripped the accumulation of market capital.

Part Two traces the origins of the household economy and the rise of the market. It also discusses the market's critics, and why the household economy is best suited to the inevitable future, if we are to have one. I also draw a scenario for coming events, illustrating possible occurrences and institutions that would manifest the dominance of the household economy. The future, surprisingly, may actually be pleasant!

The reality and size of the household economy having been established, Part Three explores the multiple factors supporting its future growth. Necessarily it shows the logic behind the decline of the market economy and the demise of money.

Part Four is a rear-guard action. It demonstrates that the favored current myth, the reality of the new industrial state, is just that, a myth.

When I began researching and writing this book, I had no didactic purpose. I must also tell you that I have never taken any particular joy in being unconventional and that I have been profoundly suspicious of those who offer themselves as visionaries.

Yet this book might easily be described as unconventional and visionary, with a didactic purpose. If that be so, it is of necessity, and I want to assure you of my basic motives. The ironic genesis of this book is its author's rather mundane attachment to convention, to loving his wife, his children, his home and all the trappings of domesticity. They are, we must admit, threatened on all sides: The technocratic sociologists and futurists offer a future society with little room for the usual matrimonial and filial bonds, while the prophets of change offer a transcendent consciousness I fail to grasp. To be caught between the two, when both are so loud, is discomforting. This book is my defense against futures I cannot accept. Perhaps it can be yours as well.

1. Ismail Sirageldin, *Non Market Components of National Income* (Ann Arbor, Mich.: Survey Research Center, University of Michigan, 1969).
2. It would be unfair to suggest that the entire profession has neglected the importance of non-money income. Most of the underlying research for this book was done by professional economists, and there has been considerable discussion and noise of late on the inadequacy of the GNP as a real measure of well-being. Two government reports have been produced: *Toward a Social Report,* January 1969, by HEW; and *Toward Balanced Growth: Quantity with Quality,* 1970, by the National Goals Research Staff.
Paul Samuelson, at M.I.T., has commented publicly on the issue, as have Professors Nordhous and Tobin of Yale. One of the earlier examinations was done by Arnold W. Sametz in an article, "Production of Goods and Services: The Measurement of Economic Growth," *Indicators of Social Change,* ed. Eleanor B. Sheldon (Russell Sage Foundation, 1968), in which he noted that real economic welfare was increasing at a substantially lower rate than the gross figures indicated. He also noted an effect that is central to this book: "The two most notable structural changes in process on the consumption side are the shift toward collective consumption and toward services. On the production side the two major shifts are toward collective (social costing) and simultaneously toward automated and toward 'domestic' (do-it-yourself) production."
It remains, however, that the definition of economic activity is clearly centered on the marketplace, however inadequately it reflects our economic condition.
3. As noted recently by John Kenneth Galbraith in *Economics and the Public Purpose* (Boston: Houghton Mifflin, 1973), when he referred to the modern housewife as a "Crypto-Servant" and an indispensable aid in maximizing the consumption of the household.

2

Workers Without Wages

IT WOULD BE DIFFICULT to overestimate the importance of work. Without it we ultimately starve. But, long before the pangs of physical hunger set in, we are shorn of identity, self-esteem, and purpose. While it may now be socially acceptable to have unusual sexual habits, be incapable of sustaining a long-term, loving relationship with another human being, or be insensitive to the needs and feelings of those not within immediate proximity of one's own age, work remains a verity, a touchstone of cultural value. Granted, the idea of work is questioned, the nature of some work is criticized, and the satisfaction of work is not so wholly self-contained as it once was. Granted also that we now have a subculture devoted to conspicuous leisure (as opposed to conspicuous consumption) and that work, like the national anthem, is greeted with some ambivalence; still, it is a fact that we are a middle-class nation with middle-class values and a doggedly middle-class attachment to the value and meaning of work.

Most of us, when we speak of work, mean work in the market economy, which is rewarded with money. Other labor, for some peculiar reason, does not count. Like the creatures in George Orwell's *Animal Farm*, some work is "more equal" than other work.

Specifically, we make a regular habit of denying the value—

even the *existence*—of work done within the household. Yet it is absolutely vital and as important to our survival as the work for which we are paid.

We are proud of the value we place on human life. When a mine shaft collapses, when a boat is lost or damaged at sea, when a plane crashes, or when a flood, tornado, or earthquake threatens, we are quick to respond and devote our full resources to saving and restoring life.

No other course of action is possible. Whether the disaster is a flood or a serious fire, the immediate result is offers of aid from every region of the country. With much sentiment and frequent tears, we are quick to declare the absolute value of human life. On a more regular basis, we devote more than 7 per cent of our gross national product to medical and health care; this is a concrete expression of our belief that the most important capital is the perishable, human variety.

Yet, in spite of the intensity of this belief or the obvious priority of human welfare, we give absolutely no economic recognition to the importance of the one single institution responsible for the day-to-day care and maintenance of human beings. The household—the family—is an institution that tends our hearts, minds, and bodies. No other institution has such clear or complete charge or such enormous responsibility. At best, every program of social care and welfare is compensation for deficiencies in some households, and there is no institution, public or private, that could be expected to assume even a small portion of the responsibility that belongs to the household.

All our lives we are told of the irreplaceability of various industries. When there is a coal strike, we are reminded of its importance to steel; when there is a steel strike, we are reminded of its importance to automobiles; when there is an auto strike, we are informed that one job in every seven or ten is dependent upon the automobile. We are now, quite dramatically, learning the importance of oil and energy. Each industry is vital, because each is interdependent with others.

The household and the labor it requires is accorded no such indispensability. Yet, we need only ask what we would do without it to know just how indispensable it is. What, for instance, would we do with our 18 million children under age five or our 37 million children between five and fourteen, not to mention

millions of elderly people? What institution would house or feed
the entire population, manage and maintain its physical property, care for its clothing, or entertain it in its leisure time?

If it requires effort and organization to create food, housing,
and cars, it also requires effort and organization to manage the
use of housing and food and to schedule the necessary work. The
household is responsible for all of this. It is a social institution.
But it is also economic in the most original and profound sense.
We are blind to the economic importance of the household because it is an article of contemporary belief that social institutions have no economic function. In fact, *our most important
economic functions are embedded in social institutions.*

I am going to show, in the pages that follow, the real economic
value of the household as it has been determined by three different studies performed at three separate institutions. The conclusion to be drawn from each of these studies is that the value
of household labor amounts to nearly a third of the gross national
product and about one half of disposable consumer income.

None of this is visible in conventional statistics. According to
the Statistical Abstract of the United States, the national income
is "the aggregate earnings of labor and property which arise in
the current production of goods and services by the nation's
economy. It is the sum of *compensation* [italics added] of employees, proprietors' income, rental income, net interest, and
corporate profits. Thus, it measures the total factor costs of goods
and services produced by the economy."

A neat and abstract figure, the national income is intellectually
"laundered" to be devoid of immediate meaning to most of us
and generally capable of inducing feelings of inferiority or boredom (or both) in most who hear it discussed. It is also a very
large number, a figure of such size that it is seldom contemplated by anyone but economists. A mere $241 billion in 1950, it
surged to almost $800 billion by 1970. At this writing, it is well
past the trillion-dollar mark. Sums of such magnitude discourage
discussion. What, after all, can they really mean for us? How,
when most of us don't understand sums much larger than our
incomes, will we ever understand billions? Cynically, we might
think that the relevance of the national-income figures is re-
stricted to those whose employment depends on their tabulation.

But the *composition* of the national income is a different matter. It is not a question of size but of content. Here, we learn that the unpaid work of mothers and housewives is excluded. This is not, as we shall soon see, a trifling matter. Not only does it work to discriminate against recognizing the economic contribution of housewives, it also distorts our perception of economic growth.

Although women are the chief victims of this exclusion, they are not alone. Virtually all work that is not rewarded with wages is excluded from conventional accounts of national income. While the household economy is, by far, the largest omission, the volunteer economy and the co-operative economy are also excluded. The common denominator of these forms of economic activity, beyond their failure to use money, is that they are organized around the idea of giving, of mutual need, and of co-operation rather than competition. They assume that productive activity is a social as well as an economic function and that the competitive drive for individual gain is not necessarily the best drive to harness in order to accomplish a given task. Perversely, our system of economic accounts excludes all motives but the competitive desire for money.

In the past, when the productive activity of the household was being drawn into the market economy by the industrial revolution, the rate and amount of true economic growth was overstated. Economic activity was not created, it was merely *transferred* from the household (where it was not counted) to the market economy (where it was). The labor of the woman who "put up" fruits and vegetables for the winter by home canning was not included in national income. When she took a job in a canning factory and purchased canned fruit and vegetables in a store, both her work and that of the clerk who sold her the goods became part of the national income. Its growth was applauded irrespective of its illusory nature.

Now similar inaccuracies are being created in reverse. As this is written, it is virtually impossible to buy home canning equipment, because the demand has run so far ahead of the supply. The Ball Corporation, the nation's oldest and largest supplier of home canning equipment, reports a surge in sales and a consumer interest dominated by the young. While their record sales will be reflected in the national-income accounts, the work of canning done in the home implied by those sales will be excluded. Nor will the labor that went into home gardens or home sewing be considered, or the consumer's labor at self-service gas stations and food co-operatives. Where once the conventions of national-income accounting worked to overstate the rate of true economic growth, they may now understate it, as work is created for the household economy but not recognized.

Finding a "home" for the household has been a problem for more than sixty years. To note that the household has an economic product—even though it may not be recorded—has been one of the clear signs of a conscientious but innocuous economist. While there is a regular flow of obligatory comment, there is little in the way of action. In more than sixty years of development, the only real allowance for non-market income in the national-income accounts is that imputed to the consumers' home equity. And even that is valued very conservatively.

This neglect in action is not a minor matter. The conventions of accounting for the national income are not a latter-day replacement for the angel-and-pin controversy. *These accounts are vital, because they are the conceptual frame through which we perceive and experience the economy.*

The impediment to measurement is the simple fact that the household, like volunteer organizations and associations, pays no wages. Because it does not operate with money, there is no direct, "objective" measure of its economic product and output. We are left with estimations and other indirect means. These, by nature, open the door to the endless discussions of methodology that provide the subject matter for graduate-thesis work, but little else.

No one has ever dared to measure the amount of work *transferred* from household to market or vice versa. At best, we have a number of efforts to measure the total product of the household. This is usually done by something called a time-budget study. Such studies are seldom directed toward conventional economic ends; the goal of most is to see how people spend and manage their time, to compare one culture with another, and to see the effects of various stages of technological and economic development on the use of time.

Once we know how time is spent, however, we can put a value on it if a corresponding job is found in the market economy. We can also pick an appropriate average figure for household tasks or consider how much the "non-working" person might be worth employed in the market, reasoning that if someone were worth more in the market, she would be there.

An informal study by the Chase Manhattan Bank, for instance, reported that the average homemaker devoted some 99.6 hours per week to household tasks. If nothing else, this study establishes the outer limits of the household economy and its credibility. The value of the housewife to be imputed from this study, assuming a minimum wage of two dollars an hour, is in the vicinity of ten thousand dollars a year. Since there are some 35 million married women "at home," we might figure, roughly, that their work is worth some $350 billion. An article in *MS* magazine, using the Chase Manhattan study, concluded that women in the home were worth $13,364 a year, a figure that translates into a national household income of $465 billion. The Chase Manhattan study, for obvious reasons, has been enormously popular with divorce lawyers and the less questioning members of the liberation movement, but the conclusions drawn from it are a trifle awkward when compared to more orthodox statistics of income. Only one family in four, for instance, had a 1970 income in excess of the amount cited by *MS* as the value of a woman's work at home. This *includes* multiple-earner families. In fact, only one man in five earned more than $13,300 in 1970.

"The Effects of Family and Housing Characteristics on Time Spent on Household Tasks"[1] is a less dramatic but more typical time-budget study, involving a sample of some twelve hundred families in the Seattle area. The study found, as might be expected, that the work week of the housewife was determined largely by the number and ages of her children. While the childless household requires thirty-five hours of work and the average household requires forty-nine hours, the household with one to three children requires almost fifty-six hours and the household with four or more children requires sixty-two hours.

Based on the average hours in this study, the unaccounted value of women's work at home, assuming a two-dollar minimum wage, would be about $185 billion. If we assume, somewhat more charitably, that the average woman is worth the wages of the average secretary ($3.75 per hour), the contribution to national income rises to nearly $350 billion. Not a small sum.

Cornell researchers Kathryn E. Walker and William H. Gauger drew similar but more elaborate conclusions after a study of some fourteen hundred families in the vicinity of Syracuse, New York.[2] The survey families were asked to keep diaries accounting for the time spent on household tasks by both husband and wife. In families with one or more teen-age children, the contributions by the younger members were also recorded.

The information was then tabulated to separate families according to the number and ages of the children, and to whether or not the wife was also employed as a wage earner. As might be expected, the value of a woman's household work was high if she had young children, and it rose with the number of children. A childless woman with no job performed household work worth about four thousand dollars, while a woman with three children one of whom was under one year old was worth eight thousand dollars. A typical young mother with two or three grammar-school-age children did household work worth about fifty-six hundred dollars a year. This is almost twelve hundred dollars more than the average employed woman was paid at that time.

The contribution of the husband to the work of the household was relatively constant. It was not, in general, found to be sensitive to the number or ages of the children and hovered, in most cases, around a value of twelve to thirteen hundred dollars. When women worked in paid employment as well as in the household, the value of the women's work at home dropped while the value of their husbands' work in the home rose.

The study also noted that the total work time for women employed in the household tended to be less than the total time (market and household work) for men. But women who held a paying job *and* did household work were found to put in a significantly longer work week than their spouses. (An abbreviated table of work-time values for the household is shown below.) None of this is exactly staggering news. It conforms, in fact, with what most people would expect if they devoted much thought to the subject.

Walker and Gauger might, at this point, have chosen another way of looking at the same information: They might have considered the household income of a family over a period of time,

FIGURE 1

Average Annual Dollar Value of Time Contributed
by Various Members in All Household Work (all values
expressed to nearest $100)

Number of Children	Age in Years	Employed-Wife Households			Non-employed-Wife Households		
	Wife	*Wife*	*Husband*		*Wife*	*Husband*	
No children	under 25	$2600	$1100		$3900	$ 700	
	25-39	2800	1100		4500	900	
	40-54	3200	600		4600	1200	
	55 and over	3200	900		4100	1600	
	Youngest Child	*Wife*	*Husband*	*12-17-Year-Olds*	*Wife*	*Husband*	*12-17-Year-Olds*
1	12-17	$3700	$1400	$ 800	$5300	$1600	$ 900
	6-11	4400	900	*	5200	1200	*
	2-5	3600	1200	*	5200	1400	*
	1	5000	400	*	5900	1400	*
	under 1	*	*	*	6600	1300	
2	12-17	3600	1300	900	5600	1300	700
	6-11	4100	1200	700	5600	1300	600
	2-5	4800	1400	900	6400	1300	600
	1	4900	2800	*	6900	1300	*
	under 1	6200	1300	*	7600	1200	*
3	12-17	2800	1200	800	5000	800	800
	6-11	4800	1200	1000	5600	1300	900
	2-5	5900	1700	*	6200	1100	900
	1	5800	2000	*	6900	1300	1200
	under 1	5200	1700	*	8000	1200	*
4	12-17	4600	1000	1000	4700	800	700
	6-11	4100	700	600	6100	1100	800
	2-5	*	*	*	7000	1200	600
	1	*	*	*	6800	1500	800
	under 1	*	*	*	8400	1700	*

Source: Kathryn E. Walker and William H. Gauger, *The Dollar Value of Household Work*.

thus determining the "life cycle" of family earnings. A young,
childless family has a total household income of about forty-six
hundred dollars. As children are born, the household income and
labor rise rapidly to about seventy-eight hundred dollars at, say,
age thirty and then recede slightly as the children grow older.
When they are in primary school, the household income drops to
seventy-five hundred dollars; in secondary school, the household
income drops further, to seventy-three hundred dollars. But the

FIGURE 2

Number of Children	Age in Years	All Workers	Non-employed-Wife Households		
			Wife	Husband	12-17-Year-Olds
0	Wife				
	Under 25	$ 2,652.3	$ 2,197.1	$ 388.0	–
	25-39	2,069.9	1,707.6	360.8	–
	40-54	11,180.3	8,909.2	2,226.5	–
	55 and over	30,927.4	21,621.7	8,348.1	–
1	Youngest Child				
	12-17	8,409.9	5,579.5	1,590.5	$ 984.3
	6-11	3,896.0	3,138.1	713.3	–
	2-5	5,723.0	4,211.7	1,126.4	–
	1	3,868.6	3,086.3	724.0	–
	Under 1	5,577.8	4,397.9	866.1	–
2	12-17	4,623.2	3,100.9	723.0	722.7
	6-11	9,216.6	7,055.9	1,581.3	290.2
	2-5	11,944.4	9,334.6	1,904.2	243.1
	1	4,915.6	3,951.7	762.5	18.2
	Under 1	5,855.6	4,801.6	783.7	4.7
3	12-17	649.3	388.9	63.0	188.5
	6-11	7,210.6	5,139.5	1,169.2	576.7
	2-5	10,362.6	7,764.2	1,416.4	557.5
	1	3,960.0	3,131.4	609.0	92.2
	Under 1	4,830.8	3,951.4	599.7	52.3
4	12-17	204.4	116.3	20.6	66.0
	6-11	3,135.0	2,369.2	441.8	233.8
	2-5	5,816.4	4,562.6	757.4	213.8
	1	2,158.9	1,656.2	376.2	58.8
	Under 1	2,338.4	1,810.5	361.1	45.1
5-6	6-11	2,394.1	1,482.0	360.3	504.6
	2-5	6,015.3	4,454.3	777.2	706.5
	1	1,816.4	1,193.5	191.0	139.3
	Under 1	2,269.4	1,634.8	329.9	213.5
7-9	6-11	25.0	18.4	1.9	4.7
	2-5	918.1	578.3	147.8	192.0
	1	567.4	347.0	49.1	133.5
	Under 1	530.5	417.1	66.7	46.7
	TOTAL	·$166,062.2	$124,109.4	$29,836.7	$6,288.7

Source: William H. Gauger, *The Potential Contribution to the GNP of Valuing Household Work.*

| | Employed–Wife Households | | | | |
Other Workers	All Workers	Wife	Husband	12-17-Year-Olds	Other Workers
$ 67.2	$ 2,857.7	$ 2,021.2	$ 817.9	–	$ 18.6
1.5	2,292.8	1,624.6	634.8	–	33.5
44.6	5,158.2	4,356.0	802.3	–	–
957.6	4,092.2	3,137.1	859.0	–	95.5
255.6	3,804.4	2,347.3	826.8	$ 484.2	146.0
44.7	1,553.8	1,219.9	254.3	–	79.6
384.9	2,316.1	1,426.8	481.3	–	408.0
58.3	1,102.1	908.0	69.9	–	124.2
313.8	443.5	274.4	169.1	–	–
76.7	2,295.5	1,195.8	421.3	585.2	93.2
289.2	3,558.3	2,319.6	679.2	265.3	294.2
462.5	3,077.0	2,051.0	609.7	144.9	271.4
183.1	1,038.8	572.8	332.7	11.6	121.8
265.5	522.3	323.7	68.4	–	130.2
8.9	390.9	167.0	70.2	145.4	8.3
325.3	2,894.4	1,911.0	464.9	423.3	95.5
624.5	2,479.4	1,723.9	490.1	79.6	185.8
127.4	536.1	306.2	108.3	26.2	95.4
227.3	472.1	313.3	104.9	16.5	37.5
1.6	245.7	118.7	25.9	95.6	5.5
90.1	900.3	637.9	119.1	103.2	40.1
282.5	1,041.1	459.3	81.1	99.7	401.1
67.7	342.1	250.4	71.2	–	20.4
121.8	407.9	236.2	161.6	–	10.2
47.3	548.0	402.4	56.3	66.3	23.0
77.3	1,018.9	599.8	189.8	169.5	59.8
292.5	164.9	125.0	16.9	23.0	–
90.2	475.7	167.9	139.3	106.1	62.4
–	–	–	–	–	–
–	368.3	229.6	59.3	73.1	6.4
37.8	–	–	–	–	–
–	–	–	–	–	–
$5,827.4	$46,398.5	$31,426.8	$9,186.2	$2,918.7	$2,867.6

income of the household diminishes most drastically when the children are no longer at home. Beginning at age forty-five or fifty, the household income of the average family descends to about fifty-eight hundred dollars and remains there unless the wife seeks employment. If she works, household income drops to about four thousand dollars.

The life-cycle earnings of the household are remarkably similar to curves that earnings researchers have found for workers in the market economy: The usual pattern of market income is a base wage which grows[3] rapidly for about ten years, then moderates, plateaus, and finally falls as the worker reaches retirement age. The same pattern is exhibited by the household. Again, this is not staggering news. But the eye falls back to those substantial figures for the value of work in the home. *Sadly, very few young mothers* feel *they are worth more than six thousand dollars as homemakers.* Yet these large sums are what intrigued Walker and Gauger.

The next step in Walker and Gauger's project was to bridge the gap between the individual family and the entire economy. They moved from micro- to macroeconomics. Having found the household income for various categories of families, they then matched their estimates with a profile of America's families provided by the Bureau of the Census. The end product is an estimate of what might be called the national household income and the distribution of household income in the United States. (See Figure 2.)

These figures indicate that the total household income in the United States was some $212 billion in 1968. Women were responsible for almost 75 per cent, $155 billion. *The largest single contribution was made by "unemployed" housewives, who were responsible for $124 billion.* These are incredible sums. Yet they are conservative, in total, because they exclude all those who are not members of a nuclear family. This estimate of the national household income excludes about *10 million* households comprising single people, groups, or families in which one of the parental figures is missing. We can put these enormous sums in perspective by comparing the earnings of the household economy with those of various sectors of the market economy.

In 1968, gross personal income in the United States amounted to $465 billion. Some $98 billion in income taxes were paid.

Research Center is responsible for monitoring consumer sentiment and buying intentions, gauging consumer confidence, and
finding most of the information used by the government to track
the consumer economy. Sirageldin's study, like the two mentioned earlier, focused on the household and the value of work
done within it. His survey of twenty-two hundred families produced results that are substantially similar to those of other researchers. Thus, while there is much methodological discourse
between those actively involved in trying to measure and account for the household economy, it is an unalterable fact that
at least three research studies conducted by three differing institutions in widely separated areas arrived at very similar conclusions. *The clear implication, no matter what the variations in
accounting and valuation techniques, is that the household
economy is about one third the size of the market economy.*

Sirageldin did not limit his survey to the value of work done
within the home. He included volunteer work and help offered
to friends as well and made some attempts at putting a value on
the services provided by equipment used in the household.

He then added disposable money income to household income
to find what he called "full income." Disposable income is the income that remains after all deductions for various taxes: It is the
income whose expenditure we can, to some extent, control. *Sirageldin found that "non-market"—or household-economy—income was almost 50 per cent of disposable income.* Three
families in four have a non-market income that amounts to *at
least* 50 per cent of their regular money income.

The table that follows shows the relationship between non-
market and market incomes as money income increases. As
might be expected, a rising money income generally means a decreasing non-money income. The family finds that it is more ad-
vantageous to hire someone for certain tasks than to do them
themselves. Non-market income does not decline sharply, however, until family money income is quite high. While one could
read this fact as implying there is some "take-off" point in money
income where the efficiency of the money economy surpasses
the non-money economy, a more likely explanation is that at
higher levels of income there is an increasing probability that
the family will have more than one earner and, thus, less time
to devote to the household. The working housewife has no

choice in decreasing the amount of non-market work she does. She simply does not have the time. The earlier figures on employed-versus-unemployed housewives and the value of their work sustain this notion.

FIGURE 4

Full Income, Disposable Income & Housework
Disposable Income, and Their Relationship
to Total Money Income, 1964

Total Money Income	Cumulative % of Families	Disposable Income	Disposable Income & Housework	Full Income	Ratio of Non Market Income to Money Income
Less than 1,000	2.9%	867	2,890	3,325	284%
1,000 - 1,999	8.9	1,686	5,506	6,095	127
2,000 - 2,999	16.1	2,674	5,812	6,455	141
3,000 - 3,999	23.8	3,666	6,875	7,334	100
4,000 - 4,999	31.7	4,535	7,588	8,169	80
5,000 - 5,999	41.0	5,436	9,061	9,581	76
6,000 - 7,499	50.5	6,575	9,939	10,585	61
7,500 - 9,999	74.7	8,216	11,835	12,517	52
10,000 - 14,999	92.4	11,147	14,780	15,531	39
15,000 or more	100.0	29,817	32,958	33,727	13
All Families	100.0%	8,115	11,638	12,045	48

Source: Ismail Sirageldin, Non Market Components of National Income, 1969; Statistical Abstract of the United States.

What are the consequences of ignoring a third of our economic product? What happens when we pretend that one of the largest areas of economic activity does not exist?

The first casualty is economic reality. The conventions of economic accounting are, in essence, a system for keeping score. The higher the score, the better off we are—in theory. Like the captain who measures achievement by an indiscriminate body count, the accounting system has a corrupting tendency. Thus we add things that should not be added to the score. We inflate the true economy by counting negatives as positive and by ignoring the ongoing household economy while adding transfers from household to market.

There is nothing horribly alarming in this. Delusion is commonplace, and exaggeration has seldom been a fatal social disease. But there is a more sinister long-term effect in the exclusion of the household economy.

Its exclusion makes it the ready victim of the market economy. Just as the market economy can expand at the unrecognized cost of the environment, it can also expand at the expense of the household. It can create false economic values. For instance, it is commonplace for women to buy highly processed "convenience" foods in order to "save time." Yet when one analyzes[5] the amount of time saved and compares it to the cost of convenience foods, it becomes apparent that this time is more expensive than the wages most women can earn in their market jobs. The market expands because the diseconomy is invisible: Household time has "no value." Only the recent terrors of inflation have diminished the sale of convenience foods.

Similarly, women are driven toward the market economy by pressing economic and social needs, only to learn that their economic needs are seldom solved by jobs, because of the cost of clothing, transportation, lunches, taxes, etc. Their social needs are thwarted there as well. In spite of this, players continue to congregate where there is a scoreboard. The market is "the only game in town."

We might be tempted here to consider the apparent destruction of the household as the inevitable end of economic development. Some writers, seeing the demise of the extended family, the increasing strain on the nuclear family, and the constant rise in transfer payments for education, old age, etc.—payments that were once incorporated in the organization of the family—have foreseen the rise of an atomistic society in which the affections and duties of filial or matrimonial bonds are supplanted by the individual search for fulfillment and self-actualization. Some see this atomism as individualism and a great boon; they reason that the psychological liabilities of the family far exceed its benefits. Others see the encroachment of the market as a final step in social disintegration.

That issue will not be resolved here. Our task is far simpler. It is to point out that arguments pro and con have a common fault. Both *assume* that the market economy is more efficient than the household economy and that it will inevitably supplant the household economy, fulfilling some notion of economic evolution.

Such a presumption can exist only because the economic import of the household is generally ignored. Once the magnitude of household labor is recognized, discussions of the decline of the family and the household economy are tempered.

We must, after all, ask if the society could even *exist* without the household.[6] And even if it could, would any other set of institutional arrangements offer greater social and economic efficiency than the household? The answer, in both cases, is a simple "No."

The enormous and unrecognized bulk of household labor that we have already discussed is only part of the reason. The rest lies in another simple but largely unrecognized fact, which we will now explore: The household can, and does, make capital investments that offer higher and more attractive returns than those available in the market economy. This fact, if we follow economic scripture, dictates that the household economy must at least hold its own against the market economy.

1. *Journal of Home Economics*, Vol. 62, No. 1, January 1970.

2. Kathryn E. Walker and William H. Gauger, *The Dollar Value of Household Work*, Information Bulletin 60 from New York State College of Human Ecology. Kathryn E. Walker, *Effect of Family Characteristics on Time Contributed for Household Work by Various Members*; William H. Gauger, *The Potential Contribution to the GNP of Valuing Household Work*. Papers presented at the June 26, 1973, conference of the American Home Economics Association, Atlantic City, N.J.

3. Interested readers should see the work of Harold Lydall in *The Structure of Earnings* (London: Oxford University Press, 1968), pp. 112–25.

4. Ismail Sirageldin, *Non Market Components of National Income* (Ann Arbor, Mich.: Survey Research Center, University of Michigan, 1969).

5. In the food industry, market labor increasingly displaces home labor as food is purchased in ever more advanced stages of processing. Consumers now spend about $200 billion annually on food. (Price inflation is such that there is no way that this figure will not be hopelessly dated between this writing and publication.) Just over two thirds of this sum is absorbed by the stores, jobbers, distributors, and processors between the consumer and the farmer. Less than a third of the total is the "farm bill." The "marketing bill" (the difference between final cost to consumer and the farmers' total income) has been rising decade after decade as food is further processed and prepared before it appears on the grocer's shelf.

In some respects, this is a great boon. The diversity of choices available in the typical supermarket, now some six thousand products, would simply not be available if there were an attempt to minimize the difference in cost between food at the farm and food at the store. Diversity costs money.

If the number of choices that are offered is large, so is the convenience. Women are no longer "chained to the kitchen" or "kitchen slaves." They are liberated. (Liberated to type, file, and labor long hours so they might pay the dry cleaners' bills and enjoy the ease and convenience of a Kraft Macaroni and Cheese Dinner.) While total food production and consumption lagged in growth, highly processed foods enjoyed a small boom. Canned- and frozen-food sales have doubled over the past decade; sales growth in prepared foods has zoomed. Yet any close analysis of the increase in cost versus the time saved in the preparation reveals that convenience foods are very dear and usually represent an extravagance on the part of the consumer.

The illustrations that follow reveal the extent to which people believe the marketplace to be intrinsically more efficient than the household and how it has displaced much labor from the household.

Consumer writer Sidney Margolius has calculated that the buyer gives Lipton $.42 to combine $.30 worth of beef and $.07 worth of dried noodles in a package of Beef Stroganoff. Similarly, Betty Crocker gets $.27 for combining $.12 worth of macaroni and $.10 worth of cheddar in macaroni and cheese, Uncle Ben gets $.12 for adding seasoning to his rice, and General Foods gets something like $1.70 a pound for adding seasonings to its Shake 'n' Bake. Examples of this type are endless and may be seen by the counter mile at any supermarket.

The economic questions are: (1) How much *time* has the household saved? (2) How much is that time worth? In many instances, no time is saved at all. None. Not a single second. Margolius even cites a few instances in which it takes *more* time to cook convenience foods than it does to start from scratch. In those instances in which time is *saved*, the extra cost of the product negates the advantage; in one typical example, the cost of the time saved computed to $4.30 an hour, almost 50 per cent more than the average secretary or factory worker earned at the time.

What, then, is the advantage? Prepared foods serve to lower the level of intelligence and skill required in the kitchen. Like navy ships, convenience foods are "designed by a genius to be run by idiots." Social rewards accrue to those with marketplace skills, not household skills. No woman has ever been cited for her skill with the vacuum cleaner; many have been recognized for their speed at the typewriter.

The irony of this is that the same woman who will search three markets to price food competitively, who will drive five or more miles to a store and spend two or three hours a week (total time) obtaining the family groceries, will then stock up on "time-saving" convenience foods. She would never think of calling a small market and having the food delivered; if she did, S. S. Pierce would not have left the retail food business. The same woman who is, in effect, paying herself two dollars (or less) an hour to drive around and buy food (compared with the more expensive service of ordering by phone and having it delivered) values her time at more than $4.30 an hour when she makes the decision to buy convenience foods! Implied or imputed economic values are beyond the ken and conditioning of most consumers. Thus, the market expands diseconomically.

6. George Gilder's recently released *Sexual Suicide* (New York: Quadrangle Books, 1973) argues that, indeed, society cannot exist without the household and that there is an "economy of eros," whose destruction would undermine the economy of the market.

3

The Rise
of Household Capitalism

WOULD YOU LIKE some good investment advice? Go long on storm windows! Now and for the foreseeable future, the homely triple-channel aluminum storm window is probably the best investment any American can make. It offers a tax-free return on investment three or four times the interest rates on the highest-yield bonds and is likely to offer a better return, over a five- to ten-year period, than most of the hottest stocks of the sixties.

How could this be? We are accustomed to thinking of good investments as things blessed by high technology (IBM, Xerox, Digital) or having special access to the dreams and desires of the masses (Disney, McDonald's, Avon). The mind balks at putting storm windows in the same league. But they belong there, and, not surprisingly, the makers of storm windows are doing a booming business. As this is written, the delivery time for new storm windows runs a minimum of four weeks and as much as eight weeks, and there is little likelihood that either consumer demand or investment appeal will decline in the near future.

The facts are simple. In early 1973 the Ad Hoc Committee on Fuel Conservation, in co-operation with several other government offices, prepared a booklet on household energy conservation,[1] in which it was announced that the average storm window recovered 13–18 per cent of its purchase price every year in fuel savings, providing only that the window was used in an area where the average winter temperature is 45° or lower—e.g., Philadelphia, Washington, Richmond. The estimate was based on late-1972 fuel prices; hence the savings have increased substantially since then as the price of heating fuel has risen, and will likely *double* by the time this book is released. In other words, the average storm window can reasonably be expected to return about 30 per cent of its cost in fuel savings every year. In effect, the storm-window buyer is achieving a 30 per cent *tax-free* return on his investment, a rate of return virtually unequaled in the world of more orthodox investments—competitive, for instance, with Coca-Cola's 28 per cent or Xerox's 27 per cent.[2]

Even when we make a tougher case and assume that the storm-window investor will sell his home in seven years (the average holding period), that the value of the storm windows won't be reflected in the selling price of the home, and that no further increases occur in the price of fuel, the homeowner's compound annual rate of return is in excess of 25 per cent! If storm windows were stocks, rather than products sold at Sears, Roebuck, we would probably pay $240 a window rather than a bit over twenty dollars. But storm windows aren't stocks. They are consumer products. That's why it makes sense for investors to sell stocks and buy storm windows.

Few household investments are so rewarding as the storm window, nor is it usually so easy to determine the rate of return, but in spite of these impediments consumers spend more each year on investments in houses and household equipment than ever before.

"Consumers," according to the 1970 *Finance Facts Year Book,* *"have become capitalists in the strictest sense of the word. In addition to wider ownership of the means of production they generally own the physical capital which provides the services necessary to satisfy many of their wants for living quarters, transportation, household services, and entertainment."*[3]

The 1970 Census revealed that some 64 per cent of all families own their home or apartment, compared to 61 per cent in 1960; 70 per cent of all those with heads over thirty-five owned a home, as did 85 per cent with incomes over fifteen thousand dollars. While the rate of advance for home ownership slowed dramatically during the sixties, because of the rapid rise in interest rates and inflation, it is still apparent that most families, given the choice between investing in the stock market and buying a home, choose the latter. This implies, if rational economic behavior is assumed, that somewhere, somehow, home buyers have determined that home ownership offers a superior return on investment. In 1970, a tough year for housing, some $30 billion was invested in new residential structures. Housing growth in the seventies is expected to be at the rate of 5.9 per cent[4] (measured in dollars of constant purchasing power), a rate almost half again as great as the anticipated 4 per cent growth rate for disposable personal income. While the primary reason for this impressive growth is the raw power of demographics and the fact that those of home-buying age (twenty-five–thirty-four) will dominate the shifts in population during the seventies, the durability of home ownership implies that it continues to make good economic sense.

We might, in fact, consider that there is a kind of "folk wisdom" behind household investment and that this folk wisdom provides better economic results than all the Monte Carlo simulations, calculations, and what-not employed by the nation's businesses and brokerage houses. It is altogether likely that the simple love of grass has led more people toward good investments than any directly rational approach. The purchase of a house, almost inevitably, leads to the accumulation of other household capital—equipment which, as we shall see, offers economic returns equal to, or better than, those offered by the market economy.

We can test this folk-wisdom hypothesis by comparing the effective returns achieved by homeowners and stock investors over the past decade. The average home, according to the Tax Foundation, appreciated at the rate of 6 per cent a year between 1961 and 1971. Since the average new homeowner was likely to have down-payment equity of about 20 per cent in 1961, his effective return on equity for the period was 30 per cent, a rate of return far higher than that achieved by the average mutual fund in the same time period, the *Fortune* 500, or any other broad-based measure of investment returns.

Purists might argue that since the homeowner's gain is largely reflective of inflation, it is illusory. After all, he has the same house and it provides the same services of shelter now as it did a decade ago, when it cost far less. But the same argument ap-

plies to the average investor. Only in rare cases has his investment brought him a real increase in purchasing power; for the
most part, he has the ambivalent experience of owning stocks
that are worth more and pay higher dividends but which would
buy not much more now than they did a decade ago.

Looking at inflation more closely, we can devise a very rough
rule of thumb for determining when the effective return on
housing investment will equal or exceed the 11 per cent return
we can expect from most industrial investments. Since the prevailing interest rate usually equals about 3 per cent plus the rate
of inflation (e.g., interest rates will average 8 per cent when inflation is 5 per cent, 9 per cent when inflation is 6 per cent, etc.),[5]
the return on housing will be equal to the cost of financing it (the
interest rate) plus its annual increase in value due to inflation.
We already know, however, that the interest rate is about equal
to the rate of inflation plus 3 per cent, so we can solve our problem by using algebra:

(1) Aver. industrial return   = 11% = Housing return.
(2) Housing return   = inflation + interest rate.
(3) Housing return   = inflation + (inflation + 3%) = 11%.
(4) Housing return   2 inflation + 3% = 11%.
(5) Solving for inflation,   2 inflation = 8%.
(6)   Inflation = 4%.

Thus, when the rate of inflation equals or exceeds 4 per cent,
the return on household investment is likely to exceed the return
on industrial or marketplace investment. Few economists expect
the rate of inflation to be *below* 4 per cent for the foreseeable
future, and many worry that it will average 5, 6, or even 7 per
cent a year. In this light, it is not surprising that the number of
shareholders decreased in 1973 while investment in durable
goods and housing boomed. But before we arrive at any such
broad conclusions, let's take a close look at the size and scope of
household investment.

The 1970 Census reported that automobile ownership had
reached almost 80 per cent and that ownership of two or more
cars had increased from 16 per cent of all families to 29 per cent
during the sixties. For the near future, whatever their liabilities,
automobiles will be a primary household investment, a virtual

necessity as the pattern of suburban living continues to spread.[6]

However impressive the distribution of these major investments is, to stop there would be to ignore the enormous diversity and growth of household capital investment. *Merchandising Week* keeps a "saturation index" to measure the market penetration of specific consumer durables (see table below).

FIGURE 5

Saturation Index of Key Products
(as of Dec. 31, 1971)

Product	Number of Wired Homes with	Per Cent
Television, B&W	65,419,000	99.8
Refrigerators	65,419,000	99.8
Radios	65,419,000	99.8
Irons	65,419,000	99.8
Vacuum Cleaners	61,879,000	94.4
Clothes Washers	61,814,000	94.3
Toasters	61,748,000	94.2
Coffeemakers	59,650,000	91.0
Irons (Steam Spray)	59,061,000	90.1
Mixers	55,324,000	84.4
Fry Pans	38,019,000	58.0
Color Television	33,496,000	51.1
Electric Blankets	33,496,000	51.1
Can Openers	31,530,000	48.1
Clothes Dryers	31,202,000	47.6
Room Air Conditioners	29,170,000	44.5
Ranges, Electric	27,924,000	42.6
Blenders	26,220,000	40.0
Water Heaters (Electric)	22,156,000	33.8
Freezers	21,435,000	32.7
Dishwashers	19,403,000	29.6
Disposers	18,616,000	28.4

Source: *Merchandising Week*, February 28, 1972.

Note that radios, television sets, clothes washers, refrigerators, irons, vacuum cleaners, and toasters can be found in virtually every home in the U.S.A. In 1971, almost 8 *million* vacuum cleaners were sold. Merchandisers found ways to sell 4.8 million can openers, 5.5 million powered lawn mowers, 8.5 million coffeemakers, 9.4 million irons, 6.4 million toasters, and almost 4.9 million electric mixers.[7]

Having been bombarded for so many years with extravagant claims for the psychic benefits that will accrue to the owner of this year's waffle-and-sandwich grill, having been the victim of countless desperate Christmas gifts of electric carving knives, facial saunas, corn poppers, and three-ounce folding travel irons; having faced the $30 charge to replace a small washer in the refrigerator and a multitude of other disasters; most of us now look on our household appliances as sources of distress rather than convenience. Curious, though, how we keep on buying them.

The same investment process that increases productivity in a business is curiously invisible in the household. Like government, the household is assumed to be immune from technological aids to productivity. Output always remains constant; only the machinery of production changes. Yet one need only attempt to make toast in anything but a toaster to experience the miraculous productivity of that machine. The problem is that the toaster's "return" is in the form of convenience and service. It fails to put money directly in our pockets.

Yet, whatever our attitude toward household capital, household-durable sales continue to grow. The consumer balance sheet, shown below, indicates the enormous size of household investment:

Figure 6

Estimated Consumer Balance Sheet
(in billions of dollars)

	1960	1965	1970	1972
Household Assets				
Non-farm home ownership	406.0	495.8	689.4	756.4
Value of consumer durables	164.8	209.2	277.4	316.2
Total Assets	570.8	705.0	966.8	1072.6
Household Liabilities				
Mortgage debts	125.1	194.6	259.5	317.9
Consumer credit	56.2	90.3	126.8	156.4
Total Liabilities	181.3	284.9	386.3	474.3
Household Net Worth	389.5	420.1	580.5	598.3

Source: *1973 Finance Facts Year Book.*

Recently, families have shown a diminishing desire to buy corporate securities but have continued to purchase homes and consumer durables at an ever-increasing rate. The appeal of household investments is so great that consumer debt levels reach new records every year. In order to have title to some $756 billion in housing, families have committed themselves to $318 billion in mortgage debt; in financing $316 billion worth of consumer durables, families have taken on some $156 billion in short-term loans, usually at interest rates in excess of 12 per cent.

Predictions of disaster are announced at regular intervals. Thrift and all the associated moral virtues of moderation and caution have been resurrected time and again by those who see the rising tide of consumer debt as a sign of future disintegration. Soon the bill collector will come and take us all away. The proud owner of a new frost-free refrigerator (with ice maker) must not only cope with the monthly payments but must also live with a nagging sense of guilt. It would have been far better, the conventional reasoning goes, if we had saved our money so that it might be borrowed by a corporation to purchase a Lear Jet to augment the productivity of corporate vice-presidents.

The problem is that few consumers see their household decisions as business or economic decisions; the household is perceived as a specialized consuming unit, never as a productive unit. *Yet a clear examination of consumer decisions indicates that families are increasingly opting to purchase the capital equipment necessary to obtain goods and services they would otherwise have to buy in the marketplace.* Implicitly, each decision for investment in household equipment and durables hints that household returns on investment are superior to marketplace returns. In fact, this is so.

The rate and amount of imputed income from housing offers the clearest comparison of household and market investments. Those who rent their houses or apartments elect to pay others for the use of their capital by paying rent. Landlords, seldom associated with philanthropy, are expected to require a return on their capital. Return on total capital in real estate (debt + equity) is usually in the vicinity of 8–10 per cent; extensive use of debt leverage can bring the return on the landlord's equity to 15–25 per cent.

Similarly, we pay interest on the money borrowed to finance

a house. A rate of 7½–8 per cent is typical in most of the United States. When the mortgage is paid off, the owner's *cash* expenses are diminished by the amount of the monthly mortgage payments. He is then receiving an "imputed," non-cash return in the form of shelter "service" equal to more than 7 or 8 per cent of the market value of the house, a return that he is, in effect, "paying" himself. His total return, as we showed earlier, is higher, because the value of his investment increases with inflation.

The homeowner's "service" return, because it avoids being monetized in the marketplace, is *tax-free*. To equal it, he would need a higher pretax return (as great as 16 per cent if he were in the 50 per cent tax bracket), a return that is far in excess of what can be obtained in savings accounts of any term, virtually all bonds, and many securities. When annual appreciation is taken into account, the return is better than can be expected in all but a handful of businesses.

It's not only better in rate, it's also larger in *total*. Equity in home ownership in 1972 amounted to some $438 billion and provided, at 7 per cent, an imputed non-cash income of some $30 billion to American homeowners, *a sum significantly larger than all the dividends paid out by all the corporations in the United States.*[8]

Few people have the capital necessary to make a clear choice between home ownership and other forms of investment; at best, most families struggle to accumulate a down payment and commit themselves to twenty-five or thirty years of monthly mortgage payments, hoping to have paid off the mortgage by the time they retire. Not surprisingly, equity in a house is the single largest asset held by most of the retired. Not infrequently, a recent retiree will buy a new house for cash, secure in the knowledge that he could not find a higher return anywhere without assuming much larger risks.[9]

While the automobile has become a social pariah over the past decade, it still remains the second-largest investment most Americans ever make. In 1970, American motorists drove some 100 million passenger cars 1,175 *billion* miles; they also buy almost 10 million new cars every year and scrap another 7 million. The absurdity of giving the automobile the amount of resources, time, and space that it demands is inescapable. Yet we must also consider the economics of transportation.

As consumers and investors, we are confronted with a choice among public transportation, taxicabs, or owning and operating our own vehicle. Deficit-ridden, declining in spite of grand public gestures by a few legislators, and increasingly dependent on the public tax coffers, public transportation usually has direct costs of four or five cents a passenger-mile. The private automobile, according to the Department of Transportation, costs twelve to eighteen cents a mile to own and operate, depending upon its size and age. A typical taxicab, excluding the initial large sum for throwing the meter and giving no consideration to time charges, costs sixty cents a mile.[10]

If the cash price were the only consideration, we would obviously choose public transportation. But we don't. Local public transit loses passengers every year. Similarly, intercity transportation is completely dominated by the automobile; more than 85 per cent of all intercity passenger-miles are in private passenger cars. The annual *growth* of private-car mileage alone is greater than the total passenger-mileage of all the nation's bus and train companies! One reason we choose private over public transportation is that the latter is seldom *point to point* and often requires substantially more time than private transportation. Intangible values also play a part—such as the fact that the automobile (after the bathroom) is one of the few places where most of us can experience absolute isolation and privacy. This is not a small benefit.

Finally, the cost of the automobile can be quite competitive. Assuming a cost of twelve cents a mile, we need only load the car with three people to compete with public transportation in price. Given the dreams of escape that most of us harbor and the limits of public transportation, it isn't difficult to see why private cars are chosen over public transportation by just about everyone, including those who qualify for official poverty status.

Service equivalent to that provided by the private automobile costs *five times as much* when purchased on the open market. In effect, the cab rider pays the driver forty-eight cents a mile for his labor and twelve cents a mile for his equipment. *Instead, most people elect to go into business for themselves.* After all, a year's driving (ten-thousand-plus miles) would amount to forty-eight hundred dollars in imputed labor income, a rather substan-

38 *The Invisible Economy*

tial sum. If the family driver averages a mere ten miles an hour, he is, in effect, making $4.80 an hour, tax-free.

While it would be absurd to assert that the imputed income the average family enjoys because it owns an automobile is in excess of five thousand dollars, the figures do indicate that *the market-place cannot possibly compete with the household for the provision of transportation services.* Similarly, public transportation as it now exists cannot compete. Faced with the absolute need for transportation, the economic choice is to "go into business for ourselves."

If we are to provide transportation for ourselves, we must have the vehicle that will do the transporting. We are again faced with a marketplace-versus-household decision. We can lease our car from a leasing company or we can buy a car; we either pay someone else for use of their capital or we can use our own. The implied return on most car leases is a minimum of 9 per cent,[11] a figure that is in line with the cost of financing a car. About a third of all new-car purchases and half of all used-car purchases are for cash. No financing is involved. Implicitly, the cash buyer is obtaining an imputed return on his investment: A 9 per cent tax-free return is fully competitive with returns in the market economy.

The total value of all the automobiles in use in 1970 was about $110 billion; automobile installment loans amounted to about $35 billion. The car-owner capitalist thus received some $6.75 billion in imputed income by virtue of his equity in this one piece of household equipment, a sum almost three times as large as the total profits for GM, Ford, and Chrysler in 1971, a good year.

American families in 1970 owned about $167 billion in other consumer durables and carried some $30 billion in installment debt to finance them. Deriving a rate of return on investment for each item would be difficult, if not impossible, since some items have no counterpart in private business. In those cases for which estimates have been made, however, household investments offer returns far higher than those found in the marketplace.

Two Canadian economists, writing in the *Journal of Finance*, did an elaborate analysis of the use of laundromats versus the purchase and use of home laundry equipment.[12] The table below shows the return on investment provided by the household equipment after allowing for the cost of electricity, water, and water heating, and assuming a number of different "utilization rates" and life expectancies. It indicates that my wife achieves a return on investment of about 20 per cent on our laundry equipment, a return matched by most mothers with young (and dirty) children. The return is slightly better than the 19.8 per cent achieved by IBM and exceeded by no more than sixty companies in *Forbes* annual list of almost eight hundred!

FIGURE 7

Return on Investment for Laundry Equipment

Years of Service	Loads of Laundry per Week		
	6	8	10
6	1.0	10.2	18.5
8	3.7	13.1	21.4
10	6.4	15.5	23.4

Source: *Journal of Finance*, December 1964.

The same economists also did an analysis of the return on investment for a TV set, assuming that if the viewer didn't watch TV he would be forced to buy some other form of entertainment. Assuming that the relative value of TV entertainment was only *one fifth* that of outside entertainment, the researchers found that the household investor's return on investment, provided the TV set lasted only six years, was 29.1 per cent. If the household had children, the return zoomed upward to 75 per cent.

A similar argument can be used to justify the purchase of a dishwasher. Assuming that a dishwasher can be purchased and installed for $250 and lasts five years while being used once a day to save ten minutes of labor valued at two dollars an hour, the machine offers a "discounted cash flow return on investment" in excess of 50 per cent.

The table below compares the return on total capital for several of America's best-known companies with the range of returns available in the average household.

All together, the total return on all consumer durables—the productive machinery of the household "plant"—was about $16 billion, bringing the total "wages of capital" in the household economy to about $46 billion. Little of this appears in conven-

FIGURE 8

Household Versus Corporate Investment Returns

%

Avon	40	TV/Dishwasher
	30	
American Home		Storm Windows
Coca-Cola		
		Gadgets
Xerox/IBM	20	
Procter & Gamble		Laundry Equipment
General Electric		Home Ownership
MEDIAN–ALL INDUSTRY	10	
Sherwin Williams, General Dynamics		Automobiles
Reynolds Metals		
St. Regis Paper		
TWA		
Celanese	0	

ROI
(Return on Total Capital)[13]

tional statistics, yet it is an impressive figure. The imputed income of household capital, $46 billion in 1970, was, for instance, *twice as large* as the net income of the entire *Fortune* 500 in the same year and slightly larger than the after-tax profits of *all the corporations in the United States.* Admittedly, 1970 was not a banner year for corporate America. But it is striking that a comparison of the total returns on corporate and household capital cannot be found in the literature of economics or sociology. In the future, a comparison is more and more likely to show the household economy to advantage. The simple fact is that the household economy is accumulating physical wealth faster than the corporate economy. As we shall see in the next chapter, it has been doing so for some time, causing a significant shift in the balance of wealth.

In a very real sense, the household has been competing against the market economy. And it has been winning. In each case above, the decision to buy a piece of equipment has meant that no comparable investment can be made by the market economy. It has also meant that labor which might have been employed in the market economy is committed to the household economy.

Conditioned as we are to think of ourselves as pure consumers, the idea that we might daily engage in competition with business, with the efficiency of corporate America, is quite alien. *But no realistic close look at our household activities can avoid recognizing that we produce goods and services in the household as well as consume them.* We can only wonder just where the process will end.

It is only logical to expect that as people become more attuned to the household as a productive organization, they will seek more opportunities to produce for themselves rather than make exchanges in the uncertain marketplace. One of the major forces behind this trend is inflation; it drives people to think of ways in which they can avoid painful and unpredictable increases in the prices of goods and services they need. Few newspapers have been without recent accounts of the vast demand for vegetable seeds, the proliferation of home gardens, the companies that provide gardening land for employees, or ever more ambitious do-it-yourself projects—not to mention speculations on an enclaved, neo-feudal society of homeowner privatism and the Swiss Family Robinson visions to be found in such books as *Inflation Survival Manual.*

One major misconception about the increasing volume of work done in the home is "rentalism." It has been noted that it is now possible to rent virtually anything. The rapid rise of this phenomenon has been cited as evidence of our diminishing attachment to things and the ever-increasing "throughput" in our lives. Extrapolated to extremes, the phenomenon poses a world in which individuals own nothing except abstract shares in corporate institutions which own—and rent—the real assets.[14]

Actually, a much more basic economic process is at work. Rentalism shows that the householder is becoming a conscious capitalist who decides to acquire an asset only when he can use it enough to justify his investment. Since there are many goods competing for purchase by our limited amounts of capital, we *economize* by acquiring that which we use frequently and renting that which we use seldom. We rent glasses for parties because we seldom have parties. We rent hospital beds and medical equipment because we hope not to have to use them too long or too often. We rent cement mixers and other tools because we do not envision their daily use. All this is nothing more than sane economics. It has little to do with "ephemeralization" or any other buzz word that codes rapid change.

While one implication of rentalism—transience—has been misperceived, another has been entirely overlooked. *The most significant aspect of the rise of rented objects and equipment is the fact that the labor usually employed in the operation of this equipment has been displaced from the marketplace to the household.* Men and women with nominal or non-existent skills are more and more often deciding that they can economically compete against specialists in arcane trades. Again, the household economy expands at the expense of the market economy.

Determining just where it will end is nearly impossible. Logic demands that some goods be produced more cheaply by the marketplace than by the home. But consider this: The Salton company now offers a fourteen dollar yogurt maker which cuts the cost of home-made yogurt (over store-bought) by 70 per cent; the apparent savings for a family that consumes one small cup of yogurt a day works out to the equivalent of a 25 per cent return on capital investment and ten dollars an hour (tax-free again!) for labor. The economics are hard to resist. The clutter that fills every garage, closet, and basement in America may yet be justified! Just as the businessman combines labor, energy, and materials to produce a product for sale in the marketplace, the householder combines his own labor with purchased energy and materials to produce a product for home consumption. He knows it is real, because he made it and consumed it. But he can't believe it, because there is no passage of money to "prove" it. In any case, home production is second-rate by definition. The properly conditioned citizen believes that work in the household economy is performed under duress, because he is not "successful" enough to have the money to hire someone.

Few, very few, can avoid fear and trepidation before exercising an unfamiliar skill. Whether it is doing an income-tax return, mastering the buttonhole attachment for the sewing machine, or reseating a toilet, the job is approached with much anxiety. We all know that others, experts, can do it well. Afterward, we must match the surprise and thrill of achievement (we did it!) against the loss of the magical happening of money. The idea that a mere scrap of paper can induce others to work and magically transform the world of things to conform with our desires is difficult to renounce.

More than $20 billion—2 per cent of the gross national product —is spent every year convincing us that we *should* be passive consumers, trusting to the magical efficiency of those who want to sell us widgets and wombats. An accumulating body of evidence, however, tells us this magical illusion is breaking down.

For a few, high incomes support the reality of money's magic. For the rich, material desire and reality are separated by no more than a wave of the checkbook or credit card. But what is reality for a few is myth for the many. While poverty may be reduced to a problem of a minority, and some degree of affluence has arrived for the majority, most Americans must still struggle to align their aspirations and desires with the limits of their incomes. Few succeed: Increasingly, those who find that their incomes do not go far enough—even those with incomes above twenty-five thousand dollars a year—turn to work in the household economy to provide services they cannot otherwise afford.

Home improvement is now a major industry. Annual sales to homeowners have been estimated at $17 billion. They are growing at 10 per cent a year; half the sales and most of the growth are attributed to do-it-yourselfers. Manufacturers vie for command of the market by turning out easy-to-install products. "Home centers," now numbering about five thousand, are growing at a rate of 20 per cent a year. The Commerce Department has estimated that 80 per cent of all paint and 60 per cent of all wallpaper is purchased by do-it-yourselfers. Retail sales of hardware and tools, $15 billion in 1970, are expected to nearly double, to $28 billion, by 1980. Few homes are now without at least a small collection of hand tools. Many are equipped with complete shops for woodworking. Similarly, the $3 billion home sewing industry is enjoying such growth that it has attracted the attention of *Forbes, Business Week,* and the *Wall Street Transcript.*

The import of these and all the other areas of household economic activity is that *private industry is becoming a subcontractor to the producing household.* The market economy is becoming an economic intermediary rather than the end of the production

FIGURE 9

Patterns of Consumer Spending

Type of Product	Per Cent
Food, Beverages, Tobacco	22.8
Food for Home Consumption	16.1
Purchased Meals, Beverages	4.5
Clothing, Accessories, Jewelry	10.3
Women's, Children's Clothing	4.7
Men's, Boys' Clothing	2.6
Jewelry, Watches	.7
Shoes	1.3
Clothing Services	1.0
Personal Care	1.7
Toilet Articles, Preparations	1.0
Personal Care Services	.7
Housing	14.5
Household Operations	14.1
Furniture, Bedding	1.4
Household Appliances	1.4
Other Housefurnishings	3.1
Household Supplies	1.2
Household Utilities	3.8
Medical Care	7.4
Drugs, Supplies, Equipment	1.4
Medical Care Services	6.0
Personal Business	5.5
Transportation	13.5
User-operated Transportation	12.6
Automobile Purchase	6.1
Gasoline, Oil	3.6
Local Transportation	.4
Intercity Transportation	.5
Recreation	6.3
Radio, TV	1.4
Toys, Sporting Goods	1.6
Books, Magazines, Newspapers	1.2
Paid Admissions	.4
Private Education, Research	1.7
Religious, Welfare Activities	1.4
Foreign Travel and other, Net	.7

Source: *A Guide to Consumer Markets*, 1971/1972, (New York: Conference Board, Inc., 1971).

process. As the economic importance of the household increases, our dependence on the market economy decreases. Not only do we do more for ourselves, but we can reduce our need to acquire money in the market economy, by increasing our personal stock of goods.

This is already happening. Consumer expenditures on durable goods expand year after year; increasingly, the family devotes a rising portion of its total cash income to the acquisition of goods it will use for long periods of time. Installment debt now amounts to some 18 per cent of disposable personal income. Mortgage-debt repayments absorb 12 per cent or more of the young home-owner's income. Analysis of consumer expenditure patterns, shown below, indicates that *more than 20 per cent of all personal disposable income is devoted to acquiring, financing, and amortizing productive goods and equipment for the household.*

Population growth (which requires an absolute expansion in the volume of goods) and the rapid wasting of consumer assets through deliberate design and technological change require that each generation begin anew the process of accumulating household capital; changes in either or both could drastically reduce the household's need for a cash income, by increasing the stock of net capital owned outright by the household economy.

Exactly how much the need for cash income could be reduced depends on the over-all rate of depreciation for household goods; a 75 per cent reduction is a reasonable estimate, assuming that an existing stock of housing could be transferred from one generation to another and that the life expectancy of major consumer durables could be doubled. This would reduce the need for cash income by about 15 per cent.

If, as present statistics suggest, we are now on the path toward zero population growth, *those who are now adults may be the last generation of Americans for whom home mortgage payments will be a way of life.* A stable population could have a much reduced need for new housing; one generation would virtually eliminate current home mortgage debt. Thus the primary household good, the home, would be removed from the market economy.

Nor do the possibilities of reducing the need for cash income end with the current configuration of goods. It is possible to substitute capital for energy. A recent *Wall Street Journal* article,[15] for instance, noted a RAND Corporation study which estimated that consumer demand for power could be reduced by 40 to 50 per cent merely by providing better insulation in new construction. The extra cost, the study concluded, could be recovered in four to seven years. Other studies, at M.I.T., have concluded that similar decreases in power consumption could be achieved in household appliances.

The same *Wall Street Journal* article commented that if Congress can legislate pollution out of automobile engines, it can also legislate a requirement for twenty miles to the gallon.[16] Since household utilities and gasoline and oil purchases for automobiles currently consume some 7.4 per cent of consumer expenditures, a 50 per cent reduction in energy requirements could reduce the need for household income by an additional 4 per cent —more than $20 billion! Achieving this annual saving, if it were to provide a return commensurate with the 10 per cent return on capital in private industry, would justify an investment of about $200 billion, almost *twice* the value of *all* new construction in 1971 and significantly larger than current gross private domestic investment. The magnitude of this figure indicates that there is considerable latitude for dealing with the energy crisis.

Most readers, no doubt, feel a bit uncomfortable with this line of reasoning. We are accustomed, after all, to contemplating making investments that will *create* income, which we can then use to pay bills (if we are lucky enough to have the capital to invest). We are not in the habit of making investments that will directly *reduce* or *eliminate* our bills. The process seems negative and a trifle niggling. Yet it is all very real and very economic. *The end of all investment is to increase the effective income of the investor, nothing more; household investments answer this requirement handily.*

The flaw in conventional perception of this proposition is a product of marketplace conditioning. We are led to believe that mere increases in throughput represent advances and increased economic benefits. The rate of technological change and the rapid depreciation of human knowledge have confronted the consumer with so many choices and so much information that he is supposed to be mesmerized and psychically dependent on the magic of the marketplace to provide goods and services. We are all familiar with the problems this has created; it would be wonderful to have a five-year moratorium on the use of the word "alienation." Yet, while there is much confusion, the consumer's *actions* speak loudly of his independence, and our rising concern with the quality of life can only work to make the "folk wisdom" of the household visible, acceptable, and intellectually compelling.

Those who have withdrawn, those in the youth culture who attempt to form communes, who buy secluded farms in Vermont or build geodesic domes in New Mexico, are attempting to supplant the marketplace entirely. By building their own homes and constructing them to minimize energy consumption, by recycling old cars or avoiding the automobile altogether, by building their own furniture, sewing their own clothes, and growing their own food, they are minimizing their need to offer their labor in the marketplace. They pool it, instead, in the extended household. Like the family in colonial Connecticut or the yeoman of England, the new homesteader can internalize 70–80 per cent of all his needs in the household; his money work is intermittent when it can't be avoided altogether.

Such wholehearted commitments are grounded in ideology; economics plays a small role and exercises no command over decisions. Orthodox notions of economy are suspended in favor of some more subtle calculus that does not lend itself to normal accounting procedures. For most of us, such commitments are impossible; the world of the future envisioned by the *Mother Earth News* and a multitude of other publications that shun glossy paper is too far out. The population of those who fuel their automobiles with methane generated by chicken droppings and cow manure and power their radios with wind generators must remain small, at least for the immediate future.

That a group may be small or extreme, however, does not mean that it cannot have significance for the society as a whole. Its efforts are the most direct and conscious endeavors to develop the household economy. As these efforts proceed, all of us will become more clearly aware of the household as a productive economic entity making the same kinds of managerial decisions and with the same responsibilities as the typical business.

According to the 1973 *Fortune* 500 list, the median assets per employee of the largest corporations in America amount to about twenty-seven thousand dollars. The average American family, with its house, car(s), appliances, tools, and various bits of equipment, operates an enterprise of proportionate complexity. While management consultants and hip sociologists prophesy the coming organizational revolution, the burgeoning ad-hocracy, and the de-structuring of American business, it is a fact that the ad-hocracy has been alive and well in the American household for decades under the skilled management of the American housewife. The household is the natural environment of ad-hocracy; corporate America is not. We are in the process of witnessing nothing less than the emergence of something that might be called "household capitalism," an economic form that must, inevitably, result in the radical reordering of society.

But while this reordering will be radical, the changes ahead will be gradual; we will be confronted with an ever-increasing number of choices that will make us opt for household-economy investments rather than for market-economy investments. Never spectacular, bearing none of the conventional signs of wealth, and augured by none of the ideological upheavals that accompany political change, the growth of the household economy will be marked by no more than a growing void in the market economy. Conventional radicalism is violent because it attempts to reform an existing economic structure with new ideas that are, inevitably, resisted. The household economy merely provides a separate economic structure and introduces a different economic process. It does not coerce, it does not depose. It merely *exists.* And grows.

1. "Seven Ways to Reduce Fuel Consumption in Household Heating . . . Through Energy Conservation," U. S. Government Printing Office, 1973.

2. *Forbes,* January annual, 1973.

3. Page 29 (my italics). *The Finance Facts Year Book* is produced by the National Consumer Finance Association.

4. Predicast, 1973. 200 University Circle Research Center, Cleveland, Ohio.

5. This relationship was posited some years ago by the St. Louis Federal Reserve Bank. While it has many exceptions, it serves the present period fairly well. For a close look at the economics of housing, read Scott Burns, *Squeeze It Till the Eagle Grins* (New York: Doubleday, 1972).

6. While it would be nice to support mass transit, the real problem is that the balance has swung so far toward private transportation that it will be exceedingly difficult to reverse it. Some observers have commented that the rising price of gasoline may do more for urban planning and architecture than three decades of sincere good wishes.

7. There has been an incredible surge in consumer-durable purchases since these figures were issued; late 1972 and early 1973 were extravagant boom periods for every portion of the consumer-durables industry.

8. Estimates of imputed income depend on the method used: The Bureau of Labor Statistics, the Office of Business Economics, and the Social Security Administration each has its own method of evaluation; most of these estimates range from $12–18 billion, depending upon when they were made; they are significantly lower than mine, because most were made in the early sixties, when both real-estate values and prevailing interest rates were far lower.

9. Alvin Toffler, in *Future Shock*, apparently concluded that this $438-odd billion in home-ownership equity, whatever its importance, was insignificant. "It might be noted," he writes in a footnote, "that millions of American house 'owners,' having purchased a home with a down payment of 10% or less, are actually no more than surrogate owners for banks and other lending institutions. For these families, the monthly check to the bank is no different from the rent check to the landlord, the ownership is essentially metaphorical and since they lack a strong financial stake in the property, they also frequently lack the homeowner's strong psychological commitment to it." While it is true that some families have modest equity in their homes, it is a fact that many have significant equity (that $438 billion . . .) and that the low-equity families are usually young families buying their first house. If these families were not committed, MGIC, a private mortgage insurer, would not have been able to underprice the FHA and "privatize" much of the mortgage-insurance business.

10. Boston rates.

11. Actually, the lessor's return is higher, because he enjoys the full markup from the effective "sale" to the lessee and may also participate in the resale when the lease is over.

12. Poopst and Waters, "Rates of Return on Consumer Durables," *Journal of Finance*, December 1964.

13. Another way to make this comparison is to compare total returns to stockholders (dividends plus price appreciation) with household investment returns. According to *Fortune* magazine, the *Fortune* 500 delivered these returns over the period 1962–72:

Per Cent of Stocks	Cumulative %	Total Return
48%	48	less than 10%
24%	72	10–15%
15½%	87½	15–20%
6%	93½	20–25%
6½%	100	greater than 25%

During the same period, home mortgages averaged 6½ per cent and the average home appreciated at the rate of 6 per cent, according to the Tax Foundation, for a total of 12½ per cent. The implication is that the average homeowner's investment, without consideration of leverage or tax advantages, outperformed at least 50 per cent of the *Fortune* 500.

4

The Changing Balance
of National Wealth

THE PRAGMATIC TEST of any idea is whether or not it succeeds. In economic matters, the usual measure of success is the capacity to accumulate wealth. We admire IBM because it has made so much money for such a long time. We worship Xerox because it has made so much money in such a short time. We think less warmly of Consolidated Edison or Duke Power, or even U. S. Steel, not because they don't provide absolutely essential goods and services but because their capacity for accumulating wealth is modest. Inevitably, they account for an ever smaller share of the nation's economic output, whatever the system of measurement.

We must now apply the same test on a larger scale. Does the household measure up? Can the household economy manage to expand its share of national wealth? Has it already done so?

So far, we have asserted that there is an enormous invisible economy, that this economy is centered on the household, that its labor, if paid, would collect more wages than any single sector of the recognized economy, and that its income from capital is about equal to the net income of all the corporations in the United States. These are not modest claims.

We have also asserted that the household economy as an economic form will dominate the future, and that the market economy, which so clearly appears to dominate the present, will decline. The institution of money will decline as well. These are large claims. But we can test them by examining the past.

Figure 10 summarizes "gross fixed capital formation" from 1900 to 1960. This represents our annual investment in new productive goods that serve to increase our wealth, collectively and as individuals. Note that single-family residential construction recently equaled business construction, whereas in 1900 it was only one fifth as large. Similarly, annual investment in major consumer durables (automobiles, appliances, etc.) now *exceeds* producer-durables investment (cranes, extruders, presses, etc.). It is apparent from these figures that the economic importance of industrial America reached its peak sometime in the 1950s. After that date, industrial America was no longer the center of capital formation and investment. Instead, the household became the focus of capital formation.

FIGURE 10

Components of Gross Fixed Capital Formation, 1900–60

| | Structures | | Equipment | |
Year	Single-family Residential	Enterprise & Multifamily Residential	Major Household Equipment & Durables	Producer Durables
1900	.27	1.44	.35	1.01
1910	.78	1.99	.92	1.66
1920	1.35	4.05	4.44	5.10
1930	1.40	4.49	4.57	4.51
1940	2.58	2.47	5.18	5.64
1950	12.15	10.15	21.87	18.94
1960	20.61	20.56	30.14	27.56

(billions of current dollars)

Source: Adapted from F. Thomas Juster, *Household Capital Formation and Financing*, 1897-1962, New York: National Bureau of Economic Research, 1968.

Some observers would describe this event as the beginning of the consumer society, in which mass markets for mass-produced products are the mainstay of economic health. We earn more, the treadmill tells us, because we consume more. This is a familiar and conventional view because it assumes that everything produced, once sold, is quickly consumed by the household and that the household uses nothing as capital for its own works.

But it is difficult to explain how an automobile owned by a cab company is capital equipment whereas it is a consumer bauble when owned by a household. The same anomalous condition applies to virtually all consumer products: the dishes and cookware in the restaurant, the sheets and pillows on a hotel bed, the furnishings of a rented apartment, the towel at the local YMCA or health club, or the glasses at the local tavern. All these things are the capital equipment of the market economy, but are nothing in the household, because the rules say the household has no economic function.

Our figures, however, are a two-edged sword. They show the incredible surge in production for the home and the development of mass markets for a multitude of products. A particularly large debt is owed to the automobile. But what is production for the factory, to be sold, becomes investment for the household. Just as the machine-tool industry makes capital equipment for the production of dishwashers, the dishwasher industry makes capital equipment for the household.

We value financial wealth most highly. We are enamored of "supermoney"; we all aspire to owning those little slips of paper representing our share of General Electric's factories, American Electric Power's generators, or American Telephone's switchboards. But *most of the wealth we see and use is household wealth.* For all but a small minority of Americans, the only important wealth is the direct and tangible stuff, the goods and equipment within the home, and the home itself. Convention says that this is consumption, that it cannot be accorded equal treatment with business investment. But convention is wrong. The stuff, stuffing, and goods of the household are *wealth*, which is very real and exceedingly relevant. Ask any flood or fire victim. This wealth has accumulated rapidly and will continue to do so; it provides, when used, necessary or desired services that would otherwise have to be bought on the open market.

This change in capital formation represents an enormous shift in the use of the nation's resources. Where half a century ago we devoted our efforts to building an apparatus of industrial production so that we might produce for ourselves and the world, we now concentrate our investments *outside* the marketplace, in both the household and collective (or government) economies.

The following figures for capital formation in 1970 can be found in the Statistical Abstract of the United States:

Single-family Residential	Enterprise-farm & -multifamily Residential	Consumer Durables	Producer Durables
30.4	35.9	88.6	60.0

(All figures in billions of dollars)

At first glance, it would appear that the rate of household capital formation has reversed again—at least for structures. But this is not the case. More than $12 billion of the amount credited for enterprise-residential construction consists of multifamily housing units. If only 25 per cent of this figure represents condominiums, the household and enterprise rates of capital formation are equal. Condominiums represented about 5 per cent of the enterprise multifamily residential construction in 1970, and cluster-development condominiums are expected to represent 50 per cent of all new housing starts by 1980. Moreover, in many of the more developed areas, e.g. the Northeast, a combination of tax-law changes and public pressure for rent controls precipitated a massive conversion of existing enterprise-owned residential shelter to condominiums and co-operatives, thus understating household capital ownership if not formation.

While the figures from the Statistical Abstract and those from the National Bureau of Economic Research are not strictly comparable, it is obvious that household investment in durables is on a par with producer-durables investment.

Logically, we can expect that a shift in capital formation will eventually be reflected in the composition of national wealth. Here we find that both the household and the collective economies have grown, while the market economy has shrunk in relation to the sum total of national wealth. As shown in Figure 11, in 1929 the household economy had 31.4 per cent of the national wealth exclusive of land, while the market economy had 32.2 per cent; by 1966 the household economy had grown to 36.3 per cent, while the market economy had dropped to 31.9 per cent. The collective, or government, sector meanwhile had expanded from 7.7 per cent to 12.9 per cent.

Our figures represent the real, tangible wealth of the nation. We are not concerned with slips of paper, certificates, or other paper instruments. We are concerned with the real and palpable.

FIGURE 11

The Changing Composition of National Wealth
(percentages of total)

	Total	1929		Total	1966	
Household	39.6			40.9		
Structures		21.8 ⎱	31.4		24.5 ⎱	36.3
Durables		9.6 ⎰			11.8 ⎰	
Land		8.2			4.6	
Market	46.1			41.7		
Structures		14.8 ⎫			12.9 ⎫	
Durables		8.7 ⎬	32.2		11.6 ⎬	31.9
Inventories		8.7 ⎭			7.4 ⎭	
Agricultural Land		8.7			5.9	
Business Land		5.2			3.9	
Collective	11.5			15.3		
Public Structures		6.6 ⎱	7.7		12.2 ⎱	12.9
Monetary Metals		1.1 ⎰			.7 ⎰	
Public Land & Others		3.8			2.4	

Source: Adapted from *Finance*, January 1967.

Some observers would note here that market wealth, ultimately, is owned by households. Or that household wealth is most often created by the market economy. These facts should not confuse or obscure our basic observation: *The power and dominance of the marketplace is receding* as its share of national wealth diminishes. Individuals increasingly find it more beneficial to invest in the household economy than in the market economy.

It is also evident that public investment has enjoyed very vigorous growth. For all the (justified) complaints voiced by liberals about the imbalance of public and private investment, the facts show a shift as powerful as that between market and household. In 1900, public non-military construction was *one seventh* the size of enterprise construction. By 1930 the gap was closing, and by 1970 enterprise and public construction were about equal:

FIGURE 12

Enterprise-Versus-Public Construction

Year	Enterprise	Public Non-military
1900	1.44	.21
1910	1.99	.55
1920	4.05	1.19
1930	4.49	2.83
1940	2.47	3.24
1950	10.15	6.82
1960	20.56	15.95
1970	35.90*	27.40

*Note: Remember, this figure is an overstatement because it contains a substantial number of condominiums, etc.

Source: Quoted in Juster; op. cit. Statistical Abstract of the United States (1970)

The implications of these shifts are enormous. While we are told regularly of monster corporations and cancerous conglomerates, while General Motors and ITT are tirelessly compared to independent (and basically malicious) sovereign states—all with some truth—there is little or no comment on the shifting balance of national wealth. The popular press offers a constant stream of reports on increasing corporate concentration; we learn that a few corporations are consolidating control of industrial wealth, but we are not told that industrial wealth is an ever smaller share of *all* wealth. Nor is much effort expended in speculating on how, or if, corporate political power will decrease as its share of national wealth diminishes. Instead, we are regaled with familiar horror stories about well-known, if slightly passé, monsters. What matter if the stories no longer represent reality? It is the comfort of the ritual that counts. No effort is spared to make certain that treasured articles of belief remain untouched by the real world.

Orthodox sociologists and economists assume that big business will be with us for some time and that it will continue to dominate our economic life. They argue only over whether this domination will be good or bad. In the darker vision of the fifties and sixties, sociologists saw America becoming a massive, consolidated corporate state. A minority—Warren Bennis and a few others—saw the arrival of an organizational revolution and a new class of facile, interdisciplinary professionals and managers who would come to dominate the economic life of the nation. We would still, this more positive group believed, require the enormous bureaucracies and constellations of power that mark the industrial state. But the ever-increasing rate of technological change would create a new work environment of freedom and flexibility. We would become "task oriented"; the new model for productive work would be small temporary groups rather than the large fixed departments so often dedicated to little more than self-perpetuation.

Both visions, however, share a belief in the continuation of large concentrations of power and intricate social hierarchies in which the highly skilled are the philosopher-kings and the arbiters of power. Corporate America, whether benign or malignant, would remain at the center of power.

There is, however, very little evidence to support this notion and much, as we have shown, to indicate that we are now witnessing a powerful shift in power. The present dominance of corporate America is exceedingly fragile, because it is little more than an accounting artifact, a by-product of a system of accounting that is insanely single-minded and excludes all non-market activity. The importance of corporate America in terms of employment* and capital formation is fast diminishing, and with it, its grip on the culture. Just as the values of the farmer have receded, so, inevitably, will the values of corporate man.

It would only be prudent, here, to speculate on the limits of this shift. Obviously, heavy industry will not disappear. Nor will the need for a variety of highly organized and very complex organizations diminish. Just as the market economy never totally supplanted the household, neither will the household be capable of totally supplanting the market.

If the market economy produces for consumers, then the obvious limit of market wealth is fixed by the limits of accumulation for the household. If the household, in turn, has some limits on its consumption (as it appears to) then the market economy is eventually self-limiting. Inevitably, the household share is greater than the market's, irrespective of the share commanded by public wealth.

We also know that technical and organizational complexity

* Discussed in detail in Chapter 18.

requires a substantial infrastructure of public investment and support. So public wealth must also expand. Thus technology drives the developing market economy toward ever greater constraint and gradually diminishes the market's share in economic activity, wealth, and, finally, the values that define the culture.

This decline may occur without explicit general recognition of the rising household economy. It may all be masked in the crisis of capitalism and the rise of socialism. But the household explains the peculiar aversion of the young for the marketplace and their nearly equal disdain for bureaucratic socialism. No reading of the daily newspaper is complete without a discussion of youthful dropouts. The disinterest of the young in business is offered as a troublesome sign. We are told that something is wrong. That we are too materialistic. Too crass. Too preoccupied with getting ahead. Too pressured. Too driven by competition and the need to achieve. Thus, dunned by daily messages of duress and despair, one wonders, finally, just what to do.

Could our despair be an illusion, an artifact created by our peculiar preoccupation with the marketplace? Yes! Viewed in the perspective of the rising household economy and the maturity of the market economy, the movement of the young to communes, co-operatives, and other forms of economic organization is not a dropping out but the aggressive pursuit of tomorrow's opportunities. Perhaps such ventures are premature. Perhaps they are predisposed to early failure. Perhaps they are too loud, too defiant, too cocky, too sure. But was it ever different?

While the young may depart eagerly for the household economy, most of us are still attached to the marketplace. Great fear attends leaving. In *Future Shock*, Alvin Toffler warns us, "Unless we are literally prepared to plunge backward into pretechnological primitivism, and accept all the consequences—a shorter, more brutal life, more disease, pain, starvation, fear, superstition, xenophobia, bigotry, and so on—we shall move forward to more and more differentiated societies." Others proclaim that the marketplace and technology are parts of a whole, that each drives the other. Having once started the cycle, there is no stopping, no turning back.

But we are, in a sense, "turning back"; the market is receding, and the household and collective economies are growing. We are moving toward a new economy of stability, and, ironically, only an unreasoning belief in the market economy will plunge us backward into "pretechnological primitivism." Sadly, such blind faith is the very danger that confronts us as we try to cope with the present and anticipate the future. The source of this blindness is the subject of the next chapter.

5

The Household
Has No Bottom Line

ECONOMIC CONVENTION tells us that producers produce and consumers consume. The respective functions are clearly defined,
mutually exclusive, and intransigently pure. The consumer is the
passive beneficiary of the producer, and while all of us are consumers, the role and title of producer is awarded with far less
generosity.

To be a consumer it is merely necessary to exist. To be a producer one must be employed. One must work for money.
Whether one is a doctor, a factory worker, or a salesclerk, the
common, shared bond is that such employment is rewarded with
money. The fact (and amount) of payment is the single accepted
test of legitimate productive work. No other evidence is accepted.
Unpaid work is generally suspect in both motivation and value.
It may even be considered subversive, since it undermines the
clear and simple causality of work: It is a treasured article of belief that work is done first, second, and finally for money.

This definitional purity of consumers and producers is a great
convenience in discussion, but it lacks much in portraying the
real world. The failure and the ideology of conventional defini-
tions and accounting are the subject matter of this chapter.

The problem of defining producer and consumer does not end
with the definition of valuable labor. We must also consider the
use of *goods* for consumption. As a consumer, I buy and consume

a wide variety of goods. But many of them "produce" in turn. They are the factors of production in the household.

As a consumer, I buy cars, dishwashers, and washing machines; as a member of a family, I use these goods to produce needed services that would otherwise be purchased in the market economy. The fact that these services are not purchased in the market economy does not mean they do not exist. I wear clean clothes. I eat from clean dishes. I move from one place to another at my convenience. The producer produces *for* the household; the consumer produces *within* the household. That is the real difference between producer and consumer.

The true distinction between producer and consumer is quite vague at this point; the rapid accumulation of equipment within the household has worked progressively to blur the distinction further. By any reasonable standard, the consumer now presides over the most vital, productive, and rapidly growing portion of the economy.

But this conventional distinction between producer and consumer is not the only problem. There are other problems of convention as well. The woman who decides to get a job outside the home hires a maid to clean her house. Both her income and that of her maid are then included in GNP and national-income accounts, because they involve the exchange of money. In reality, the only *real* addition to the economic product is the job outside the home, not the cleaning within the home. The work of the maid is included in the GNP not because it is *done*, but because it is *paid for*. Similarly, a painter may propose to paint my house for nine hundred dollars. If I hire him, the GNP will increase by that amount. If I do the work myself, its value becomes invisible: The work has been done and the value produced, but this value is excluded from measures of GNP. I might also, say, restore a vintage car, thereby creating value and an economic good. But the value remains invisible until the car is sold.

Everything I do for myself or my family and everything they do for me are excluded from accounts of national product and income. Everything I do for money, however dubious its intrinsic worth or utility, is added to GNP and national income. The value of a friend's services on his own car is excluded from GNP. But the cost of his accident, ambulance ride, and hospital stay is not. Indeed, a multitude of entirely negative economic events—the cost of police, prisons, pollution, accidents, etc.—are included in GNP, while the value of home production, volunteer work, and the services of consumer-owned capital are excluded.

Most of our economic statistics do not exist to demonstrate and quantify our real economic product but to trace the growth of exchange, of the market economy. We are not interested so much in economic welfare as in the circulation of money, as evidenced by the curiosity of the Internal Revenue Service about the earnings of the Mafia, assorted prostitutes, bookies, and car thieves. Crime, because it involves the circulation of money, will be included in the statistics of income long before the output of the household is considered.

This is now a familiar complaint. We are no longer happy with the GNP. Some economists have suggested that we replace the statistics of GNP with "NEW," or "Net Economic Welfare," so that our figures will more accurately reflect the economic condition of the nation. No doubt, a more reasonable compilation would be useful. Yet even these suggestions, however strident and radical, ignore the household economy. The NEW, instead of measuring the volume of *all* economic activity that requires the passage of money, would measure only *some* of the economic activity that requires the passage of money, and the household economy would still remain invisible, because its economic activity occurs without benefit of money.

To some readers, this may seem like a technical problem. But it is ideological as well. The household, since it pays no wages or dividends, presents a problem of valuation. How much is a service in the household worth if no one pays for it? No one knows.

The use of money offers no such problems. If someone willingly paid to have a specific service performed, then it must have been worth it. Why? Because market price is the test of value. Thus, the exchange of money, by definition, authenticates the legitimate value of any work. In effect, the market ideology says, "I was paid for, therefore I am."

As we have already noted, this is a questionable proposition. After all, *much of our economic activity occurs without market choice.* We start with employment and unemployment taxes, federal and state income taxes, obvious and hidden sales or excise taxes, local real-estate taxes, and then consider compulsory automobile insurance and medical insurance, long before we ponder the wages essentially extorted by the nation's plumbers, electricians, and carpenters (as is well known), not to mention its surveyors, stockbrokers, lawyers, doctors, and other closely bound professionals.

In many of our economic transactions we literally have no choice, and in many others we have no *effective* (or economic) choice. In a regulated and controlled economy in which an ever rising portion of all economic activity is controlled by political rather than individual market decisions, the circulation of money becomes an increasingly poor measure of economic welfare. At this writing, more than 30 per cent of the average family's income is expended through political decisions by way of taxes. Yet the money-value convention prevails, because we still believe that the market is the ultimate arbiter of value.

The problem of the household, in larger terms than its lack of a currency, is that it has never been included in the ideology of the market economy. It has no "bottom line." Its social purpose is not profit but sustenance. Thus, little effort is devoted to exploring and understanding its economy.

According to the 1970 Census, there were some seven hundred thousand accountants in the United States, all devoting their life's effort to recording the transfer of money from one party or institution to another. Every year, more than a hundred thousand degrees are conferred in accounting, business, and commerce. Another twenty thousand are awarded in economics. There are, in short, veritable legions of people devoted to the administration, management, and control of the institutions of the money economy.

The economy of the home attracts much less attention; a mere ten thousand degrees are awarded annually in home economics, a discipline that is still largely concerned with the quality of cake frosting and exploiting the versatility of the sewing machine.[1] The household economy suffers from neglect.

Some might note that we are not predisposed to feel that the attention of accountants and business managers is a wonderful event. They are not customarily cast in the heroic mold, and they are offered up, most often, as the bearers of intolerable boredom or as embarrassing reflections of the mundane creatures we become upon turning thirty. Seldom are they displayed as the Ministers of the Market Ideology, the Custodians of the Ledger

Scrolls, or those select few whose tireless ministrations to the dollar provide the Rosetta Stone of all economic achievement, the Bottom Line.

But they are very important people. They constantly test our faith in a desert of ledger-sheeted tedium. Like God, they work their will in mysterious ways that more-common mortals fail to understand. Only they can explain the sublime mysteries of profit and loss. And we regularly offer tribute by providing them, year in and year out, with billions in new computers and calculators—not to mention submitting our books for blessing and certification.

The orthodox and faithful business communes with its accountants and auditors regularly and devotes much of its resources to elaborate accounting for the "factors of production". It has cost and profit centers, internal and external charges, transfer prices, business plans, program and variance budgets, inventory controls, receivable controls, pro-formas, tax accounts, and shareholder accounts; it has, in short, a bewildering perplexity of measures and controls, all predicated on the idea that productive capital is scarce, labor dear, and management spread thinly. All are in need of constant economizing. Indeed they are. The same techniques could be applied to the household, but they are not, and the contrast is instructive.

A tour of the nearest business establishment might reveal the following: A large manufacturing space is filled with impressive machines, much noise, and the appearance of productive toil. In one area a new and larger machine is being installed. It is rated at thirty thousand widgets per hour. In a distant corner the old machine gathers dust. Nearby, the completed product is boxed and stacked in a storage space; electric fork lifts facilitate the rapid and efficient movement of boxes from production to storage to shipping. Outside, an assortment of trucks and cars deliver and pick up, aid salesmen in making calls, and provide necessary transportation for indolent executives. In the office itself, an assortment of dictating machines, typewriters, files, switchboards, adding machines, electric pencil sharpeners, and ball-bearing swivel chairs all mark the office as a place dedicated to getting the job done. It must be done quickly and efficiently, with the least possible waste. This is the primary charge of the market organization.

Once a year, inventory is taken: The adding machines are

rolled out, computer terminals plugged in, accountants gathered, and the sum value of all the equipment is found. The cost of labor is totaled, as is the cost of raw materials. Internal Revenue Service guidelines are consulted in regard to the useful life of carpeting, partitions, desks, and wastebaskets. Someone may guess at the expectancy of good will. Finally, the depreciation of all directly productive capital equipment is tallied and charged against income.

The IBM salesmen arrive around the same time, wishing to discuss the high cost of word processing; Diebold and Kodak visit to acquaint the president with the high cost of information storage and filing; Dictaphone drops by to undersell IBM, and Pitney Bowes suggests that now is the time to stop licking stamps and typing addresses. Another salesman may argue with the purchasing agent over the savings to be found in buying longer rolls of toilet paper, Dura bulbs, and Quick Reply stationery.

What each of these friendly visitors has in common is the desire to install or replace a piece of equipment. Something "more productive" will be added. Time will be saved and payroll costs cut. Capital can profitably be substituted for labor. The final argument is that the existing equipment has already been depreciated; it can be discarded with little harm to the balance sheet or income statement. The bottom line will be enlarged. Amen.

Depreciation charges by American businesses now amount to some $80 billion annually, an amount that would almost support the Department of Defense. There is little alarm over consuming capital at this rate. Depreciation is a regular and justified cost of doing business; indeed, a high rate of capital consumption is often taken as a measure of business efficiency and progressiveness. In the stock market it is awarded high price/earnings multiples. No prize is more valued.

The justification offered for all this is that depreciation reflects the demands of the real world. One way or another, whether through old age or technological obsolescence, income-producing equipment is bound to lose its value. The losses suffered now by the massively depreciating company may be nothing compared to what they will inflict on their competitors *later,* when they introduce their New Product. The end of technological competition, quite simply, is the destruction of old capital and the conservation of labor.

66   *The Invisible Economy*

None of this is viewed with horror. It is a condition of existence in a competitive, technological society. Whatever it costs on the balance sheets or employment rolls of business, the price is assumed to be justified by the long-term benefits of the process.

The accounting labors that describe this process reveal the close calculation required to meet the needs of the bottom line. Labor, capital, and energy are all juggled to bring as much of the economic product down to profit as possible.

Businesses that fail this ritual of performance are sacrificed, slowly or quickly bled to death by the passage of red ink. Only the strong and valued remain, as the market meant it to be.

No such attention is devoted to the household economy. Its laborers punch no clocks. Experts do not monitor the efficiency of the housewife with stopwatch and clipboard. Mass production does not exist. And whatever the physical reality says, depreciation of capital goods does not exist. As any social worker or lawyer knows, the average family does not even keep a record of its expenditures, let alone a rational and businesslike accounting of its activities. It does not record its profit and loss, and seldom knows (to the delight of insurance salesmen) its net worth, current debts, or current assets. Indeed, a small industry of personal financial counseling has grown on the recognition that the most efficient, hard-nosed, and profit-oriented business executive may have the financial affairs of his household in an absolute mess. The household economy is operated in almost perfect ignorance, a fact attested to by some two hundred thousand cases of personal bankruptcy every year and by estimates that millions of families are constantly insolvent but don't know it.

Perhaps the clearest example of this economic ignorance and myopia is our attitude, as consumers, toward household equipment. Cars are expected to last forever. So are washing machines and dishwashers and everything else used by households to provide necessary services. Alas, we are consumers in the household, not producers; what businesses call depreciation justifiably incurred in the course of daily work, we call waste.

No doubt much of what we call waste is just that—the premature loss of value due to planned obsolescence, short design lives, or just plain poor construction. But that is a separate issue.

The problem of the household is that it has no easily defined bottom line. It is excluded from the ideology of the market. It does not produce to sell; it makes no attempt at a "profit." It merely acquires such goods as will provide services it deems "necessary." The idea that they might be providing a "return on investment" is unthinkable.

The cab driver who regards his taxi as a capital investment used for the production of income is likely to consider his personal automobile as an inconvenience that must be endured. Similarly, the man who operates a laundromat will likely see the regular replacement of his machines as the most efficient route to profits. But he will also resent the inevitable deterioration of the same machines used by his wife at home (even if they did, while in use, provide a return higher than that achieved by IBM). The need to replace household equipment at regular intervals prevents us from acquiring other goods and services we so urgently need.

Household investments produce returns in services rather than cash. We are trained, somewhat justifiably, to recognize only those returns that are in cash, for cash, after all, is the most flexible form of return. It facilitates exchange and trade. A cash return allows us to buy whatever we may want. Or we may just choose to accumulate the cash. A washing machine offers nothing but clean clothes in the here and now. And the ultimate service of a car, whatever its psychic satisfactions, is delivered in miles, not dollars. Household investments, by nature, are discrete and real. They lack entirely the magic of capital. Their returns are rigid, immediate, and non-transferable. The phenomenon of compound growth does not exist in the household, a fact we will consider at greater length when we discuss the future stationary state.

Having seen that there is a household economy, that it controls substantial capital and is accumulating more, and that it employs more labor than any single sector of the market economy, we must now turn to the historic relationship between the household, the market, and collective economies.

1. Fortunately, there has been some change in the literature of home economics. Awakened (and challenged) by the women's liberation movement, the profession has done much soul searching of late, and its journals now regularly contain attempts at formulating a reasonable analytic structure for household economics.

Part Two

The Past and Future
of the Household Economy

The historic forms of economic organization; the rapid rise of
the market; the market's critics; and the awkward path to the
future: a modest utopia

6

The Natural Economy

NATURE HAS AN ECONOMY of its very own. While we do our best to ignore or disguise it, the main purpose of human society is to cope with the very real demands of the natural world. The currency of this natural economy is not the dollar, the deutschmark, or the mystical gold bar. It is the simple calorie. If we don't eat, we die.

Nature's economy is swift and absolute; no society can exist without an ample supply of calories, and the achievements of a society are usually a function of how efficiently it has organized to produce calories. Beggars do not attend operas and the starving do not discern between ratings in the Michelin Guide.

Three categories of organization suffice to describe the economic life of virtually all societies: the household, the collective, and the market. No single form of organization is intrinsically superior to the others, and there are few examples of societies in which any one form entirely supplanted the other two.

Primitive societies are often strongly collective, not because we once were friendlier, more giving, and smarter, as romantics believe, but as a necessary response to the basic adversity of life. In primitive societies, where nature has not provided abundant food, it is absolutely necessary that most energy be devoted to searching for it. Worse, the yield on the search for food is so erratic that regular eating habits can be maintained only by *pooling* the total product of the community. In a sense, early communal societies are organized around the insurance principle: Survival requires that risk be shared.

In such a society, there is little surplus and a minimum of durable goods or capital in any form. Shelter is often communal, because this is the most direct way of minimizing the communities' expenditures on that need. Similarly, clothing is minimal and simple, education is nominal, and unproductive members are seldom tolerated. While such societies can have very complicated structures of authority and decision, as well as peculiarly concentrated distributions of capital, it remains that collective organization is primarily based on the scant margin for survival offered by nature. Production is so perilously low and the returns on individual effort so tortuous and uneven that only communal or collective economic organization can sustain a viable culture and society.

The household is the smallest unit of economic organization. Although it is the polar opposite of the collective economy in size, the household economy serves many of the same purposes. Like the collective economy, it is self-perpetuating and provides a social institution and structure for the redistribution of the economic product of labor. The household, like the collective, is responsible for nurturing and educating the young and sustaining the elderly.

But the household can exist as a major, economically productive unit only in societies where the yield on economic activity is regular enough to insure that the family can be self-sustaining most of the time. Thus, hunting societies are largely collective, while the household is the dominant economic institution in societies devoted to primitive agriculture.

The word economy itself is derived from the Greek "oiconomia," which means "householding" and reflects the organization of a unit to produce for its own use. We are much attached to this idea; to some humanist writers, the agrarian household economy represents a kind of Eden and the industrial revolution is the equivalent of the Fall; having bitten the apple of compounding and capital, man is cast out into the unfriendly world of alienation, anomie, and exploitation.

But the important fact is that the household economy is primarily an agricultural one organized around families and ties of kinship in which each unit produces largely for its own consumption. Thus, the romantic frontier family had little to do with the outside world. It had to be self-sufficient, to sustain itself, make for itself, deliver its young, bury its dead, and operate, for the most part, as though it were alone in the world.

A colonial family of 1770, in a settled area such as Connecticut, made its own shelter, provided its own fuel and light, raised its own food, and slaughtered its own animals. It also made most of its own fabric and clothing. Money was scarce because there was little need of it.

According to economic writer Stuart Chase, such a family produced about 75 per cent of its own needs within the household. Another 20 per cent were obtained in the immediate community, usually by means of exchanging a percentage of the excess produced on the farm. The miller received no coins; he took a portion of the goods he processed. Money was needed only for those things that could not be produced in the area, e.g. glass, kiln-fired brick, tools, and fabrics. These items required a degree of constant demand or relatively large plants and investment.

In colonial America, cash-crop farming was rare, something undertaken with reluctance in order to obtain the few essential goods needed from the outside world. Indeed, large-scale cash-crop farming did not prevail as the model for the agricultural world until the beginning of this century.

Where the household economy is large, the collective economy is likely to be small. This circumstance is not the product of any ideological decision, but simply that at preindustrial productivity levels the surplus of the household economy is too small to support collective services beyond those assuring survival. Many services are best provided on a collective basis (for example, fire and police protection and welfare for the indigent were first organized as volunteer actions). In colonial America, because of a high degree of volunteerism, no levies against the incomes of families were required. As in the wholly collective economy, the function of the collective economy in the era of the agrarian household was largely one of distributing risk.

That the number of services in the collective economy has grown to include health, education, sanitation, highways, transportation, the maintenance of monuments, and the pursuit of interplanetary travel is often cited as an example of how far we have fallen from the ideal of self-sufficiency and the spirit of co-operation and generosity, not to mention the tougher virtues of self-reliance, fortitude, and so forth. No doubt there is some truth in this. It is sadly ironic that our sensitivity to others is in inverse relation to our ever-increasing interdependence. But these issues, which are the usual grist for confrontations between left and right, are not our concern here.

Our concern is the unique properties of the market economy, the organizations that it creates, and its current but failing domination of our economic perception. As we have already noted, both the collective and the household economy are so structured that it is impossible to disentangle the economic aspects of these organizations from their social and biological functions. They are exceedingly natural economies, evident in the operation of wolf packs, bees, and porpoises as well as of human societies.[1]

The market economy, on the other hand, is uniquely human. It has no counterpart in the natural life of other species. This is neither a blessing nor a curse—but it should signal caution.

While the market organizational form is uniquely human, the activities of the market economy overlap and compete with the activities of the household and collective economies.

The difference between the market and other economies lies in the attitude toward risk. Entrepreneurial activity has always been defined by uncertainty and risk. The usual business litany *praises* the risk undertaken by individuals and quasi-individuals (corporations) and argues that the social whole benefits from the risks taken by individuals. Hence, risk takers should be liberally rewarded. "Marketives," to use the terminology of economist Robert Theobald, constantly weigh the perceived risks against the possibilities for gain, and the incentive for this gain leads to better mousetraps, breakthroughs, advances, and other goodies.

The important word here is *gain;* market activity makes the unique assumption that it will result in a competitive benefit to those who indulge in it, that it is possible to accumulate wealth, and that one may, by virtue of that accumulation, change one's relative position in the society. No such attribute can be attached to the household economy. And collective economies are usually organized to *maintain* the relative positions of individuals. Indeed, *most societies are constituted to preserve a given social order.* The organization and power of the collective economy is the apparatus by which that order is preserved.

One might argue, at this juncture, that our government does not fit this mold, since it purports to promote equal opportunity and maximum social mobility. Those on the political left would call this very assertion farcical, trotting out the long history of oppressive governments and class warfare. Those on the right would note that government now operates to give mobility and status without merit. No amount of discussion will resolve these differences.

It *is* abundantly clear, though, that the institutional structure of our society is such that mobility is offered to very few, while those who have achieved power and wealth have every means of government at their disposal to protect them from downward mobility. The tax structure, industrial and agricultural subsidies, corporate perquisites for executives, and the structure of our educational apparatus from the primary schools through the colleges, all serve to preserve and protect the existing social order.

It is only reasonable to expect that this would be the circumstance. While the renunciation of pre-emptive status, power, and privilege is a sacrifice that entitles its maker to become a folk hero, a prince of romance, it remains that we do not seriously expect those with wealth or power to renounce their dividends or positions voluntarily. We are inclined to think well of them if they stoop to becoming governors or senators.

The higher social functions of the collective economy, however, are not at issue here. Rather, we are concerned about distinguishing between the market economy and the household or collective economy. The uniqueness of the market economy lies in its having no natural boundaries, no biological or natural constraints. It is a Faustian instrument, divorced from nature, with no inherent capacity for recognizing self-limiting factors. It is, in fact, ideologically predisposed to ignoring limits and is often proclaimed as the instrument for *abolishing* limits. The market offers freedom. The household and collective do not.

The benefits of this freedom from ritual are all around us. An explosion of invention, innovation, and what is usually called progress must all be credited to the incentives of the market system and the strivings of individuals freed from earlier bonds to the other economies. Until recently, the general consensus has been that these benefits are an unadulterated good and that the growth of the market economy should be encouraged at the expense of the other two. Now there is some doubt.

Environmentalists are particularly critical of the market economy, asserting that it is blind and destructive, incapable of recognizing inherent limits. Yet the environmental movement has failed to win a broad and powerful constituency, not because it has no ideology but because it has been forced to offer all its arguments in the language of the market.

The market economy dominates our expression in both ideology and language. We have no vocabulary for any other form of economic experience and, thus, little perception. Just as the Eskimo has forty words for the varieties of snow because it is vital to his life and experience and only one word to describe flight, we have a multitude of words to describe our experience in the market economy but none to describe our experience in the natural economy.

Yet this natural economy, ultimately, will determine whether we live or die and whether, en route to survival or extinction, we will manage to maintain social and political forms that are compatible with the real and natural world.

At the moment, few of those who administer organizational and technical power can see beyond the language and experience of the market economy, and virtually none of our political leaders can do so. We are now witnessing a collision between this almost universal deficiency and the demands of reality. The natural economy, in the end, will determine the relationship among our three human economies.

Our current task, however, is only to see that there *are* three economies and that they are held in balance by a combination of social belief, natural circumstances, and technology. A change in any of these factors can cause a dramatic shift in the economic institutions that dominate human society. As we shall soon see, it was our capacity for a series of technological advances that brought about an abrupt and radical shift in the balance between the household and market economies, a shift that has now reached maturity and is, of itself, reversing.

1. Reading in economic anthropology can hardly fail to impress the reader with the variety of cultures that have managed very happily without a large market economy. A modern *systemic* view of the natural economy, far larger than the constraints of the market, can be found in Howard T. Odum, *Environment, Power, and Society* (New York: Wiley-Interscience, 1971).

7

The Incredible Rise
of the Market Economy

No EVENT IN HUMAN HISTORY has been more dramatic than the rise of the market economy. While trade has existed for millenniums, the idea of using the market economy as the life blood of society is relatively new, dating back no further than two centuries ago, when *The Wealth of Nations* was published. Nor did the dramatic rise begin with the articulation of the idea; the market economy didn't have a complete grip on the institutions of Western culture until the 1830s, the decade identified as the economic "take-off point"[1] for English and American society.

Karl Polanyi likened the growth of the market economy to that of a virus, a germ that multiplied so quickly that it destroyed centuries of social institutions before anyone grasped its true meaning. We had, he thought, subordinated "the substance of society . . . to the laws of the market," an event that would result "in the demolition of society."[2]

We now live in a market-dominated (and largely demolished) society. Whatever protests some make about the growth of government, etc., our underlying rules of action and assumptions are economic; the structure provided by geographic monarchies has absolutely disintegrated, religion is in great disrepair and largely moribund, and the family has been threatened and reduced. We are, in fact, almost incapable of imagining any social arrangements other than those dominated by the rules of the market-place. We have become institutional chauvinists.

There are some powerful reasons for this bias. Even if we can escape the constraints of our immediate experience and wax philosophical about the more distant past, it remains that we, our parents, grandparents, and great-grandparents are the products of the most profound period of economic growth ever seen. It is difficult to see this as anything less than final and absolute.

In less than a hundred and fifty years, we have moved from a society in which the measure of effort and energy was the capacity of a single man or farm animal to one in which each worker controls the energy equivalent of a small army. Where, a hundred and fifty years ago, resources were abundant and industry was scarce, we now face problems of where to sweep our mounting industrial output and where to obtain the resources for further expansion. In less than two centuries, the relation between the market economy and the traditional household/collective economy has completely reversed. Two hundred years ago, the market was of little importance to anyone. Now the market is predominant, to the virtual exclusion of the original and more natural economies.

The illustration below presents the relative dispositions of the three economies at different historic periods. In primitive societies, as we have already noted, there is virtually no market economy. Much of the work is done collectively and co-operatively (fishing, preparing for crops, taking in crops, hunting, etc.). How the economic product is distributed is a matter decided by the structure of the social order.

The mercantile economies of the seventeenth and eighteenth centuries witnessed a development of the household economy that is difficult to classify. "Cottage industry" was precisely that; households organized to produce goods at home . . . but for the market. Merchants arranged for materials, contracted with households, and found buyers for cloth. The work was irregular, overhead was virtually nonexistent, and nominal capital was required. Household workers didn't depend on their cash products for sustenance but worked small pieces of land for their food—land that was usually owned by the nobility. The great mass of people were strongly attached to an established social structure and had

FIGURE 13

The Changing Dominance in the Economic Triad

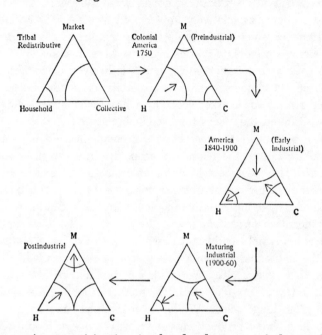

only a minor participation in the development of the market-place.

Colonial America is unique in that it combined, by historical accident, mobile labor and free land at precisely the time when it could most beneficially be organized around a household economy. Our ideals of self-sufficiency and independence throve in this environment; we were a frontier nation built on the energy and product of independent households.

The single limitation of the household economy is that it must, by definition, remain simple, generalized, and uncomplicated. It must produce small quantities of many things. We can eat only so many potatoes and carrots, wear only so many shirts, burn only so many candles, sit in only so many chairs, sleep in only so many beds. To produce for personal use is to be committed to unique, singular production. Under such circumstances, economies of scale are impossible. Nor is it possible to make use of much in the way of capital equipment or to harness large sources of energy to mechanize production. Note that we are talking about producing goods rather than services. As long as our attention is focused on producing goods, we must regard the household economy as relatively limited and inefficient. It is difficult and time-consuming to make a candle or a bar of soap at home, let alone contemplate fabricating a washing machine.

A society that is starved for goods is likely to concentrate its best efforts on overcoming that scarcity of goods. Hence the rapid rise of the market economy when technological developments offered the means for overcoming scarcity.

The growth of the market was accompanied by an equally rapid attrition of the household economy. In nineteenth-century America the movement of one man from the household to the market economy meant an enormous increase in output; between 1860 and 1900, industrial employment tripled but industrial *output* increased *fifteenfold*.

The industrial trend has continued since 1900, but the attrition of the household economy has peaked and subsided. Where once there was a clear abandoning of production in the household in favor of production in the market economy, the relationship is no longer clear. While the marketplace makes dramatic assaults on home production in some areas (such as food preparation) and continues to lure workers into the labor market, households are making somewhat less dramatic inroads on the usual preserves of the marketplace, particularly in the area of services.

The market and the household have now reached an unhappy standoff, marked by the growth of consumerism. The household is beginning now to regain lost ground. Meanwhile the collective economy has also enjoyed very rapid growth, usually at the expense of the marketplace but sometimes at the expense of the household.

After nearly two centuries of violent growth, the market economy is reaching maturity. The next stage of development will be the re-emergence of the household economy. This should not be interpreted as a regressive step. The household economy of the future should not be confused with the household economy of the past. We are not about to return to the agrarian past or re-enter the sylvan age of yore. Life will not be filled with meadows and sheep, butter churns, and homespun; we will see a *new* household economy.

The growth of the market economy has created the conditions necessary to make the household, once more, a viable economic institution whose visibility will increase as the market economy matures and declines, the victim of its own success.

The household has not been a competitive economic institution since the industrial revolution. That transformation removed men from the household and sent them looking for work in the marketplace. It initiated a more complicated and indirect production process, in which a family no longer worked directly for itself but sold its labor in exchange for cash.

One of the indirect effects of this change was to leave women in charge of an institution that no longer served a clear and overtly valued economic purpose. The household became a "cost center" rather than a "profit center," and all those associated with it, mainly women, lost status, power, and self-esteem.* This is not a small, side effect. It has brought with it, over nearly a century, an ever-mounting conflict between the sexes that is now seen as direct competition for jobs, salaries, and the power and self-esteem attached to "productive" work. Fortunately, the re-emergence of the household as an economic institution may end the competition engendered by the dominance of the marketplace.

Our capacity to see and accept this change—the re-emergence of the household—is constrained by nothing more than our attachment to the marketplace and our even greater attachment to the notion that the marketplace represents the last step in the economic development of the human race.

In fact, the market is, again, only one of three economic forms and (like most viruses, perhaps) it is self-limiting. The market economy is not the end of economic development; it is only a stage—and one that has always had a number of harsh critics.

Some of these critics and their conceptions of alternative futures are the subject of the next chapter: Their thoughts and

---

* Significantly, women are most often employed in "cost," or overhead, centers rather than in production, or "profit," centers; even excluding the predominance of women in teaching, nursing, etc., women in corporations often have jobs in public relations, administration of personnel, etc.

the accelerating loss of public confidence in business give us our first inkling of the self-limiting nature of the market economy and how it must compete with the household.

1. Walt Rostow identifies the "take-off point" for a developing society as that junction in history where the annual rate of capital formation exceeds the annual rate of population growth, thus beginning the process of compounding that brings on dramatic increases in per-capita income.

2. Karl Polanyi, *The Great Transformation* (Boston: Beacon Press, 1957), pp. 71–73.

8

Critics of the Market, Defenders of the Household

No SOCIAL INSTITUTION has suffered more strain over the past two centuries than the household. Once the fundamental building block for agrarian society, the family was responsible not only for transferring the values, ideals, and expectations of the society from one generation to the next but also for sustaining those too young or too old to fend for themselves.[1] The extended family, in which three generations lived under one roof along with this or that maiden aunt or uncle, has been reduced to the nuclear family of parents and children. Now even this small group is recognized as a volatile, rather temporary combination. Clergymen ruminate at length on its decline, and the media voice the public concern by capturing the disintegration of an American family on Public Television. Rhetorically, we ask if the Louds represent us all.

Yet, for all its current liabilities and whatever jeopardy sociologists claim for it as an institution, the household and the family are part of a long tradition of independence and strength that has been tragically clouded by the development of industrial society. The brief history of those who were advocates of the household and thus, perforce, critics of the market, is the subject of this chapter.

Marxists blame the apparent decline of the family on capitalism, claiming that monopoly capitalism, in its endless search for larger markets, sees the extended family as an impediment to

multiple sales of dishwashers, cars, and TV sets; if only one item
is likely to be sold per family, the reasoning goes, then the interests of capitalism dictate that we must have more and therefore smaller families. Moreover, the same diabolical machine that
needs ever more consumers to absorb its production also requires mobile workers to flow without ties from one company to
another. The social and economic functions of the family, according to this line of thought, must be sacrificed in the interest of an
efficient economic system. Thus, the market economy, together
with the rapacity of capitalism, is seen as the primary force in
the disintegration of traditional society.

Capitalists paint a curiously similar picture of the evils of socialism and communism. The good, Christian capitalist regales us
with tales of families being broken up to serve the needs of collective agriculture or of state child care as an instrument for at-
tacking motherhood and undermining the healthy psychological
development of children. The usual scenario, as presented in
countless articles in the 1950s, offers that once the child has been
taken from the influence of his parents he can be molded to appropriate subservient form by the state. Inevitably, this is seen
as a crushing human tragedy, a situation that contrasts sharply
with the individual freedom and personal development fostered
by the American family in our free-enterprise system.

In short, each economic system claims that the other is responsible for the demise of the family.[2] What happened, in fact, is
that large-scale industrialization outstripped the economic productivity of the household so that it became, in the scramble for
affluence, an institution with no credible economic function under
either system. Thus, the family and household declined from the
middle of the nineteenth century to the present.

Happily, singular dedication to any ideal is doomed to failure.
Now, after a full two centuries in which the market economy was
in the ascendant and the household existed in the cold shadow
of economic progress, we are witnessing the restoration of the
household economy. This event is occurring because the household has become, once again, a competitive, viable *economic*
entity as the marketplace has matured. Happily, we can note
that the household economy has *always* been the institutional
mainstay for those who sought a democratic, egalitarian society.

Among the Founding Fathers, Thomas Jefferson was attached

far more to the household economy than he was to the market-place. The ideal of Jeffersonian democracy was an agrarian state with a wide distribution of property. Ownership of property and the security it provided, combined with an absolute minimum of government, were the keys to a nation that could be run sanely with maximum benefit for all. With land of his own, a man could be independent; he was not subject to the coercion of his employer. As long as land was the only significant asset and could be acquired easily, there was little chance that society would become harshly stratified or that power would fall into the hands of a few. These are the roots of Populism.

But Jefferson's dream was doomed from the start. Early on, his ideals were tainted. The Louisiana Purchase itself, while it provided land to fuel the dream of homesteading, also served to launch the acquisitive dreams of Manifest Destiny. Inevitably, the struggle for property became competitive. The dream of a simple, good nation composed of secure yeoman citizens, each the lord of his own productive property, ended before it could begin.

Even if such a society could have been established, it could not have survived more than half a century before technology would have negated its foundation; by 1840 the industrial revolution was under way, and the possession of land was no longer the primary measure of economic power. The household economy could not compete with the marketplace. By 1900 the last frontiers were closed, homesteading had become an institution of the past, and the United States was fully committed to becoming the world's largest industrial power.

All this did not occur without protest. Urban America had doubts about itself. Idealists disdained the crass and corrupting features of the city. Arcadian dreams abounded, as did talk of "getting back to the land" and pilgrimages "back to nature."[3] Intellectuals asked disturbing questions about the development of the market economy and the enormous concentrations of industrial power.

The marketplace was viewed with much distrust, and it became safe to say, in general, that urban, market-oriented life was as intrinsically evil as rural, household-oriented life was intrinsically good. Much attention was devoted to the effects of environment on the human character. Since people were continuously being displaced from the land and accumulating in the big (and bad) cities, guilt was as rampant as economic opportunity.

The panic and depression of 1907 did much to relieve the guilt and reawakened discussions of returning to the land. One writer, Bolton Hall, wrote two popular books, *Three Acres and Liberty* (1907) and *A Little Land and a Living* (1908), extolling the virtues of farming on small pieces of land. Committees were formed to put the unemployed to work on vacant city lots,* and charitable organizations offered to set up entire families on farm homesteads if the family would leave the city. Both books abound with figures indicating that a single acre of land, carefully cultivated, could feed and provide for an entire family. Hall's thesis was that virtually anyone could make a living by growing vegetables and that those who could not obtain employment otherwise would be well advised to take up farming.

Interest in such plans tends to be in inverse relation to the health of the market economy. When business is good, only the most dedicated will forge their beliefs into action and leave the marketplace. When business is bad, there is much less to lose.

The most prolific advocate of the household economy has to be Ralph Borsodi; virtually unread today,[4] his books developed the reasons for "dropping out" of the marketplace and pursuing a life in the household economy.

Beginning in 1923, with *National Advertising vs. Prosperity,* Borsodi held that the growth of national advertising did much for the manufacturer and nothing for the consumer; in the same book, he postulated that the savings achieved in mass production were lost in the rising costs of distribution, an idea he developed more fully in 1927 with the publication of *The Distribution Age.*

Here Borsodi anticipated Ralph Nader by forty years. It is impossible to read his work without concluding that he may have been the grandfather of consumerism. "When we come to the practices which today prevail," he wrote, "in buying for ultimate consumption, we find that less than one hundred years of divorce between production and consumption has almost entirely destroyed the consumer's capacity for measuring quality."[5]

And later: "With the manufacturer no longer forced to meet the critical judgment of the consumer, it is perfectly natural for

* An idea that has been revived and modified by an English counterculture group called The Street Farmers.

the manufacturer to develop methods of marketing which will yield him the highest net profit, regardless of the intrinsic value of his product."[6] In such statements lay the genesis of truth-in-lending laws and all the consumer advocacy martialed by Betty Furness and Virginia Knauer.

By 1929, Borsodi's complaints had become something of an ideology. *This Ugly Civilization* announced to an enthusiastic audience that "the factory system" was a temporary artifact of the steam engine. Electricity meant that production could be returned to the home, where it belonged. In example after example, Borsodi showed that the household economy can compete with the marketplace in the production of food, shelter, fuel, clothing, etc. At no time, however, did he argue that the marketplace should be avoided altogether. Rather, he stated that it is more *sane* to live in an inexpensive house in the country (where the family can provide for much of its own needs) than it is to live in an expensive city apartment while being committed to specialized employment that is unstable and insecure.

Few of our newspapers and magazines have been without some account of a family that has come to the same conclusion in recent years. At least one book, Irving Price's *Buying Country Land,* has become a best seller by catering to thoughts of "returning to the land." Similarly, Helen and Scott Nearing's books, *Living the Good Life* and *Maple Sugaring in Vermont* (both accounts of creating a non-money, household economy), have been brought out in paperback to meet popular demand.

Borsodi's dream was to have an economy in which the household provided the means of subsistence while intermittent participation in the marketplace provided luxuries. The only problem is that the present system doesn't work that way: Employment, by and large, is all or none. One is available forty hours a week or one cannot take the job. Intermittent employment is something to be avoided, for it means layoffs and unproductive time, as many carpenters, auto workers, and other tradesmen can testify.

The inflexibility of employment was not a problem for Borsodi and his ideas through the thirties. He found a ready audience among the unemployed. He founded the School for Living, in Suffern, New York, where household arts were taught. Still functioning today, it might be considered a kind of "halfway house" for urban families in their exodus to the country. During the depths of the depression, Borsodi established an experimental community in Ohio; its object, similar to those homesteads established by the followers of Bolton Hall, was to take the unemployed off welfare at the cost of investing in the basic tools of a farm. Each family was provided with three acres and a modest home; co-operative cottage industries were initiated to provide other goods and services difficult for the single household to produce.

There isn't a single commune in America today that does not owe an unrecognized debt to Ralph Borsodi; considering the burgeoning interest in returning to the land—from members of the counterculture to tired computer salesmen—Borsodi's continued and almost total obscurity† is amazing. Part of the reason for his obscurity lies in the peculiarity of his subject. One must suppress a desire to ridicule comparisons of the manufacturing might of General Motors with that of the rural household; moreover, Borsodi seldom documented his case quantitatively, letting it rest on assertions and requiring, finally, that the reader make a leap of faith. Such leaps are best made from sinking ships. As troubled as the U.S. economy was and is, it is still generally conceded to be better than most alternatives.

Borsodi's significance, however, extends beyond consumerism and the household. He was the last theorist to advocate agrarian living as a general way of life. Those who followed him have forsaken direct advocacy of the household farm, and beginning with Paul Goodman, have stated their case on the macroeconomic scale.

If the restoration of the household economy lacked universal appeal even in the thirties, few observers could escape recognizing the absurdity of our economic arrangements. Writing in 1934, as millions of men were unemployed and thousands of factories stood idle, Stuart Chase identified a fundamental issue that would preoccupy socioeconomic thought for the next four decades. "Presently," he wrote, "the Western world will split between the Scarcity men and the Abundance men; between those who act in one culture and think in another, and those who think

† As this is written, he is still alive at age ninety, living in Exeter, New Hampshire, and has recently invented an alternative currency that is inflation-proof.

as they act. . . . It is not money which makes the mare go; it is oats."[7] Just as the instability of the economic machine led some to want to abandon it, others found the juxtaposition of poverty, hunger, and deprivation with the acknowledged abundance of machinery, materials, and able-bodied men absurd. Thus began the search for some social arrangement that combined the productivity of industry with the assumed stability of the household. *Communitas* is the best-known product of this search.

In *Communitas* (1947), Percival and Paul Goodman wrote: "Starting from the human goods of subsistence and luxury, the increment of profit was reinvested in capital goods in order to earn more profits, to win for the enterprisers more luxury and power; this is still human motivation. But in recent decades the result has been that the center of economic concern has gradually shifted from either providing goods for the consumer or gaining wealth for the enterpriser, to keeping the capital machines at work and running at full capacity; for the social arrangements have become so complicated that, unless the machines are running at nearly full capacity, all wealth and subsistence are jeopardized, investment is withdrawn, men are unemployed. That is, when the system depends on all the machines running, unless *every* kind of goods is produced and sold, it is also impossible to produce bread. . . . Full employment is the device by which we flourish; and so the old curse of Adam, that he must work in order to live, now becomes a goal to be struggled for, just because we have the means to produce a surplus, cause of all our woes."[8] Little has changed since 1947.

Rather than organize production around the household, as Borsodi planned, Goodman concluded that the existing economy should be divided between the "subsistence share" and the rest, which was that enormous aggregation of activities that served the "desire for variety, convenience, luxury, emulation, power, and wealth." Rather than reorganize the means of production, he proposed a change in accounting. Subsistence would be "free"; it would no longer be part of the market economy.

At any previous time, such a proposal would have been ridiculous. Most human labor *was* devoted to subsistence. If it requires the constant labor of every member of the society merely to keep body and soul together, subsistence cannot be "free." But in an economy in which the subsistence fraction is an ever-diminishing part of the economic whole, it becomes absurd to base the operation of the entire apparatus on the assumption of basic scarcity. The abundance of goods requires that subsistence be removed from the economy; it is no longer an *economic* subject but a social one. "Subsistence is not something to profit by, to invest in, to buy or sell."[9]

Goodman estimated that only one seventh of all the labor then employed in the United States was involved in the production of subsistence goods. The total, he believed, might be as small as a tenth and could be made significantly smaller if production were truly arranged to provide subsistence goods as he envisioned them. When he re-estimated for a new edition of the book, in 1960, he felt comfortable with the thought that only *one tenth of all labor* was required for subsistence goods. Since then, productivity has increased by about 40 per cent, indicating that the subsistence economy could be supported by about *one fourteenth* of the work force.

At first glance, these estimates seem rather strange and unbelievable. But we need only consider agriculture to see the enormous productivity of our system. Farm employment dropped by almost 50 per cent between 1950 and 1970. Total population, during the same period, increased by more than 50 million. It now requires the labor of some 3.6 million people on farms to produce all our food. Another 1.6 million are employed in "food manufacturing" and an additional 1.6 million in retail stores. All in all, some 7 million workers produce the food for 210 million Americans.

By no stretch of the imagination could American eating habits be called a "subsistence diet"; the average adult is overweight and must constantly avoid the mountains of salted, processed, oiled, low-cholesterol calories shoved at him every day. Subsistence does not include the business lunch, the maraschino cherry, or the garlic-and-barbecue-flavored oyster cracker.

The labor of one person now provides the food for thirty. Another way of stating the same relationship is that about *two and a half years of labor could produce enough food for a lifetime of eating.* A subsistence diet would require much less. Similarly, about two years of labor[10] will produce lifetime shelter for four persons, indicating that a half year of labor would entitle someone to lifetime housing exclusive of operating costs. Again, these are not "subsistence" ratios but apply to present housing costs in all but the most expensive urban areas.

Three years of labor, then, will provide food and basic shelter for life. Other ratios can be created at will; e.g., twenty years of education can be had for one year of labor if the average class size is twenty students, etc. Whatever we finally decide to include in the subsistence economy, *the ultimate arrangement requires that the individual exchange a certain amount of time for the guarantee of a lifetime subsistence.* In essence, Goodman advocated that we exchange the subtle, or often fierce, hunger-directed coercion of a money economy with all its competition, anxiety over maintaining employment, "progress," etc., for a limited amount of very clearly defined, explicit coercion. After a period of contractual labor, the individual would be free from the demands and uncertainties of the money economy and guaranteed subsistence for life. Not a bad deal at all. Using Goodman's one-fourteenth estimate, such a "contract" would require two or three years of contractual labor.

As a proposal, the idea might take form as a kind of national service corps which enlisted the service of every citizen for two or three years beginning at, say, age eighteen. This public army would do the work necessary to provide subsistence for the entire population, and diminish at once the incarceration of some (e.g., minority labor on farms) in employment that does not pay a living wage.

Some, no doubt, would picture such an arrangement as a monstrosity, thinking that after completing this contractual work to achieve subsistence, many people would retire to enjoy decades of indolence and sloth. But, in fact, such an arrangement would give people a more open choice between the non-money economy and the money economy. Those who sought conventional things would be free to pursue them; others would be free to do what *they* pleased. They would have "paid their dues." Having broken the relationship between the money economy and physical survival, the household economy might achieve cognitive parity with the marketplace. It would be recognized as a satisfactory alternative. Millions of women who now work without pay in and out of the home might no longer feel so pressed about getting a paying job and the self-respect believed to be included in the weekly pay envelope. Having achieved subsistence, people would be free to choose between the generalized work of the household economy and the specialized work of the marketplace.

The social benefits of such a change would be enormous. Exclusion from the money economy by way of retirement often means a painful loss of self-respect for people who have worked all their lives. The abrupt and arbitrary change in a person's status from productive citizen to "has been" is a strain with which an ever-growing portion of the population must live as the nation ages and retirements come earlier than ever before.

Many would choose household production, because it offers everything that is lacking in marketplace production: *Fortune, Psychology Today, Newsweek, Time, U.S. News & World Report,* the *Atlantic Monthly,* and a horde of other magazines have all carried articles about "blue-collar blues." There is no end to discussions of the horrors of GM's Lordstown plant. Other articles suggest that collar color is not a barrier to worker depression and boredom; the happiness of clerks, middle managers, and embattled corporate presidents has all been subjected to examination.

Worker alienation and the import of production-line horrors can be exaggerated, of course. When reading accounts of such misery, it pays to remember that only one worker in twenty is a slave to the mass-production line. Yet, in the end, whatever discount we apply to the protests of the socially concerned, we must agree that production is organized for efficiency in output, not for worker pleasure. As Daniel Bell noted in *Work and Its Discontents,* "the engineer conceives of efficiency in technological terms alone." Thus the modern factory is efficient for everything but the mental health and well-being of the worker.

Organizing the marketplace for efficiency imposes external costs on the worker. These costs are psychic as well as economic. Given a choice, the workers might avoid marketplace work wherever these externalities are too oppressive. We might see entirely new patterns of production. In a different economic environment, there is no way of estimating how large the household economy might grow or what relationship it might finally bear to the marketplace.

Imagine, for instance, how it would feel to know, at age twenty-three or twenty-four, that you have done the two or three

years of national service and are now free—with the sure knowledge that you will never be hungry. Some might argue for an
end to all "progress," believing in the fundamental laziness of
people, but I find it much easier to imagine a forcefully innova-
tive, vibrant society, because the last economic chains would
have been removed.

Free Men and Free Markets (1965) is economist Robert
Theobald's contribution to the reformation of our economic relations. His proposal of a guaranteed income is a mechanism for
creating Goodman's split economy. A guaranteed income, after
all, is a guaranteed subsistence. Again, the right to live is removed from the economic realm; it becomes a social function, an
inherent part of our institutional arrangements.

Like Goodman, Theobald uses the stick of depression and unemployment as well as the carrot of utopia to win his audience.
Abundance, he argues, creates problems entirely different from
scarcity. Our insistence on using policies appropriate for scarcity
in an environment of abundance can lead to nothing but disaster.

Given a guaranteed income, Theobald assumes that people
will organize differently to produce goods above and beyond
subsistence. "Marketives," the traditional organizations of production, will be complemented with "consentives," organizations whose primary goals cannot be defined on a balance sheet
or an income statement. Informal, with no need to seek constant
expansion; subject to no hierarchy of power and ownership—
the inevitable accompaniments for the marketive—the consen-
tive could produce all the goods and services that are now "too
costly" or "unprofitable." Production would no longer answer to
the bottom line.

There would, of course, be some problems associated with such
an economy. As things are now, distasteful jobs are generally accompanied by low wages, while attractive jobs often have
equally attractive wages. Given a guaranteed income for all, this
condition would not survive.

The wages of those who clean toilets in Greyhound bus stations
might then compare favorably with those of vice-presidents at
International Telephone. Jobs that were intrinsically unpleasant
would require higher wages, because the supply of people who
would be willing to take them would diminish. Absolutely no
one could get household help, alas, and all the meek who wait on

tables, collect garbage, or distribute hand towels in expensive hotel washrooms would negotiate for their just deserts in *this* world rather than the next. You can bet, in the words of Guy Grand (*The Magic Christian*), that it would "cost a pretty penny to get out of that one."

To some, no doubt, this is a prediction of disaster. Obviously, no recognizable aristocracy of wealth, power, or ability could exist under such arrangements. Yet it makes great sense also, for as long as unpleasant work is poorly paid, there is little incentive to eliminate it. As things are now, we often eliminate those forms of employment which are pleasurable or give pleasure. We displace the higher forms of craftsmanship and art because of the harsh demands of economics, while thousands of lives are committed to the drudgery of washing hospital floors and hawking newspapers. Such is the logic of our economics.

It is important, at this juncture, that we recognize our hidden biases and beliefs. While many talk about the need to have a free, egalitarian, and democratic society, few believe deeply. Most are content to believe that a few, inevitably, will exercise power over others and that freedom consists in having this power exercised in benign forms.

We believe intensely, for instance, in modern management, in the efficacy of installing a few in positions where their decisions are absolute and must be followed by many others. Such sacrifices, we believe, must be made in the name of efficiency. And lest we forget, we would not be "where we are today" without efficiency. Discussion tends to be lost in a morass of superstition: There is a natural aristocracy; inevitably, a few will have much and many will have little. Without leaders and decision makers (oh, never forget the decision makers!) we would be starving, broke, and unemployed, and the portable steam iron and electric toothbrush would never have been invented, let alone mass-marketed.

So it is that those who wish to rise in the hierarchy of social power send their sons to Harvard Business School, and large corporations identify the man with a destiny by having him attend special seminars in decision making and risk taking at M.I.T.'s Sloan School or Stanford's Business School. The only possible social structure, it would be offered, is the pyramid. Without it, all social thought would disappear because we could not

afford it. Special power, in other words, is justified by its productivity. In the end, we choose not to bite the hand that feeds us.

It would be difficult to overrate the strength of this managerial
myth. It is responsible, in part, for the embarrassment we feel at
comparing the operation of the household economy with that of
General Motors and for the disdain offered to small businesses
and a wide variety of volunteer organizations that fail to conform
to our belief in the productivity of concentrated power. This belief, overt and covert, in all its forms, is the largest single impediment to a restructuring of our economic and social life.

Fortunately, evidence is accumulating that "power is productive" is a myth, and that large hierarchic organizations have no
monopoly on efficiency. Industrial economist Seymour Melman
investigated the productivity and profitability of a variety of
comparable manufacturing firms in Israel. Some were traditionally managed firms, with a strict hierarchy of power and decision
making, while others were co-operative.

The conventional wisdom demands that the productivity of
the managed enterprise be higher and that in the course of time
the co-operative enterprise be superseded by the more efficient
form. Melman found, however, that the co-operatively managed
firms were more efficient, more productive, and more profitable.
And all without giving the boss a special parking spot.

"The people working in the kibbutz enterprise," he found, "are
motivated to feel needed and wanted within the context of the
total community. Such feelings, among people who share in a
common task, are powerful motivating forces for individuals to
give their best in the performance of shared responsibility. The
participation, voluntary cooperation, and mutual control: these
are democratic communities that operate internally without
coercion (no courts, no police, no jails), and without money."[11]

Melman concludes by noting that most of our social observers
offer us a choice between a "value oriented" society and one that
is "technologically determined." "The assumption is," he writes,
"that the latter means individual incentives, inequality, social
stratification, and elite rule in the name of technological advance
and efficiency. Value oriented is taken to mean egalitarianism,
humanism—meaning, necessarily, anti-technology." Between the
lines, we are to read that we have a choice between the technology that brings us abundance and the idealistic freedom that

guarantees our future want. In the conventional view, abundance and freedom are considered mutually exclusive.

In fact, this isn't so. Nor is it necessary to travel as far as Israel or to read articles in the *Journal of the Union of Radical Political Economists* to find support for the notion that co-operative enterprises are often more efficient than enterprises guided by authority. Testimony has been sold monthly through no less stolid an organization than The Fortune Book Club in the form of *The Human Side of Enterprise,* a book by management professor Douglass McGregor. Without recourse to ideological ground, McGregor offers "Theory Y" to replace authoritarian management "Theory X." Because the modern organization has limited means of coercion, McGregor argues, authority has a very limited value in management. Instead, managers must rely on co-operation and persuasion and on their capacity to enlist the desire of the individual to express himself through the goals of the organization.

Such reasoning is far short of heresy. McGregor and "Theory Y" are not alone in the wilderness. What is lacking in public consciousness—or even in the literature of management—is recognition that the decline of authority is a consequence of far larger events than faulty child rearing, permissive schools, the power of the local union, and the other popular hobgoblins of disorder. The larger fact is that the economic drive which justified (or at least sustained) the hierarchic structure of industrial society has matured. As a result, all that would support the continued existence of powerful hierarchies, from the organizations within the market economy to the market economy itself, is disintegrating. The day of large organizations and small elites is at an end.

To many, this notion may seem at odds with the obvious evidence of current experience. We see on all sides the ineffectiveness of individuals and the conflicts between large blocs of power. Public and private labor are well organized. The nation's largest corporations regularly flex their muscles, arousing displays of conspicuous opposition from the nation's regulatory agencies, and the general outcome for most of us is a constant sense that we are powerless in a world of giants.

This is not an illusion. We are far more conscious of our dependence on the market economy than we are of our household power. But, as we have shown in earlier chapters, the power and importance of the household economy is rising, while that of the market is decreasing. The critical event that stands before American society is whether or not we can resist a coalescence of market organizations and collective power to form an oligarchy of feudal capitalism. This pessimistic vision enjoys some popularity.[12] Worse, the events of the past decade offer little evidence to support a more positive view.

Yet it remains that the real but little-recognized forces discussed in this book are constantly at work to increase the power of the household and decrease the power of the market economy. We must not forget that it was the rise of the market economy and of the industrial society, that led to the eclipse of the household and the ideals of Jeffersonian democracy. Jefferson's idea of an egalitarian society was forced to live in an institutional and economic vacuum: There has been precious little in the developing structure of industrial society to support our historic egalitarian ideals.

As the household economy grows and the market economy matures, this will no longer be the case. The circumstances that supported Jefferson's dreams are returning, albeit modified by two centuries of technological advance.

It would be a pleasure, here, to announce that the household economy will rise Phoenix-like from the ashes of the agrarian economy and that we will, at any moment, witness a "household revolution."

But revolutions depend on a homogeneous and monomaniacal vision. The real world is not like that. It is heterogeneous beyond comprehension. What is happening is a change in economic *equilibrium,* almost invisible, a change that has already reversed the ascendancy of the market economy and now limits the size of new enterprises.‡ Ultimately, it will result in the decline of money. The household economy, as it gains economic strength and recognition, will become the driving institutional force behind a truly democratic society.

One sign that this revolution is occurring, beyond both the economic facts presented in earlier chapters and the rising volume of criticism, is the recent and powerful changes in public attitude toward the business community in particular and the market economy in general. Nationalization, unthinkable once, is pro-

‡ The size of new enterprises in relation to economic growth is discussed in Chapter 18.

posed regularly for problem industries. Economist Kenneth Galbraith makes a case for nationalizing the defense industries in the New York *Times Magazine;* ecologist Barry Commoner argues for nationalizing the railroads in *Harper's*. The nationalization of medicine is an almost inescapable subject, particularly among those who have paid recent hospital bills.

We no longer trust the nation's businesses to be fair and honest, and we no longer have much faith in the market economy or the price system. Inflation, controls, and government regulation have done more to create new radicals and dissenters than decades of proselytizing true believers.

It is, in fact, not possible to have experienced the sixties without a palpable sense that the market economy is no longer an object of reverence, that the public feeling against business runs higher than a distaste for Babbitts or embarrassment at the overzealous pursuit of profits. The *depth* of the turn in public sentiment is amazing. A Harris survey revealed that public confidence in big business slipped dramatically between 1966 and 1971. If there is any consolation for business leaders, it is that public confidence in just about *everything* disappeared in the same period.

FIGURE 14a

The Decline of Public Confidence

	Per Cent of Confidence	
	1966	*1971*
Banks, Financial Institutions	67%	36%
Big Companies	55	27
Local Retail Stores	48	24
Scientific Community	56	32
Mental Health, Psychiatry	51	35
Medicine	72	61
Education	61	37
Organized Religion	41	27
The Military	62	27
Congress	42	10
Executive Branch of Government	41	23
Supreme Court	51	23
The Press	29	18
Advertising	21	13
Television	25	22

Source: *Business Week,* June 17, 1972: Harris survey, copyright Chicago *Tribune.*

A majority or near majority now favor the breakup of large companies, controls on corporate profits, and government control of prices. Moreover, it is generally believed that the consumer receives more value for his money from regulated industries.

FIGURE 14b

Values offered Consumers

	Most Value	Least Value
Electricity	62%	5%
Telephone Service	50	7
Life Insurance	23	12
Major Appliances	21	7
Grocery Products	16	38
Automobiles	13	19
Gasoline	11	19
Home Furnishings	9	15
Prescription Drugs	8	29
Automobile Insurance	8	27
Cosmetics, Toiletries	2	31

Source: *Business Week*, June 17, 1972, Opinion Research Corporation.

All this augurs a dark and embattled future for business in America. The public no longer believes that the answer to its hopes and problems lies in business enterprise and the marketplace. If one is to believe these foreboding surveys, the only thing that prevents a wholesale shift toward the collective economy is that most people have little confidence in *that* either. Which leaves us with the household.

There are reasons far more compelling than a tradition of critics and present discontent for the fall of the market economy. The market, as we shall soon see, is incompatible with the stability necessary for our survival.

It is unlikely, however, that this will ever be a general and agreed conclusion invested with sufficient public power to change our institutions. While political leaders offer new social and economic agendas, change still comes into the world ad hoc, piecemeal, and tortured, and our happy future, if we reach it at all, is likely to be the product of a nearly endless series of accidents, crises, and terrifying problems. After ten years of government by crises, we cannot expect less. The possible nature of these crises and how they lead, inevitably, toward the household economy and the stationary state are our next subject.

1. As a vehicle for economic transfer payments, the vital importance of the family cannot be overestimated. Family transfer payments *dwarf* the explicit payments made by the federal government via Social Security, etc. Education alone, for instance, involves the transfer of at least $40 billion a year from parents to children. For further comment, read Kenneth Boulding, "The Household as Achilles Heel," in *The Journal of Consumer Affairs,* winter 1972.

2. Unhappily, the assault on the family does not end with the political dimension. Now, for every conventional psychologist who offers mastery of the Oedipal problem as the crucial experience in forming the human personality, there are radical psychologists who offer that the family is a psychological concentration camp, a kind of unique horror in which malice and suffering inevitably prevail and which serves to prepare us for the (even greater) social horrors to be perpetrated by the institutions of government.

Just as Polanyi saw the development of the marketplace as a kind of virus that destroyed the necessary institutions of social relationships, the radical psychologist sees the pursuit of individual destiny as something that cannot be constrained by the "givens" of the family. The pursuit of either or both leads us to anarchism, to complete disintegration of all social institutions, and to a world without givens, or constraints of any kind. It leads us, in short, to a kind of vacuum, to an atomism in which an individual, without benefit of past or future, must posit his own identity and validate his own experience. Few can confront this prospect with anything but anxiety.

We find ourselves, rather suddenly, at a peculiar philosophical intersection. Historically, debates over the prominence of the household or marketplace economy have been grounded in the pursuit of individual freedom, and our intersection reveals itself to be a kind of Möbius strip, in which one side, pursued far enough, inevitably becomes the other. Those who argue for the marketplace and the individual freedom it provides seldom see that the aggregations of economic power it creates negate the freedom sought; in becoming the singular, all-powerful force in our experience, it robs us of our freedom in the very act of expanding the range of economic choices. Similarly, the pursuit of freedom from familial structures ends in a kind of nihilistic vacuum, the kind filled with existential despair, blessed with dubious significance.

3. See Peter J. Schmitt, *Back to Nature—The Arcadian Myth in Urban America* (New York: Oxford University Press, 1969).

4. In researching this book I found that none of his books have been taken out of the Boston Public Library or the Boston Atheneum since the late forties, and virtually all have been put into the most obscure storage.

5. Ralph Borsodi, *The Distribution Age* (New York: D. Appleton, 1927), p. 219.

6. Ibid., p. 225.

7. Stuart Chase, *The Economy of Abundance* (New York: Macmillan, 1934).

8. Percival and Paul Goodman, *Communitas* (New York: Vintage Books, 1960), pp. 188–89.

9. Ibid., p. 192.

10. Based on the usual rules of thumb that people can afford to buy a house that costs two to two and a half times their annual income.

11. Seymour Melman, "Industrial Efficiency Under Managerial vs. Cooperative Decision Making: A Comparative Study of Manufacturing Enterprises in Israel," in *Studies in Comparative Economic Development* (Beverly Hills: Sage Publications, 1969).

12. This rather dreary prospect has a widely diverse group of supporters. Those on the left see an oligarchy of the robber barons. Those on the right assume that capital is in decline and knowledge is in the ascent; the combination of the former with the latter will produce a fearsome world of technical bureaucracy, as portrayed by Daniel Bell. The alternative to Bell is to embrace the dated robber-baron/Populist camp or to rise above it all with the liberationist camp of R. Theobald, Marcuse, etc. We often reject the liberationist camp because it is a world without constraint and, therefore, often without form; but this reluctance does not mean that the world offered by Daniel Bell is inevitable. The household economy has real dimensions, scarcities, and constraints. But it offers far more than the sodden technocracy proposed by Bell and more popular exponents such as Alvin Toffler.

9

Our Accidental Future
... and How It Might Happen

ALTHOUGH IT DID NOT SEEM so at that time, the seventies is rather funny in retrospect. No other era of human history so conclusively proved Murphy's Law: "If anything can go wrong, it will." While armies of economists, lawyers, and consultants of all persuasions plotted, planned, programmed, and legislated, reality consistently refused to work according to the ideas by which it was so neatly described.

The unusual inflation that accompanied the recession and unemployment of 1970 prompted wage and price controls in 1971. Then, as the economy improved, consumers went on a two-year buying splurge to acquire new homes, automobiles, and appliances. Business investment increased dramatically, and world demand for agricultural products outpaced supply. By mid-1973 the economy of the United States was running at full capacity. Auto workers complained of unending weeks of overtime, interest rates skyrocketed, and suddenly absolutely everything was in short supply. Purchasing agents could get no materials and employers could get no purchasing agents. Grain prices doubled. Wood was scarce and expensive. Cotton, paper, natural gas, heating oil, gasoline, and plastic sheeting were all in short supply or unavailable. The steel companies closed their order books for 1973 before the autumn leaves had fallen from the trees, the price of turkeys doubled, chickens became scarce, and it was rumored that there would be no butter in the supermarkets by Christmas. In spite of all this and an inflation rate that had seldom been equalled in U.S. history, unemployment remained relatively high, barely dipping below 5 per cent in late 1973, before it crept up toward 8 per cent in the recession of 1974. Several economists noted that if unemployment remained high at a time when most of the nation's plants and factories were operating around the clock, it was apparent that a much higher rate of domestic investment was necessary to create new jobs. So the investment credit was expanded and new tax measures were hotly debated: Liberals pointed out that while corporate profits had grown at 20–25 per cent a year, the average worker's purchasing power had actually shrunk during the last months of the 1972–73 expansion and that a large reduction in corporate taxes was the last thing the American worker needed.

The reduction would probably not have passed if it had not been for the continuing problem of the Penn Central Railroad and further mismanagement at the Lockheed Corporation.[1] Both were nationalized in late 1976, following recognition that the closing of either would bring an abrupt end to the economic recovery.

Liberals and conservatives traded, tit for tat, and the tax reduction was passed. Very few leaders or legislators read the future in the events of 1976, but it became clear in 1977, with the passage of the Special Capital Bank Act. Thus the Congress created the largest investment banking house in the world, virtually overnight.

The reason for the bank was simple: The return on total capital in many heavy industries was below the market rate of interest on high-quality bonds. The major utility companies had suffered from level or declining earnings for several years, and the steel industry (among others) had enjoyed a limited return in 1974, its best year. The business of the Special Capital Bank was to subsidize the interest rate on negotiated loans, bonds, and debentures needed by the ailing heavy industries to expand plant and production. The net effect of the lower interest rates was to lower costs and increase profit margins. The steel industry, for instance, became competitive on world markets and improved its profitability sufficiently so that it could float new stock issues, something it had been reluctant to do when its shares were selling at five and six times earnings. The utilities no longer had to face angry consumers to ask for rate increases; instead they tapped the "cheap money" at the Capital Bank. Rate increases, thus, came very indirectly through interest-rate subsidies that were, in the end, financed through general revenues faithfully collected by the Internal Revenue Service.

The labor movement celebrated the bicentennial by negotiating for a nearly universal "30 and out" contract, allowing workers to retire with at least 50 per cent of their preretirement wages after thirty years of service, regardless of age. Public employees won similar terms of employment, and the Mobile Labor Act of 1977 extended similar terms and protection for the growing labor force employed in relatively small service organizations.

The Tax Reform of 1978 was passed with much fanfare from the Democratic administration, but it was widely admitted in private that it was, as the earlier reforms had been, largely a device to compensate for the effects of inflation. In fact, the national rate of taxation was still significantly higher in 1978 than it had been in 1971.

The demise of the Highway Trust Fund was touted as the greatest coup of the year—perhaps of the decade; it was accompanied by a five-year moratorium on new highway construction and the transfer of all highway funds to NAGTA, the National Ground Transportation Agency. It was generally agreed, however, that the agency was necessary to prevent public displays of absurdity and to maintain the mobility of a labor force that had witnessed the escalation of automobile operating costs. New-car sales had been stalled since 1973. The only reason the actual number of registered automobiles had not declined was the rapid rise of the automobile "recycle" industry, which had come into existence under the price umbrella offered by the inflation of the mid-seventies.

The year 1978 had another peculiar milestone: The birth rate had consistently been below the replacement level since 1975; economists and sociologists began to speak very seriously about the leveling of the population and the long-term effects of a static condition; more than a little hysteria attended this observation, and the business community found itself divided into two camps.

Leaders in the staples and commodities industries formed BAB (Businessmen Acclaim Babies), collected a $500-million war chest, and praised the three-child family in word, song, and deed. The three-child family appeared prominently in the advertisements of insurance companies, cereal manufacturers, and dairy products, a sharp contrast to the offerings of travel agents, hi-fi manufacturers, and the purveyors of luxury goods. Despite much public comment and soul searching, the birth rate remained low. Wags suggested a need for procreative pornography.

By 1979, virtually all the heavy industries in the United States were claiming economic hardship and seeking entry into the vaults of the Special Capital Bank. The nation's utilities no longer made regular public offerings, and the bank had supplied a substantial portion of the debt capital for the steel, aluminum, copper, oil, gas, communications, and transportation industries. The demands on the Special Capital Bank, however, had also grown large enough that they were highly visible in the national budget, and it had become clear, to some, that price increases the public did not pay voluntarily were being administered less obviously through the subsidy program. Marxists noted that this was "just another expression of monopoly capitalism." The government had become a mechanism for supporting high rate of return on investment. Conservatives argued that if such mechanisms did not exist, investors would very likely begin hoarding evaporated milk, wine, and antiques rather than committing their capital to the certain losses they would incur in the market. Inflation, after all, was still rampant.

Somewhat belatedly (the major years of large annual additions to the labor force being over), the Social Security Administration lowered the retirement age to sixty, an age quite compatible with "30 and out," and made provision for those who retired at fifty-five.

By 1980, unemployment had been reduced to tolerable levels (about 5 per cent), but inflation continued at 5–6 per cent. The growing army of the retired and semiretired, who had to fight to maintain their purchasing power, consolidated as a political force. The net result was a rapid escalation of the employment tax and increased pressure on corporate earnings, as everincreasing amounts had to be earmarked for corporate pension funds instead of for dividends.

The stock market wavered and drifted lower, but a major panic did not occur until August of 1982, when the Western Union Corporation filed for reorganization under the Bankruptcy Act. It was learned then that a combination of poor earnings, under-performance of its investment fund, and prior unfunded pension liabilities (amounts committed but not actually paid in) had combined to make the pension fund's claim on corporate assets exceed the assets of the corporation, thus wiping out the stockholders' equity and precipitating the crisis that culminated in reorganization.

In the months following the Western Union debacle, virtually all the operating railroads in the United States were nationalized to prevent a series of bankruptcies; a wave of quick calculation on unfunded liabilities culminated in the stock-market collapse of Christmas Week, during which some $300 billion in capital values disappeared. The losses were still more horrendous in the new year.

The collapse of the stock market was more than a matter of casual interest. It involved the future of virtually every corporate worker in the country. Worse, the anxiety provoked by the failure of Western Union and the railroads, as well as the obvious problems engulfing a veritable horde of other companies, had created a selling panic far worse than the blackest periods of 1929 or 1931. Insurance companies and banks, who were managers of billions in pension funds, found themselves trapped by an illiquid market.

The Big Ten trust companies attempted to stem the selling panic by declaring a moratorium on stock sales. They reasoned that since their net inflows of new cash were almost in balance with necessary cash outflows to pensioners, they could reduce their corporate bond and Treasury holdings, if necessary, and ride out the panic. While this was reported in the newspapers, along with declarative full-page advertisements in the New York *Times,* knowledgeable observers noted that the big financial institutions really had no choice but to be heroic: It was patently impossible for all the institutions to liquidate their equity positions simultaneously, because, in fact, there were no buyers.

Thus the banks watched helplessly while small mutual funds and individual investors sold out their equity positions. But what was a selling panic in one market was a buying panic in another. The money removed from investment in corporate stock rapidly found its way into Treasury bills and notes, producing a precipitous drop in interest rates. As government-issue yields dropped, corporate bonds became more attractive. It was reasoned that in most cases corporates would not be victims of the pension crisis, since the claims of the bondholders superseded the claims of both the pension fund *and* the shareholders.

It appeared, in the early spring of 1983, that the big banks and insurance companies might win their gamble: While their common-stock portfolios lost value, their bond portfolios were gaining value through the upsurge in bond prices. On balance, the more traditional and conservative banks were in reasonable shape.

While no one knew where the stock market was going—or even where it *should* go—it appeared, for a few weeks in spring, that the crisis was over.

Very likely it would have been over if the Big Ten had been able to stand together. But one Washington bank with a particularly large portfolio of vulnerable cyclical stocks found itself under pressure. Worse, the union for which it managed the large fund was in the peculiar position of having a declining membership and thus being committed to getting more money from fewer workers to support a growing number of pensioners. The only alternative for the bank was to obtain a high yield on its portfolio. Thus, the vulnerability of its securities augured disaster if the Big Ten ever broke ranks.

The union told the bank that if they didn't start liquidating, the account would be removed and the union would liquidate the securities on its own.

The Last Panic began a few months later, when it was discovered, in spite of the bank's efforts to disguise the sale of the securities, that one of the Big Ten had violated the moratorium. In one day, the stock market virtually disappeared. Trading was suspended not in one, ten, or a handful of securities, but in *six hundred.* Then the New York Stock Exchange closed. When it opened, three months later, the United States Government had become the "investor of last resort" and the United States had become a peculiar, but de facto, socialist state.

After the panic and general angst faded, it was recognized that what had happened was a kind of economic implosion in which all the heavy commodity industries and vital supplies of daily goods and communications were incorporated into the federal economy, leaving a market economy composed of two kinds of enterprises: those relatively small and local, and national but very specialized businesses. It was some time before the general public realized that there really *was* something left of the stock market, and some of America's largest (and only) remaining fortunes were preserved or made by decisive movement in this period of absolute confusion.

The strangest feature of this economic crisis was that, in spite of its enormity, it transpired in a nation that was peculiarly insulated. Although there had been abundant fears since 1970 that another depression was due, or overdue, no such event occurred. The economy continued to run at near capacity, employment was satisfactory, and the large and relatively recent increase in the number of retired persons had created an army of people willing to work part time, at relatively low wages, performing tasks and services that the regular market economy had not been able to perform for more than two decades. When the pension crisis put the earnings of corporations in doubt, they simply borrowed more from the Special Capital Bank.

Even small companies, which had had enormous difficulties in obtaining financing for more than a decade, suddenly found their positions improved, because the flight of capital from the major corporations had filled the commercial banks with demand and savings deposits, and glutted the government and corporate bond markets. Conditions had not been so favorable for small, private business in more than half a century. Money was cheap and highly available, a fact that was a joy to many and a curse to a few; the sudden flow of capital from equity to savings markets had resulted in interest rates at or below the rate of inflation. Most investors thus chose between lesser evils and resigned themselves to a loss of purchasing power.

While these circumstances were painful for large investors, who were few in number, they were "business as usual" for most Americans. They had been buying government savings bonds since World War II and had regularly seen that their savings, between inflation and taxation, could not maintain their purchasing power. Since pension funds and social security had obviated or at least reduced the need to accumulate large amounts of capital before retirement, most Americans had become dedicated consumers. With small exceptions, they had committed more of their income, in amount and proportion, to the acquisition of "consumer durables"—goods that helped the household produce goods and services for itself. While the fifties, sixties, and seventies had seen the growth and near saturation of the conventional household-goods markets, the late seventies saw technological developments that made it possible to expand dramatically the "capital equipment" employed by the household. The most important development, reaching consumer markets in large numbers in the early eighties, was the "total energy" plant for the single-family home. These units made it possible for the homeowner to generate his own heat, hot water, and electric power at a highly competitive cost and to choose between alternative energy sources. While oil was often chosen (of necessity), wind served large areas on the East and West coasts, sun served in the South and Southwest, and the Biometh Corporation pioneered in the production of methane from feedlot wastes in the Midwest and Maine. Then Biometh moved into developing municipal sewage-energy plants. Oil-distribution co-operatives grew as rapidly as food co-operatives had grown in the early seventies, and the Biometh technology accelerated the municipal takeover of local electric utilities. Public takeovers were particularly rapid in urban areas, where the contrast between the freedom of the suburbs (via the new generating equipment) and the monopoly of the centralized utilities was most pronounced. Leftist papers announced that this was only one more instance of the central cities' being held captive by private capital and that, in typical capitalist fashion, the people were going to be forced to pay for the energy extracted from their own collective excrement.

Thus, while it was not yet visible in the Crisis of 1983, it was already a fact that private investment beyond the household was a perilous undertaking. The notion of public purchase of corporate securities, i.e., socialism by default, was readily accepted. Indeed, at the prices paid by the federal government, there was a long and clamorous line of eager sellers, hardly befitting the dignity usually required of the nation's leading bankers.

By 1985, the crisis had passed and the nation found itself with "The New Capitalism," a structure that had many "capitalist" planets orbiting a large socialist sun, the federal economy. A portion of the enormous cost came out of savings found in eliminating the interest subsidy on the Special Capital Bank loans when the industries were recapitalized with lower-interest-rate debt. Except for the larger consumer-product companies, the private companies that remained in the market economy—still a substantial number—tended to be very private, having bought in their publicly traded stocks through the seventies.

The burden of federal debt was further reduced as new policies of taxation evolved. These involved a slow escalation of estate taxes on Fed-Corp securities as the capital requirements of the federal economy diminished and could be met with internally generated funds. It also provided an incentive to invest in new market-economy ventures, which were risk-ridden but largely tax-free. An enormous volume of capital, however, was invested in the household economy, accelerating the resurgence of local control and independence. By the year 2000, the average home was self-sustaining in terms of energy; it produced a small (but growing) portion of its food and some clothing, and had become affiliated with a growing number of producer and consumer cooperatives. While there was no denying the existence of an enormous apparatus of public production, the emphasis and culture of American society had shifted from the concern with centralization and power that had dominated it for more than a century to the study of small groups in relatively small communities, often arbitrarily defined because of urban concentrations.

No great plan, no charismatic leader, and no powerful new ideology directed this transformation. One thing seemed to lead to another. Inflation and the deterioration of the market economy led people to look for stability and opportunity outside the market. A little effort and energy applied in the home turned out to be surprisingly productive. A little technology made it even more so.

Indeed, one of the greater discoveries of the period was that big technology was not inevitably efficient and that it was as much the product of big capital as it was of the drive for efficiency. Small capital was highly competitive and it liberated small technology for the productive household.

While it was still necessary to have large plants to produce steel and other vital materials, it was increasingly possible to bring economic production within the boundaries of the community and the family. Long before the end of the century, economists had calculated that the ordinary family's income in the developed household economy would be derived from a combination of three sources: About 25 per cent would be derived from an existing stock of inherited capital goods—houses, household equipment and energy machines, etc.; another 25 per cent would be produced collectively; and 50 per cent would be produced by some combination of household and informal communal work, the exact ratio of household to communal to be determined by the habits and mores of the area.

Two ironies of the crisis attracted much comment from sociologists. What amounted to a revolution had transpired peacefully, quite obviously in answer to a variety of market forces, and quite clearly being instigated and controlled by older Americans rather than young ones. It was joked that the rallying cry of revolution was, "How secure is my pension?"—a phrase that suggested few barricades and little drama.

Yet these were the facts. Those who predict the future are cautioned to observe that even small changes in the demography of a population can be revolutionary. Such was the change that occurred in the United States in the seventies; the elderly grew by number (and by fiat) as the age of retirement was lowered. The young did not. It was the graying of America—not the greening—that brought about the fall of the corporate state.

The second irony is that the crisis might have passed if events could have been stretched out a few years. By 1990, most of the circumstances that had created the chaos of the seventies were waning.

The largest single influence on the Calm Nineties was the final slowdown in the rate of population growth. Although it would, inevitably, continue to grow for another fifty years, the *rate* of growth began to fall. Just as the seventies had seen a temporary oversupply of both primary teachers and classrooms, the nineties began with a growing but *permanent* oversupply of teachers and classrooms. Local school taxes, after decades of·increases that had outpaced the growth of the economy, started to plateau. State subsidies to education dropped, and the enormous apparatus of state teacher-training colleges came under taxpayer fire. Municipal and state demands for capital began to drop.

Through the nineties, as young families (spenders) became a smaller proportion of the economy while older families (savers) grew in proportion, the supply of savings grew so great that the temporary drop in interest rates that had characterized the transformation of the late eighties became permanent.

The level of consumer debt plateaued and then began to fall; the general level of inflation subsided as wages stabilized, and interest rates dropped to levels that had not been seen for sixty years. The last years of the century witnessed what historians have since called The Last Land Grab. The effect of low interest rates was to increase the amount of money a family could spend in acquiring land and a house. Thus, those who owned real estate before 1990 benefited from a windfall profit.

As a result of the inflation in real property and durables prices, it became obvious, by the year 2000, that there was enormous wealth that was not accounted for in the usual statistics. Towns frequently had nominal debt in relation to the size and degree of municipal improvements owned by the town; states owned enormous amounts of property without any debt; and the federal government, aside from its shrinking but still cumbersome portfolio of corporate bonds (issued to replace stock in the crisis of 1983–85), was busily refunding the national debt by internal purchases among the various agencies.

If the nineties were a period of economic calm, they were also a period of frenzied experimentation by psychologists and sociologists. It had become abundantly clear by then that the conventional patterns of work and play were quite obsolete. The man and woman who worked hard to age fifty-five or sixty became a "social problem" overnight when retired. They either competed for existing jobs, sank into depression, or became part of a rapidly growing "invisible economy" whose size and complexity had begun to chafe against the edges of the orthodox economy.

The "phased work plan" became general in the nineties, with an average twenty-five-hour work week over a working life of twenty-five to fifty years, depending upon sex and occupation. While weekly hours varied from fifty to zero, the norm for the bulk of the population, those between twenty-five and forty-five, was the twenty- or twenty-five-hour week scheduled in a week of *eight* days so that each family had four days at work and four days at home. The work week was increased after the major years of child raising. It increased to a maximum of thirty-five hours until age fifty-five, when it began to decline to a maximum of ten hours a week at seventy. Making it a deliberate public policy to provide employment for the elderly was a sharp reversal on a trend that had climaxed in the mid-eighties. While part of the program was absolutely necessary as part of the Nationalization Program, it had also become clear, by then, that the elderly were a valuable national resource that could not be ignored.

One of the more peculiar by-products of the decade was the National Time Trust, an institution that could only have come into being as a means for consolidating an otherwise bewildering array of time and income arrangements. Recall, for instance, the problem of Welfare and the numerous plans for a guaranteed annual income that were proposed throughout the sixties and seventies. Consider also that the nationalization of the basic industries created the peculiar situation of an established but relatively stagnant portion of the labor force and economy having its financial security underwritten by the public at large while the most rapidly growing portion of the economy, the services, was so constructed as to make public ownership or control impossible—not to mention basically undesirable.

The solution was to realize the essentially arbitrary nature of the financial instruments that composed the retirement and welfare system and to replace it with a system of time credits not subject to the vagaries of the market, technological progress, or industrial change. Thus, in exchange for three or four years of work with the National Time Trust, every citizen achieved a guaranteed subsistence for life. Since it included the compulsion to work—at least for a few years—the Trust satisfied the demand of conservatives; in providing a mechanism that allowed individuals great latitude in choice between work and leisure or material goods and leisure, and participation in the regular, market economy or in the developing, "free" economy, it also made dreamers happy, although they were bitter about the compulsory aspects of the program.

As a practical matter, the Time Trust proved to be the answer to one of the most vexing problems of the earlier "affluent society": Who would do the dirty work? The problem of finding people willing to do menial jobs was solved by requiring that *everyone* do them for a year.

The National Time Trust began registering citizens in the year 2000. Since only new entrants to the labor market were to register, it was widely assumed that the transition from a financially based economy to a time economy would take at least thirty years and perhaps as many as forty. In fact, fully 90 per cent of the labor force was fully credited before twenty-five years had passed, because so many older citizens, habituated to work and long hours, applied to work for the trust, assigning their credits to their children.

During the same twenty-five-year period, consumer and public indebtedness continued to be reduced. By the year 2025, long-term mortgage debt was relatively rare. Public debt was virtually non-existent. In both instances, the debt that remained usually represented the cost of modernizing or replacing existing facilities and equipment rather than the cost of entirely new facilities.

If economists had reluctantly conceded that the money/market economy was no longer an accurate measure of economic activity in the nineties (for by that time the national product was understated by a full 50 per cent rather than the 25–33 per cent of 1975), the real death knell of the money economy came with the establishment of the Time Trust, for it eliminated subsistence from the money economy and allowed people to form new kinds of economic organizations that did not employ money. Thus, all the crafts that had been threatened with extinction in the first half of the twentieth century were reborn in the first quarter of the twenty-first century. And the household, or family, economy, having reached its nadir in the late nineteen fifties, became the model for future economic development.

It would be impossible to list, in a short space, all the positive events that accompanied the rise of the household economy and the decline of the market economy. Perhaps the most important is that the substantial increase in the capital employed by the household and the fact that it was no longer part of the market served to make two positive social ends possible. First, the stabilization of population and the accumulation of household capital worked to tie one generation to the next and restore family bonds that had been eroded during the early-industrial era; second, the pure intractable bulk of this household capital and the mechanisms by which it was passed from one generation to the next forced people to cease thinking in isolated, linear terms and to begin thinking of their own lives and the lives of their children as part of a cycle, a whole, a system in which means and ends were indistinguishable. Nature was no longer seen as something to conquer. Creative attention was no longer focused on bald, unending output, but on the benefits created by all the capital employed by society. As the competitive, exploitative culture that had been the inevitable by-product of a market-dominated society lost ground, the early resistance to the transformation faded and new, co-operative institutions arose.

There was, of course, a constant expectation of revolution and counterrevolution during the entire period. Impatience was a product of the era, as well as a peculiarly complete lack of historical perspective. While the entire transformation required no more than the passage of fifty years, it was the constant expectation of most of those then alive that revolutions, by definition, were violent, abrupt, and immediate. Yet fifty years, in retrospect, seems a short time to accommodate the construction of a brand-new human society.

The future may not happen this way. It may be quite as horrible as some suggest, or we may have no future at all. But if we are to have a future worth raising children for, its shape and content must be similar to the events offered.

A major institution cannot fall without another to rise and take its place. This is not fate or cynicism, it is compelling necessity. We are busy, complicated, and very faulty creatures; our lives are not changed easily, let alone transformed. Whatever the final circumstances of the change, it will be our fate to witness the decline of the market economy and the rise of the household. The end of this development is a peculiar creature ambivalently known as the stationary state. Our attitude toward it and its happy compatibility with the household economy is our next concern.

1. This was written before the energy crisis in the fall of 1973, an event that promises to accelerate the scenario offered. Specifically, Lockheed is now in deep trouble and there seems to be no resolution for the problems of Penn Central. Solar heating is now a common newspaper topic, complete with cost estimates, and numerous articles have appeared suggesting, in effect, that cattle dung and chicken droppings are two of our greatest national resources. The stock market decline of 1974 nearly brought on the envisioned crash as insurance companies were forced to sell stocks in autumn to have adequate reserves, and many securities analysts are worrying about the effect of the drop on future pension contributions vis-à-vis corporate earnings.

10

A Modest Utopia

WE ARE MOVING toward something called the stationary state, a condition of human society in which almost everything—population, production, consumption, and investment—is stable and constant. It might also be described as a modest utopia, a society that falls far short of the futuristic dreams found in the Sunday comic section.

There will be no hourly rocketship departures for Mars, no robots to command, no cities under the sea, and no afternoon jaunts to Australia. Nor will our modest utopia offer two or three automobiles per capita, opportunities for consumption that would make Caligula blanch with jealous rage, or orgies of electronic sexual satisfaction programmed by Muzak. All this—and all the other daydreams of omnivorous consumption—will be missing. Instead, we will live and love well and long, a fate that is deceptively simple in appearance and probably far less modest an achievement than most of us would like to believe. The lesson of the sixties, which we have yet to fully absorb, was that it is a lot easier to achieve some of those Sunday-funnies predictions than to add to the receding reservoirs of human warmth, compassion, and understanding.

This modest utopia is not a long way off. It is not something that will occur in five hundred years. Or three hundred. Or two hundred. It will occur soon, or it will not occur at all. By soon

I mean that within fifty years the bulk of the changes in our social and economic institutions will have been made and those born thereafter will consider the past, our present, as curious and unimaginable. Within twenty-five years we shall see many of the enormous (but largely accidental) changes that will lead to the disappearance of most of what is familiar to us now.

We will not ascribe these changes to "future shock" or to any other sociomedical malady. Nor will it mark the inevitable triumph of Marxism or the sad expiring of the free spirit. We will merely note that there has been a major reapportionment among the three sectors of human economic activity: The household economy will achieve dominance as a result of the success of the market economy in a finite world.

The reason our future will be so different from that offered by the usual prognosticators is simple: Most prediction assumes that the market economy will dictate the shape and content of the future. In fact it will not, because the ethos and operation of the market economy, with its emphasis on accumulation and growth, is mutually exclusive with the idea of a stationary state and, like it or not, the stationary state is a requirement of human survival. This does not mean that market-economy institutions will cease to exist, it means only that they will play a much diminished role in future human society and exert virtually no influence on how we think and feel. Instead, economic institutions that are compatible with the idea of a stationary state will prevail. It just happens that the household economy has the necessary compatibility.

The important difference between the market and household economies is that the former is committed to the idea of compounding, to the perpetual doubling and redoubling of capital, and the latter is concerned with the creation and use of capital in the present. The return on market capital is magical, Faustian cash, a substance that is infinitely exchangeable, compoundable, and otherwise flexible to meet the most extreme of human wishes. Capital in the household economy provides returns in services. These services are non-transferable and cannot be accumulated. I may own the goods and equipment that will provide me with a roof over my head, a dry shirt, a warm meal, or a visit to a friend. It remains that the return is a non-transferable service, something consumed in the here and now or not at all. A moment's thought will reveal the enormity of this difference.

It will also reveal why there is so much passionate hostility toward the idea of the stationary state. The simple fact is that the market economy is a hard act to follow, largely because it offers so much opportunity for fantasy clothed in "realism." It lies at the center of dreams of wealth and power, however pathological; it sustains greed; it offers unreal solutions to real problems; it provides a route of escape from facing the immediate limits of most human beings. These are "real" virtues, assets that we are ill inclined to lose.

In truth, it would not be too much to consider our attachment to the market economy as a kind of addiction that must be overcome before we can understand the requirements of our future society.

The first requirement is a stable population—"zero population growth." And no other issue so clearly reveals the growth neurosis. Several years ago, for instance, an article in *Architectural Record*[1] threatened architects with unemployment if we achieved the goals of zero population growth.

That an otherwise reasonable publication, backed by a company with one of the largest economic research units in the United States, can offer such threats and anxiety to its readers is one indication of how dearly we cling to the idea that babies are good for business. The fact is that population growth increases the demand for basic commodities and, in doing so, bails out the perennial overinvestment in production facilities. Without a growing population, there would be no hope for the otherwise inept businessman. His mistakes would catch up with him too soon. And they would most likely be fatal.

Similarly, the growth of population creates opportunities for personal advancement that otherwise might not exist; a doubling of the population doubles the number of management jobs. Population growth, in short, underwrites investment errors and provides job mobility for many who might not otherwise be able to obtain it. It eases the harsh edges of competition. Motherhood is sublime.

These benefits, and the employment of a few architects, are small losses when weighed against the long-term consequences of a stable population. It now requires more than two thousand dollars a year to raise an average child, a sum that makes no allowance for orthodontics, attendance at Harvard College, psychotherapy, and other goodies some consider necessity. If the one million new families that will be formed *this year* decide to have two children instead of three, they will save some $40 billion over the next twenty years. So will the million new families who make the same decision next year. Nor will the economic benefits end at direct savings. Smaller families need smaller houses and smaller cars, consuming less fuel and paying less in the way of taxes. Fewer children per family mean fewer new schools, fewer needs for new buildings of all sorts, and fewer interruptions in traffic to install larger pipes for water, sewage, telephone, and gas lines. Fewer children means that the pile-up of families in our urban areas will abate, reducing the pressure on land values and, indirectly, allowing us to keep buildings longer instead of tearing them down every thirty or forty years because the land under them has become so valuable.

In the orthodox view, these events raise the fear that the rising tide of affluence and ever-increasing personal savings would result in a glut of investment capital that would soon bring on world depression and make the thirties look like the golden years of Western civilization. The problem is that the market view insists on seeing all capital as being commanded by the market economy rather than by individuals within the household economy.

A stable population of smaller families would not only bring the benefits cited above, it would also set the stage for a rapid increase in the household economy by supporting a high rate of household investment. The rapid accumulation of household capital and the resulting decrease in consumer dependence on the market economy would set the stage for the larger social and economic changes that would create our modest utopia.

Between a relatively large accumulation of household capital and basic sustenance provided by participation in a system like the National Time Trust, the way would be cleared for an era of very rapid social change, dominated by the following trends.

A defocusing of social goods and values. Most of the issues that arouse so much passion and pain today would wither away from neglect and popular indifference. The entire issue of social mobility and social opportunity would be diffused (and defused!)

throughout a system that no longer focused entirely upon achieving a commanding position in the market economy. It would be possible to pursue divergent values and goals without having to make the extravagant sacrifices now required.

A leveling of incomes. As people found that they could make good trade-offs between the market and household economies, they would experiment in non-market economic activities. Cash income, in effect, would no longer be an accurate measure of standard of living, a circumstance that would serve to reduce crime and the appeal of robbery, theft, extortion, and fraud. It would also stimulate more varied and creative uses of people's energy, as achievement could be tied to something more flexible than dollar income.

A sweeping decentralization of higher education. It would be reorganized as a virtual "cottage industry," providing contact on a tutorial or apprenticeship basis—a kind of intellectual guild system—rather than trusting to large, central institutions granting increasingly irrelevant certification. The new, local organization would reflect the needs of the decentralized society. In a sense, this has already occurred in some of the avant-garde colleges. The pressure to provide closer student-teacher contact and a more varied curriculum is part of the current crisis in financing our institutions of higher education. As our economy becomes ever more service-oriented, it will become increasingly difficult for our present institutions to prepare people for the job market. The new institutions will be based on some widely distributed public facility, such as the public library.

A general decline in large hierarchic organizations. As the scale of human communities becomes more manageable than it presently is, people will reject the control large corporations can exert. It's very likely that the only large organizations to survive would be some of the heavy industrial companies contained within the federal economy.

A general rebirth of community and a restoration of neighborhoods. With the emphasis on economic and social mobility detached from the corporate economy, people would be free to rebuild the sense of community lost in the past century. Few aspirations have a larger constituency than this one. It is the constant plea of TV commentators, and its decline has been exhaustively examined by sociologists of all bents and persuasions. The hunger for community is where the radical right and radical left join hands and become almost indistinguishable. It is an underlying goal in Murray Bookchin's *Post-Scarcity Anarchism* and a treasured theme in the writings of such social reformers as Robert Theobald. Its lack is the constant theme in the books of Vance Packard and one of the many sources of social pain in Alvin Toffler's *Future Shock*.

The only cure is the one that is inevitable: the decline of the market economy and the monolithic structure of social values that it creates. The rise and strength of the household economy will allow people to refocus their energy and aspirations on the world that is immediately at hand, the household and community, rather than making them live in two worlds, as most of us do now.

A proliferation of new organizational forms. There will be an enormous surge in producer and consumer co-operatives, interest-group networks, neighborhood centers, and extended families. Writer Upton Sinclair envisioned such a society of co-operatives during the thirties but saw the co-operative movement decline as economic health was restored. Today's co-operative movement has its roots as much in the desire for community as in economic necessity. It is likely to expand, whatever the economic circumstances of the immediate future. The largest impediment to its further development is the dominance of the market economy; as that recedes, new forms of interchange, based on co-operation rather than competition, will thrive.

A refocusing on the present rather than the future. Some writers, such as Herman Kahn, see this process as an "increasingly sensate, hedonistic" society auguring a breakdown of puritanism, ethical values, and so forth. But such visions are constrained by the limits of the market economy: The household economy, on the other hand, lives in the here and now; it does not "mean" or become, it *is*. It will restore immediacy, contact, and consideration to our daily lives as the barriers, attenuations, and abstractions of the market economy disappear.

A reintegration of age groups. The market-dominated society divides people by degree of economic function; only those who are full participants in the market economy are accorded complete recognition as human beings. Others are somehow deficient: The elderly are viewed as functionless and useless, children as objects that must be trained, and mothers as rather dull-witted unfortunates, worthy of condescending sympathy, reminders of the most common fate worse than death. We segregate children from the adult world until they enter it; we build singles complexes for the unmarried, garden apartments for young marrieds, housing developments for the growing family, leisure villages for "empty-nesters," condominiums for the retired, and nursing homes for the aged. By exercising a nominal degree of care, it is entirely possible to avoid contact with anyone not within a few years of one's own age. This unnatural and exceedingly costly condition will end as the household, rather than the market, becomes the focal point of our social and economic life.

A general and very impressive increase in economic efficiency. In a market-dominated economy, our notion of efficiency is becoming increasingly distorted. Because the market economy is built on *exchange,* every effort is made to increase money income, the mechanism of exchange. Thus, the capitalist attempts to increase sales and profits, while the worker hopes to increase his paycheck. Both measure the degree of their success by *flows of income* rather than stocks of goods—by an ability to *meet* expenses rather than a *lack* of expenses. We can best see this by examining an area where the market and household economies meet.

Suppose the useful life of the average piece of household equipment were doubled. What would happen? Logically, we might expect consumer expenditures on such durable goods to edge down from the $90 billion a year currently spent to, perhaps, $45 billion. As a result, our GNP would decrease and jobs would be lost as all those employed in the production and distribution of the $45 billion in unproduced durables joined the unemployed. No doubt, presidential commissions would be formed and Congressional hearings held. There would be a cry for special programs of vocational retraining. Union officials would protest the loss of employment, executives would close down factories, and a lot of shareholders would miss their dividends.

But where would the real losses be? Certainly not among those who bought the new equipment! They would enjoy the same economic good for twice as long, with no increase in expenditure. Obviously, the consumer would benefit. Better yet, the economy would benefit, because it would now have available labor and equipment that formerly were occupied replacing worn-out goods. In a logical, reasonable world this would be called progress; increasingly, we call it disaster. Thus the consumer is often asked to support the deliberate destruction of household capital in order to provide employment and return on investment; in return, he is guaranteed similar support should economic efficiency ever threaten *his* job.

All of this is logical, familiar, and necessary in an economy in which there is no alternative to the market and an absolute need exists to maintain cash incomes and sustain a given level of economic activity. Economic welfare, in such a system, is measured in "throughput" rather than in the amenities that accrue to individuals. We are all familiar with the result: waste. What Ralph Borsodi complained of in the thirties was still with us in the forties, when the Goodmans wrote *Communitas;* it had become worse by the time Vance Packard wrote *The Wastemakers,* in 1960, and set the tone for a decade of rising consumer anger. In a market economy, the producer and the consumer are bound to become enemies in a war that neither can win.

The market economy is not a creature suited to an environment where materials and energy are increasingly scarce. The market is geared to "more and more," not to more from less. Yet the reality of our limited natural resources requires precisely that: more from less. The household, not the market, is the institution for such a condition.

It would be difficult *not* to describe our future society as a utopia, because it contains virtually all the elements prescribed by those who have wished for utopias. There will be peace, freedom, a general improvement in human relationships, leisure, economic efficiency, and a real—if peculiar—variety of luxury. What more could we want?

This is not a rhetorical question. Some people feel a compulsion to translate "stationary" into "stagnant"; they proclaim that the market economy is our only hope. This belief is absolute insanity, yet those of us who would welcome a more stable world are made to feel a certain embarrassment.

The protests of the growthies rekindle our secret Faustian dreams of wealth and power and make us worry that the human race may not be able to get along without murder, rape, swindle, theft, arson, general and perfidious greed, hate, anxiety, ulcers, and the subtle new forms of terror yet to be devised by the Department of Defense. Without crime, horror, and misery, TV would have no programming, hence no advertisers, and Faustian America would be a depressed nation terrorized by roaming bands of the bored, malodorous, and unemployed.

Life in the stationary state, no doubt, will lack the excitements we now have. It might no longer be possible to lose a week's sleep because of the evening news, or your job and home because of a recession, or your family because it was necessary to choose between them and a career. No doubt there will be much strain because we will all have to find new things to worry about, new causes of concern, and more subtle sources of pleasure. We are talking about a modest, a very modest, kind of utopia. But it certainly beats what we have now, and it is very likely, when the facts are clear, that it will have far more joiners than exiles.

Having dreamed of glory, we are reluctant to accept a future that requires us to count our pennies, to turn our collars, and to quietly measure our lives away in teaspoons. But we must. And let me tell you, it really won't be so bad. We may even learn to enjoy ourselves, a capacity bordering on the vestigial. *Stationary doesn't mean stagnant.* It means different. Something none of us has ever experienced. Yet it is almost never mentioned without a certain defensiveness, beginning as far back as John Stuart Mill, who commented: "It is scarcely necessary to remark that a stationary condition of capital and population implies no stationary state of human improvement. There would be as much scope as ever for all kinds of mental, cultural, and moral and social progress; as much room for improving the Art of Living, and much more likelihood of its being improved, when minds ceased to be engrossed by the art of getting on."[2]

Very little can be offered to allay anxiety and defensiveness about a stationary society. They are as strong now as they were in the nineteenth century. Since no binding logical argument and no definitive proof of its quality obtain, our view of the stationary state is largely a matter of belief. I believe that the world is finite, and that we had best learn to live within its limitations and our own. I think also, for reasons just given, that life in such a society will be better, not worse.

But, rather than argue, let's consider the alternatives. Assuming the world is finite, if we continue on our present course we will have a massive, head-on collision with that finite reality. Millions, even billions, will die, and all the very real progress of the past two hundred years may be lost in a decade. This prediction is not an unfamiliar reading of the future. We have an abundance of Cassandras. If the bombs don't get us, the environment will. And if that fails, there's always Godzilla.

On the other hand, if the world turns out to have more room and more valuable goodies than it now appears to have, the future offered by a market-dominated economy is still pretty grim, because it requires an ever greater loss of personal freedom. Why this is so is the subject of the next chapter.

1. "Economy—Ecology—and Zero Population Growth," *Architectural Record,* August 1970.
2. J. S. Mill, *Principles of Political Economy* (New York: D. Appleton, 1890).

11

The Dreary Alternative

IRONICALLY, *the growth of the household economy and the arrival of the stationary state may be all that separates us from a social hell.*

More than four decades have been devoted, with varying degrees of dedication, to the ideal of building a free, egalitarian, technological society. We have programs to end poverty and deprivation and laws to enforce equality of opportunity. We convene regularly to change the distribution of income and wealth and we suffer the public declarations of a horde of legislators, national and local, all proffering their allegiance and identification with the poor and middle class; we berate the waste of money and resources on defense and praise conservation in all forms, save that which threatens local employment; and we offer to practically everyone (including the intellectually infirm) the social talisman of a college education. All this (and more) is the baggage of conventional liberalism; yet only in 1971 did someone consider what would happen if all the usual, unfair impediments to social equality were removed.

Writing in the *Atlantic Monthly,* Harvard psychologist Richard Herrnstein offered the following syllogism:[1]

"1. If differences in mental abilities are inherited, and
 2. If success requires those abilities, and

3. If earnings and prestige are dependent on success,
4. Then social standing (which reflects earnings and prestige) will be based to some extent on inherited differences among people."

At the moment, differences in social standing are determined by "artificial" factors—by the possession of inherited wealth, for instance, or by being graced with a favored tone of skin coloring. The history of manners and society is a record of the efforts most of us make to achieve pre-emptive social status in this or that situation. We dream (perhaps covertly) of achieving special dispensation to exert unchecked power over others. All these efforts and dreams may come to an end.

Herrnstein observes that once the social and legal impediments to social equality are removed, our social structure will be controlled by innate, genetic differences. There will be no opportunities to redress the social balance, because we will have transcended all the crass institutional, man-made barriers to status. But such barriers will be replaced with intrinsic, natural ones. "Greater wealth, health, freedom, fairness and educational opportunity," Herrnstein writes, "are not going to give us the egalitarian society of our philosophical heritage. It will instead give us a society sharply graduated, with ever greater innate separation between the top and the bottom, and ever more uniformity within families as far as inherited abilities are concerned."[2]

Those at the bottom will no longer be able to carp about the rapid rise of the boss's idiot son; Irishmen will have no recourse to tribal affiliations. Indeed, the rigid, genetically determined egalitarian society of the future offers all the social possibilities of the beehive or the anthill; while fascinating to observe, it is fixed and changeless. In retrospect, the pockets of favoritism, the rich veins of social power, and the small pools of privilege that characterize the imperfections of modern society may seem like oases of comfort on our completed march to a natural order.

While Herrnstein's syllogism has provoked anger and near violence in some of his colleagues, it is not necessary to believe in his syllogism to expect a future in which immense power accrues to a very few. The vision of society as molded by enormous and oppressive intellectual bureaucracies can be found as well in Daniel Bell and Herman Kahn. It is, in fact, the best offering of most intellectuals who have not embraced this or that transcendental vision. As numerous articles regularly warn us, the technical apparatus for the superstate is rapidly being put in place. Data banks, computer dossiers, the distance of the public from most decisions, the absolute power of the police, the "normative" powers of the public schools, and virtually all large and necessary organizations have been under attack because of the power they wield. The world of *Nineteen Eighty-four* may arrive even sooner than expected.

The strength and inevitability of these visions of intellectual bureaucracy depends on how fully our future society and institutions are geared to markets and specialization: the greater the dependence, the more fully we may realize an oppressive, "natural" feudal society. Such a world is the real future offered by the pursuit of Faustian dreams. It is not a very pleasant one.

My analysis here implies, however, that this basic belief in the market economy and specialization—in large bureaucratic organizations and in ever-increasing social and political control over individuals—is unjustified. A new and revitalized household economy will serve very well as a buffer between individuals and the larger society. Herrnstein's frightening syllogism, in short, may be irrelevant to the future form of economic society. Similarly, all the conventional projections of a future "knowledge society" are predicated on economic organizations that are largely incompatible with our need for stability.

So far, we have seen that the market economy is only one of three forms of economic organization, that something called the household economy exists, has substantial size, and is currently growing faster than the market economy. We have seen that non-money household income from labor is almost 50 per cent of disposable cash income. We have also seen that imputed household returns on invested capital exceed those found in the marketplace.

Yet these realities are virtually absent in the economic and social theories that direct important decisions. And public policy regularly assumes that only the market and collective economies exist. Economists continue to assume that labor displaced from the marketplace vaporizes. Social scientists continue to assume that all the perceived evils of industrial life—factory boredom, blue-collar blues, loss of ego, alienation, etc., etc.—are inescapable accompaniments of a technological society, amenable to no more than compensatory measures and half-witted palliatives. Small wonder, then, that we are in the midst of a national crisis of confidence, and that there is an increasing credibility gap between the testimony of experts and the gut feelings of more ordinary mortals. Most of us, after so many years of crisis, feel that the future is unlikely to bear any relation to the plans of experts and technicians. *The household economy, in spite of its invisibility, may be the only instrument for creating a positive and livable future.*

Fortunately, as we shall soon see, time and nature are on the side of the household.

1. Richard Herrnstein, "I.Q.," *Atlantic Monthly,* September 1971.
2. Richard Herrnstein, *"I.Q. in the Meritocracy"* (Boston: Atlantic Monthly Press, 1973).

Part Three

Why the Market Economy
Must Decline

The reasons for the inevitable decline of the market economy—
the logical outcome of a natural process

12

Inflation and the Dilemma of Investment Return

THE MARKET ECONOMY is not, as some would have us believe, a failed and evil institution. It is merely the mature product—and victim—of its own success. It has created an environment that will no longer support either its continued growth or its dominance of our social and economic institutions.

The most prominent sign of this changed environment is inflation, and the likely consequence of a long period of intense inflation will be the bankruptcy of many individual firms and some industries, and the emergence of an ever larger and more powerful federal economy. Inevitably, the market economy will shrink. Necessarily, the household economy will expand.

The only known cure is more destructive than inflation itself. With the possible exception of a few pure capitalist types, few are willing to accept more unemployment in lieu of continued inflation. Large unions aren't alone in feeling that unemployment is a poor cure for inflation; many businessmen share the concern that unemployment is at least as dangerous. Pragmatically, the businessman sees that he has a choice of reduced profits because of lower sales or reduced profits due to lower margins. The difference is more political than economic, and since unemployment can cause discomforting displays of public starvation and want, the bias is to coexist with the more democratic affliction.

Whatever the consensus, however, it remains that if inflation continues at its present rate, the basic industries of the United States—and most of the industrialized world—will be in a shambles. The simple fact is that, as presently constituted, they cannot continue to function in the current, inflationary environment. Small companies can, and do, close down and disappear without a trace. Large companies do not. They are not allowed to close, because they are vital to maintaining some measure of full employment, a goal usually considered more valuable to the social and economic whole than the survival or extinction of any firm or industry. The increasing public need to exercise preemptive collective power, together with the inflation which creates that need, is precisely the bind that augurs for the growth of the federal economy. Penn Central and Lockheed are symptoms of the future.

Inflation is not new. In the past, it has been a mild problem, one that could be isolated to such specific sources as wars and government deficits. It ambled along at 1–2 per cent a year, a hardly perceptible rate, and it was rumored to cause some harm to business. But no one could prove it. It was also thought to lessen the losses suffered for some business misjudgments. On balance, its effects were generally considered neutral.

Mild inflation was one of those nebulous things that traditional Democrats argued for and traditional Republicans argued against. The argument achieved some ritualistic value, and the disappearance of such a trustworthy but largely irrelevant subject would probably have been more unsettling than the consequences of resolving the dispute.

We'll never know for sure, however, because inflation is no longer mild. Nor is it specific and isolated, an event to be blamed on an unwanted war, an extravagant Congress, or crop failure. Now it is general and rampant. While it is very easy to point to other nations with even greater inflation problems, the differences are of degree. We all have the same malady, but some have it worse than others. The cure is socially and politically unacceptable, and, worse, is no longer certain. We now know that inflation and unemployment can live with each other—even if we can't live with them.

We hear—as we should—much noise and complaint from consumers. We hear much less from the investor and capitalist. Yet it would be difficult to determine who has suffered more because of inflation. As this is written, the Dow Jones Industrial Average stands approximately where it stood five years ago, having provided investors with a dividend return of about 3 per cent a year during the entire period. The wider market averages offer even poorer results, and the other exchanges are areas of near disaster. The smart investor was one who kept his money in Treasury bills, because interest rates were attractive during the entire period. Alas, even the smart investor is not a richer investor. At best, he has preserved the nominal value of his capital while losing actual purchasing power. Since the goal of all investment is the creation, preservation, and increase of purchasing power, the investors' choices were between lesser evils. They still are.

Very little sympathy is extended to the investor, since he is part of a privileged minority group. The man who loses a million dollars in the stock market wins little sympathy from those who had nothing to lose; he has no shoes, but the rest of us have no feet. This single fact—that the investor is far outnumbered by those with little or no market capital—has led to the creation of public policies that favor the attrition of the market economy and the growth of the collective and household economies. When these two conditions become more universal and significant, the left, no doubt, will feel it has achieved a moral victory; the right will consider that it has suffered a great and crippling defeat. In fact, only the inevitable restructuring of the human economy will have occurred. How and why the market economy's attrition is inevitable is not a simple matter, but it is an important one; and understanding begins with the idea of economic health.

One direct and crass measure of economic health exists: corporate profits. Here we find that profits are only now returning to the level achieved in the late sixties, and stock prices, after price collapses that placed the optimistic investor high on the endangered-species list, are returning to levels previously achieved. They do this with regularity. Fear reigns supreme, leaving little room for the usual displays of investor greed. Angst prevails: When prices are up, new projections of yet higher prices come to the fore; when prices are down, dour predictions of utter collapse abound.

If we dispense with the psychodrama of investments, the investor and the general public face the same dilemma that confronts business managers and government officials. *Profitability determines the value and viability of any enterprise.*

In choosing among investments, the financial analyst will usually look for two things: first, for a high return on invested capital, on the actual equity put up by the investor; second, for a high return on *total* capital, which is a measure of the amount of interest and profit generated to service all the capital (including borrowed money as well as equity) employed by the company. Finding high returns on both, he is likely to recommend the security. His observations may then be reflected in a high price/earnings ratio for the stock. A high ratio is presumed to indicate rapid growth, while a low ratio is presumed to indicate slow growth.

IBM, because it has a return on stockholders' equity of nearly 20 per cent and an annual growth of about 20 per cent, has an earnings multiple of around 20; a more typical company, with an 11 per cent return on stockholders' equity and an annual growth of 4 or 5 per cent, has an earnings multiple of 6 or 7. For fairly obvious reasons, investors and corporate managements want high and (they hope) rising earnings multiples for their stocks.

The price of stocks is based on expectations of future performance, a fact that leads the stock market to some rather peculiar juxtapositions. According to the 1973 *Forbes* annual, for instance, the Coca-Cola Company was worth more than the *entire* steel industry. It was also worth more than the entire air-transportation industry, almost $3 billion more than all the supermarkets in the United States, and $3.5 billion more than the entire aerospace and defense industry.

"In today's consumer oriented economy," the magazine noted, "heavy industry ranks relatively low in market value. The whole metals industry—steel, copper, aluminum—you name it—came in at under $20 billion. Chemicals was only slightly better at $27 billion. Transportation was just over $17 billion. And industrial equipment, the very sinews of our economy, was $10 billion. Taken all together, heavy industry, with its massive plant and sophisticated technology, was valued by the stock market at $50 billion less than the companies that package drinks, soap, and cosmetics."[1]

Market values are very much a function of profits and rate of return. Coca-Cola, with its return of 27.8 per cent, is obviously more attractive than International Harvester, with its return of 5.7 per cent. Profitability and growth in the market economy clearly lie in serving the needs of the consumer and the household economy.

Evidently, the stock market is telling us that the traditional industrial state has a limited future, because the heavy industries *are the least capable of responding favorably to an inflationary economic environment.* The proof is in their poor profitability. The burden of inflation, which is reflected in interest rates, weighs heavily upon these industries, making their future prospects dim.

The basic reason for this is that the prevailing interest rate in the open market is higher than the rate of return on total capital in most of our heavy industries.

Forbes rankings of return on total capital and return on stockholders' equity, by industry, are shown below. The median return on total capital for all industry was 8.5 per cent, not far above the yield on long-term bonds and substantially below the rates that could be found in short-term money-market investments in recent years. While most of the industries that served direct consumer needs enjoyed returns in excess of 9 per cent, the steel industry provided a return of 4.5 per cent. This is less than the interest rate on passbook savings accounts at the local savings bank. And unlike the local savings bank, U. S. Steel cannot induce new investment with offers of free electric blankets, hair dryers, and sterling serving platters. In 1973, a year in which U. S. Steel had more orders than it could fill, return on stockholders' equity was 9 per cent, an amount significantly below the prime interest rate for most of the year. Industries that serve the consumer directly have no such problems. They may complain about reduced margins for profit or the unnecessarily high cost of debt, but it is still quite worthwhile to take the risk of being in business. The return justifies the risk.

The closer an industry is to the consumer, the higher its probable rate of return. The consumer is nothing less than the life blood of the modern economy. Industries that are far removed from the consumer and the household are very likely to have little to offer the investor in the way of either growth or return on investment.

Why the Market Economy Must Decline

FIGURE 15

Industry Returns on Total Capital 1967–72

Industry Group	Return on Total Capital	Return on Equity
Consumer Goods: Health	16.0	17.7
Consumer Goods: Personal	11.8	15.7
Finance: Banks	11.1	12.3
Finance: Insurance	9.8	10.5
Consumer Goods: Food & Drink	9.7	13.0
Distribution: Wholesalers	9.5	12.3
Consumer Goods: Household	9.5	12.2
Electronics	9.5	11.9
Metals: Non-Ferrous	9.4	12.2
Information Processing	9.3	11.5
Distribution: Supermarkets	9.2	10.9
Distribution: Retailers	8.6	12.8
Leisure & Education	8.6	12.7
Industrial Equipment	8.6	11.3
Energy	8.5	10.9
MEDIAN	8.5	11.4
Building Materials	8.4	10.5
Automotive	8.3	10.1
Construction & Drilling	8.3	14.2
Consumer Goods: Clothing	8.0	10.1
Chemicals	7.4	9.5
Aerospace & Defense	6.8	7.8
Utilities: Natural Gas	6.7	12.7
Forest Products & Packaging	6.5	9.1
Utilities: Electric & Telephone	5.7	11.9
Metals: Steel	4.5	5.0
Surface Transportation	4.4	5.9
Air Transportation	3.5	4.9

(vertical annotation spanning the 8.6 to 6.8 range of the Return on Total Capital column: "Range of Bond Returns")

Source: *Forbes*, January 1973.

The situation obviously is most perilous for industries with a return on total capital that is below the rate of return offered to bond investors.[2] Specifically, this means air and surface transportation, aerospace and defense, steel, forest products, the utilities, and some chemicals. To these we might add the automotive and the construction industries, at this juncture, each for different reasons that ultimately can be traced to the rate of inflation.

Since it is expected that high interest rates will prevail for some time, industries with low returns are unlikely to be able to raise capital for expansion or replacement of worn equipment. One result is the wild proliferation of materials shortages that began to appear in 1973. Another result is the increased lobbying by heavy industries for special and subsidized sources of capital. (If you can't raise prices, lower your costs.) In the past few years, the electric utilities and the steel industry have both offered plans of government-subsidized debt, and Congress has recently created "Fanny Rae" to finance our ailing railroads with government-backed commercial loans. *The net effect of all these plans and inevitable shortages is to force our heavy industries ever closer to government control and regulation.*

The basic cause of this problem is inflation: The heavy industries are least capable of passing on inflation-induced cost increases.

Economist W. Halder Fisher of the Batelle Memorial Institute, for instance, analyzed prices in different industries over a twenty-year period. His work, presented in *Scientific American,*[3] indicates that the closer an enterprise is to final consumer demand the more likely it will be to pass on its increased costs in the form of price increases. Basic heavy industries have been responsible for very little of our price inflation. The major burden lies with the service industries.

Some of the effects of these trends are now clearly visible, particularly in the profit margins of commodity producers. The basic dilemma that each producer must face is that wages and other costs are rising faster than productivity and prices. If wages rise at an annual rate of 5–6 per cent a year and productivity increases at 3 per cent, the producer has got to find some way to accommodate that gap. His options depend on his business.

The commodity producer really has no options. While his costs of production are up, he cannot raise the price of his product without losing business to competition. Inevitably, his profit margin shrinks and his return on total capital falls.

There are many options, however, for the producer of consumer goods. Faced with rising costs, he can re-engineer the product and cheapen it. He can eliminate assembly or finishing work, thus passing some labor on to the consumer; since it is precisely this work that is least amenable to productivity increases, passing it on to the consumer allows the manufacturer to concentrate his efforts on those parts of the productive process where

FIGURE 16

Inflation Trends 1953–75

PRICE INDEX (1960 = 100)

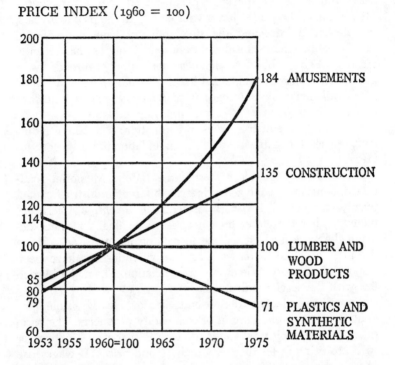

SAMPLE PRICE TRENDS are plotted for four sectors of the U.S. economy for the period from 1953 to 1975. All follow a linear trend except amusements. Approximately the same ratio holds throughout the economy. Of 82 productive sectors, 26 have non-linear trends.

Source: *Scientific American*, November 1971.

productivity increases might match wage increases. *It becomes, thus, an economic necessity to promote the growth of the household economy, by providing it with an ever-increasing amount of work.*

Opportunities for creating work for the household do not end at the factory. Since the cost of production is usually less than half of the final cost to the consumer, rising manufacturing costs can be compensated for by reducing the costs of distribution.

The prices of many consumer products have remained stable because consumers have patronized low-margin, discount stores and supermarkets rather than traditional retail stores. Again, price stability is more apparent than real, because the cost of service has been shifted to the consumer.*

Pure service industries lie at the far end of the economic spectrum. Faced with rising wage costs and limited productivity increases, they usually opt to increase their prices. Hence the rapid increase in the direct-cash cost of services.

These tendencies are not speculation. They are observations of what has happened over the past twenty years. But what about the future? Can we see a pattern? Is there something in these facts that indicates the shape and form of future economic activity?

The future for consumer goods and consumer services will show a continued displacement of labor from the marketplace to the household. In the case of consumer goods, the manufacturer will ask us to do an ever-increasing share of the work at home; in services, we are likely to do more and more for ourselves. In reality, we already are doing so.

In the future, we will do more within the household economy. *How much* we do will depend on our income relative to the national average, the markup on labor costs required by the specific service in question, and the cost of acquiring the information or skill necessary to perform the service.

So long as inflation prevails, the household economy will enjoy a substantial and growing advantage over the market economy. Ironically, *the only way the marketplace production of goods and services can maintain its nominal health (i.e., return on investment and profitability) is to provide for the continuous expansion of the household economy.*

The commodity industries, because they are incapable of displacing labor at a rate sufficient to maintain profitability, will drift closer and closer to government and the collective economy. As the return on total capital approaches or sinks below the prevailing rate of interest, and the opportunity for providing an attractive return to equity investors declines, the appeal of

* This is discussed in more detail in Chapter 15.

regulation will increase, since it may be the only way to provide a return to investors.

In a sense, the heavy industries have been caught in a sea of rising interest rates, a sea that has risen so far and so fast that these industries are now threatened.

It might be argued, at this point, that none of this would happen if the market system were allowed to operate unhampered by government intervention and regulation. If prices were allowed to rise, the argument goes, industry returns would also rise, and they would be competitive, once more, in our newly inflationary environment.

However, a more profitable stance for industry is unlikely, because it would require rather significant price increases. Since most of our troubled industries require at least fifty cents of capital investment for every dollar of sales, and most typically require close to a dollar, it would be necessary to increase sales prices significantly, an increase that would then multiply through the rest of the economy. The end effect would be more inflation and an effective reduction in the standard of living. Reducing the standard of living means increasing unemployment; people would be buying less. In the end, the resulting recession would probably have the effect of decreasing demand and thereby reducing the commodity industries' profits to where they had been when the entire process started. All of which means that an increase in basic industry prices is likely to produce a net loss for the entire economy.

No such liberation of the free-market price mechanism (as economists call it) is likely to occur, however, because we have witnessed a large shift in power between labor and capital over the past twenty years.

Return on investment has fallen, profit margins have shrunk, and profits as a percentage of national income have plummeted. Nor does there appear to be any turning back. As painful as high interest rates are, the alternative is an absolute lack of consumer demand fostered by unemployment. If we look once more at the spectrum of returns on total capital in Figure 15 and contemplate these in light of a long siege of high interest rates, we see a case of "the devil take the hindmost."

The investor in heavy industry is faced with the prospect of seeing his capital dissipated or else of seeking to protect his return through government regulation—he has no other choice. Unlike the oil industry, few other areas of heavy industry have the resources or crass clout to survive a long siege of real or contrived scarcity. Nor will the public tolerate being held hostage by one industry after another, even if a reasonable case for higher investment returns can be made. In the end, our heavy industry will, by default, be absorbed by the federal economy.

Year by year, the distinction between government enterprise and private enterprise diminishes. What, after all, is the Lockheed Corporation? Who, at this point, has more at risk, the investors in the stock of the company, with their $320 million in equity, or the American taxpayer, who has cosigned loans for $250 million? And what about Penn Central?

Is there a difference, we might ask, between an intentional non-profit enterprise and an unintentional non-profit enterprise? Is there a difference between United States Steel and Blue Cross, the local hospital, our universities, or any of the entire spectrum of non-profit organizations that have enjoyed such health in the past decade? Yes. There are a lot of very unhappy investors in the steel and chemical industries. Lacking shareholders, non-profit institutions have no such problem.

Day by day, the distinction between collective enterprise and large marketplace enterprises grows more obscure. The automobile industry, for instance, enjoys *de facto* regulation; the degree of government control and intervention in the pricing and development of automobiles suggests that Ford, if it is not officially regulated, might as well be.†

The theory of capitalism and the marketplace offers that the pursuit of profit, of gain, leads money to be invested where gains are possible. Gains are possible only where a legitimate need exists, *ergo* capitalist investment is the most efficient instrument for meeting the needs of a free people. In theory, the railroads, airlines, metals, chemicals, and other suffering heavy industries should then be showing an attractive profit. No one, after all, is about to assert that steel is not vital. We would miss United States Steel, Du Pont, and International Paper far more than we

† Consider it in relation to most other industries; how many have product changes scheduled by Congress or prices adjusted by Presidential comment?

would miss McDonald's and Disney Productions, yet both of the latter are far more esteemed in the stock market and far more profitable than the heavy industries. We must all face the fact that the marketplace values McDonald's hamburgers a cool $750 *million* more than all the girders and plate of the United States Steel Corporation.

So what happens? Where do we go from here? Confronted with the choice of being a dead capitalist or a regulated one, which does one accept? One accepts regulation or moves on to other areas. The form of marketplace activity is kept, but the content is removed.

We are moving toward an era of *de facto* public ownership of basic industry, toward the slow attrition of the market economy. Just as England maintains a decorative royal family to preserve traditions and dress a rather drab, administered world with a few grand ceremonies and hints of divine power, we shall one day soon enshrine the shareholders of Continental Can and Kaiser Steel.

FIGURE 17

The Attrition of the Market Economy

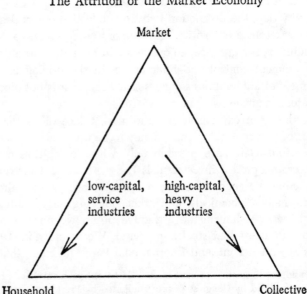

Market

low-capital, service industries

high-capital, heavy industries

Household   Collective

No formal ceremony will accompany the event. Conservatives will continue to believe that everything would be all right if the government would just leave them (and private enterprise) alone. Liberals and radicals will still protest the dividends received by the holders of AT&T stock; the wealth of the nation *is* poorly distributed. And the stock market may continue as before, though it may no longer be the last playing field for the products of fine eastern prep schools.

It may even be possible to maintain the illusion that nothing has changed. But it has. Slowly, imperceptibly, and by none of the routes predicted and recognized in other nations, the early, hard core of American industry is now being incorporated into the collective economy. Its continued appearance as a collection of independent, private companies is largely an illusion maintained in the interests of tradition.

Our new reality is simply this: *The real marketplace is quietly shrinking.* As the securities of heavy industries come more and more to resemble those of municipalities and government agencies—as they must—there will be more money chasing fewer genuine marketplace opportunities.

Simple supply and demand tells us that the price of what remains in the real marketplace must rise; hence the growing gap between the growth-industry stocks and the heavy-industry stocks.[4] It also tells us that some of that money is not going to stay in the marketplace. It will go looking for another game, one played in the household economy.

But this exodus, dramatic as it may seem, is really no more than a side show, a diversion from the fact that most Americans have been household investors for decades, that to be so has made economic sense for decades, and that it will continue to make sense in the future. *The household economy grows on the conflict between labor and capital,* a conflict that is ever more likely to be resolved in favor of labor. In a very real sense, only household capital is a good investment, a fact illustrated by the returns shown in Chapter 3.

We can understand the effects of this changed balance of power by examining the problem of "managing" the economy. The basic goal of this management is to achieve some kind of happy balance between employment opportunities, business profits, and inflation. The political problem begins not at granting the principle of management but at calibrating the last steps of the process, the final trade-offs between inflation, jobs, and profits.

If we were to imagine such a calibration, it would look something like the illustration below. The illustration assumes, as most business economists do, that increasing employment is likely to bring increased wages. In turn, higher wages are assumed to decrease the profit margins of business operations and, ultimately, to decrease the rate of return on invested capital. Conversely, decreasing employment implies decreasing demand, which translates into decreased sales and lowered profit margins as a smaller volume of business is forced to carry a fixed overhead cost. Again the result is a lowered return on invested capital. At the moment, the optimum point is presumed to occur at an unemployment rate of about 5 per cent.[5]

FIGURE 18

Business Profits *vs.* Unemployment

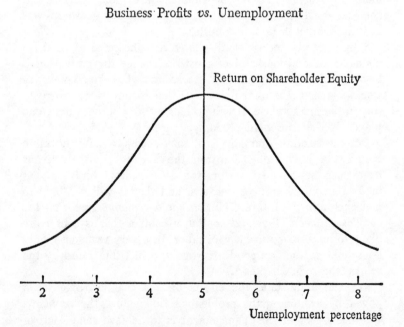

Return on Shareholder Equity

Unemployment percentage

In practice, the debate between return on investment and employment is never presented as it is above. Instead, public debate usually focuses on a relationship known as the Phillips curve, in which unemployment and *inflation* are shown to be inversely related. The choice presented is a bitter one, for it inevitably pits one group against another. Again the world of lesser evils prevails. If women and teen-agers, who tend to have relatively high rates of unemployment, want an abundance of job opportunities, they can have them only by subjecting the elderly to devastating inflation. Those who work can negotiate higher wages; the elderly, retired, and disabled, who live on fixed incomes, have no such recourse.

At the moment, the curve tells us that we can have approximately 3 per cent unemployment if we accept 5 per cent inflation, 4 per cent unemployment with 4 per cent inflation, and 5 per cent unemployment with 2 per cent inflation. (The curve is shown below.) Although this curve is by no means fixed and ironclad, research to date has indicated that as the economy matures the curve deteriorates: It requires more and more inflation to maintain the same degree of employment.

None of this would be a problem if inflation affected all concerned parties in exactly the same way. We could adjust to it, just as we could adjust to deflation. The problem is that it *does* affect all constituencies differently, including different industries. One of the main reasons for this differential effect is interest rates, because some industries require more capital than others.

Inflation increases the cost of borrowing money. The higher the rate of inflation, the higher the interest rates to be found in the money market. So it was in 1969, with inflation running at 5–6 per cent, that interest rates on long-term bonds were 8–9 per cent, and now, after a brief respite in 1971–72, rates are high again.[6] Since interest rates are tied to inflation and inflation is inversely related to unemployment, *the end result of a national policy of full employment is to reduce the economic viability of heavy industry, thereby forcing it to reach for regulation and government protection.*[7]

The result is a "no lose" situation for the household economy. As long as full employment is a prime public policy, traditional economic forces will work to push ever more labor out of the market economy and into the household economy, which obviously will continue to grow.

In the unlikely event that our policy of full employment is

FIGURE 19

The Phillips Curve

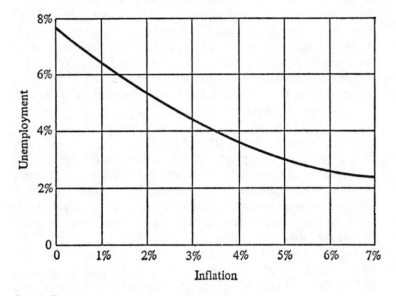

Source: *Fortune*

abandoned, we must consider what would replace it. It would
be politically impossible to substitute for it anything less than a
guaranteed annual income or some other system of income maintenance that would allow millions of people to become full-time
"employees" of the household economy. They might be "unemployed" so far as the market were concerned, but to accept this
description as truth would be inexcusable myopia. As soon as
orthodox employment is no longer the prime economic goal of
society (and dropping the full-employment policy would indicate
such a change), other economic forms will grow. And their
growth will be stimulated by direct and absolutely necessary
subsidy from the market economy.

The household economy can't lose.

1. *Forbes,* January 1, 1973, p. 33.
2. At this juncture, understanding the difference between return on total
capital and stockholders' equity becomes very important. If a business with

no debts can have net profits of 10 per cent on total investment, a still higher
rate of return *to the investor* can be obtained by borrowing at a lower interest rate to obtain *leverage* (otherwise known as the bitch goddess of high
finance). Two companies in the same industry, with identical sales and returns on *total* capital, can provide their owners with different returns on
equity.

EXAMPLE:

$1,000 Total capital	$1,000 Total capital
×10%	×10%
$ 100 Net return or 10% on equity	$ 100
	−30 Less interest on debt of $500 at 6%
	$ 70 Net return on stockholders' equity of $500 = 14%

The greater the difference between the interest rate for borrowed money
and the return on invested capital, the greater the potential for significantly
leveraging the stockholder's return. If the total return is 10 per cent, and the
cost of borrowed money is 5 per cent, the return on equity is 15 per cent when
one dollar is borrowed for every dollar of equity and 20 per cent when two
dollars is borrowed for every dollar of equity. How much leveraging is done
depends on the judgment of the companies' managers and the wisdom of the
lending bank. Note in Figure 15 that the return on total capital falls faster
than the return on equity; this is evidence that as the total return falls, managers substitute debt for equity in order to maintain the return on equity.

Unfortunately for the steel industry, there is a limit. Leveraging works for
you only when there is a *positive* difference between the return on total capital and the cost of borrowing money. If the return on total capital and the
cost of borrowing money are equal, nothing can be gained by substituting
debt for equity.

Worse, if the return on total capital sinks *below* the cost of borrowing
money, leverage then works in reverse: The return on stockholders' equity
is diminished by the need to service the corporate debt. Under these circumstances, the shareholder sees the value of his stock shrink until the actual cash
return provided meets investor expectations. Thus, the price of "income"
stocks is usually very sensitive to interest rates, for the dividend is constantly
measured against the prevailing rate of interest. Not surprisingly, few lenders
are eager to loan such troubled enterprises money, because there is little assurance the interest payments can be made.

In reality, the process described is far more complex. The electric and telephone utilities, for instance, show a return on total capital of 5.7 per cent,
considerably below the cost of currently borrowed funds, but they also show
a return on equity of 11.9 per cent, certainly an attractive figure. The industry
received a high return because most of its borrowed money had been obtained
years earlier, when interest rates were low. Rather than see its earnings crip-
pled as interest rates rose, part of the burden of inflation was shifted to the

earlier bondholders, who had loaned the company money years before at 3, 4 and 5 per cent and saw, consequently, the market value of their bonds drop as interest rates rose. In effect, a portion of the burden was transferred to the holders of debt rather than of equity: The bondholders saw their capital dissipated. Unlike the shareholders, they have no recourse to a rate increase, so the real market risk in regulated industries often accrues to the bondholder. This circumstance is likely to prevail in the future as well. As the companies expanded and needed new financing, they had to borrow at prevailing market rates. The net effect was to raise their average cost of debt closer to the current market rates, thus beginning a squeeze on net profits that resulted in the utility rate-increase requests seen all over the country in the past few years.

Any inconvenience experienced by public utilities can usually be remedied by an appeal to the local department of public utilities. Consumers will protest, of course. Some will note that they feel no need to carry the cost of a utility's advertising and public-relations campaigns as part of the cost of electricity. Other "waste" will be discovered and aired; much spleen will find expression in letters to the editor of the local newspaper. It is even possible that a few members of the regulatory board will make dark statements about the electric company's callousness toward the consumer or inquire why the telephone company needs more money to continue providing a declining quality of service.

But, in the end, the rate increase, or most of it, is approved. The return on total capital is maintained. The company elects to borrow a bit more. And all those poor widows and orphans who are the sole recipients of utility-company dividends are again assured that their income will go onward and upward unimpaired. (This is not to say that some utilities are not desperately pressed because their need for new capital and the cost of capital are such that they need large rate increases in order to operate with a margin of safety.)

No such remedy exists for unregulated industries, such as steel. The head of U. S. Steel cannot apply to increase his rates and, therefore, his return on total capital. The recent round of price controls had little meaning for steel, chemicals, and paper. Price competition alone was sufficient to keep prices stable. In fact, this is precisely the problem. Heavy commodity industries find it difficult or impossible to pass on cost increases to their customers. When a steel manufacturer raises his prices, he must contemplate losing business to foreign imports. American steel manufacturers complain with some justice that Japanese steel underprices American steel because the industry benefits from low-interest government loans and debt-to-equity ratios of as high as 20:1, astronomically higher than those in the U.S. steel industry; thus the price of Japanese steel is artificially low. Not surprisingly, the steel industry is now lobbying for government aid for the $2 billion it will need for capital equipment, etc., over the next decade (*The Wall Street Journal*, February 28, 1973). If foreign imports are no problem, materials substitution may be: Instead of buying steel, a contractor may elect to use concrete; a manufacturer may elect to use aluminum. So the steel man doesn't dare raise his prices —at least not much.

3. *Scientific American,* November 1971.

4. This effect has been called "the two-tiered market"; a number of investors and institutions have called for a more balanced investment policy from pensions, trusts, etc. But the fact is that even though the "vestal virgins" stocks (otherwise known as the "Nifty Fifty") have suffered large drops in price and price/earnings ratio, the rest of the market has fallen even farther.

5. Late in the 1970–71 recession, government economists tried to rationalize the continuing high unemployment rate by noting that unemployment among married men was extremely low (about 3 per cent) while it was over 10 per cent for women and teen-agers, a result, they offered, of the high influx of teen-agers and women into the work force during the decade. Such workers, the argument continued, could not be considered as being deeply distressed, because they were not the "breadwinners" of the nation. The debate touched off the longest series of articles and letters in *The Wall Street Journal* this writer can recall. Actually, we have a very rapidly changing labor force, and no single measure, of unemployment or anything else, has ever proved satisfactory. Other economists, noting the low unemployment among married men, forecast that inflation would be worse than expected when it resumed because the labor market was actually much "tighter" than it appeared under the 6 per cent unemployment figure. They were right.

6. The St. Louis Federal Reserve Bank, in a research paper, concluded that the "true" rate of interest was 3 per cent and that market interest rates tend to be equal to the true rate plus the rate of inflation; thus, in 1971–72, with inflation at 3–4 per cent, interest rates ran 6½–7½ per cent. This formulation has been criticized, but it does serve as a reasonable, if fallible, measure of interest rates and inflation.

7. It is now frequently argued that the social costs of inflation are balanced by ever greater social benefits and that we should, therefore, accept a relatively high rate of inflation (4+ per cent) as one of the costs of providing employment. In *Retreat from Riches* (New York: Viking Press, 1973), Peter Passell and Leonard Ross argue that the cost of maintaining the usual and traditionally bearable rate of creeping inflation (2–3 per cent) would be an unemployment rate of 5 per cent over all. But even this rate, they offer, understates how devastating our concentration on a "sound currency" can be, because a 5 per cent over-all rate may translate into a rate *three to five times as high* for young Blacks, teen-agers in general, and women. It would be better, the book argues, to accept the high rate of inflation, enlarge production and employment, and compensate those on fixed incomes for their losses. Some of this has already occurred. Soon Social Security payments will be automatically boosted when the cost-of-living index increases, and several economists have suggested that the U. S. Government float "inflation bonds" that carry a rate of interest and an inflation adjustment so that those who are savers rather than investors will have a protected savings outlet. As it is now, the poor and middle-income family that saves at 5–6 per cent is doomed to seeing its savings lose the race against inflation.

All this implies that some degree of inflation is absolutely inevitable and that interest rates will remain high for the foreseeable future; thus the profitability of American industry will remain problematic at best, and if such instruments as the "inflation bonds" do come into existence, it will be exceedingly difficult to distinguish between an investment in a regulated industry and an investment in a government debt issue.

13

Why Taxes Are Depressing

TAXES ARE VEXING, incomprehensible, and hideously unfair. This is common knowledge. It is also in the nature of things that no issue in taxation is ever resolved nor a solution ever accepted, because no way has yet been found to make taxation palatable. These facts, and all the endless debate that usually surrounds the subject, usually suffice to obscure the observation that is the subject of this chapter.

Taxation—the need to raise the public revenues necessary for supporting the social and political institutions that make a complex industrial society possible—inevitably creates a desire to employ one's time and capital in areas outside the market economy. Like inflation, the necessity of taxation is a self-limiting factor in the development of a market economy.

Since it is only reasonable to assume that most of us will go to some lengths to maximize our comfort and benefits, it is also reasonable to assume that as the burden of taxation increases, the effort we shall expend to avoid it will also increase. Unless one is extravagantly wealthy and can afford to hire the requisite experts, it is difficult to avoid taxation by participating in the exchange economy. Whether we employ our labor (all that most of us have) or our capital, the reward is generally in taxable dollars.

Crime is one obvious avenue of tax freedom. So is the art of
waiting on tables, the vocation of the scavenger, and the pre-
ferred cash fee obtained by some lawyers. But these are special
cases, at best, and most of them are liable to criminal prosecu-
tion if discovered. Only by moving out of the market economy
can labor and capital legitimately avoid taxation. Taxation, in
other words, favors the household economy; high taxation favors
it strongly. The greater the burden of taxation, the greater the
temptation, on the part of both workers and investors, to avoid
the marketplace. The household is a reasonable and readily available alternative.

Taxation is not an academic matter, and its burden is not small.
For most people, any reduction in federal income taxes provided
by the reforms of 1962 and 1970 was quickly absorbed by the
rapid escalation of the employment tax. State governments were
ready to absorb any inconvenient new surplus by instituting new
sales and income taxes. Whatever survived *these* new burdens
was absorbed by increases in the local property tax.

The average white-collar worker, according to the Tax Foundation, paid out some $1,707 of his seventy-five-hundred-dollar
annual income in taxes in 1960. By 1970, his income had risen
to eleven thousand dollars but his total tax bill had increased to
$3,475. Adjusting for inflation, we find that his private purchas-
ing power did not increase at all.

FIGURE 20

Taxation and John Q. Public

	1960	*1970*	*% Change*
Total Income	$7,500	$11,000	47%
Federal Tax	831	1,525	84
State Tax	204	508	149
Local Tax	672	1,442	115
Total	1,707	3,475	104
As % of Total	23	32	—
Net Income	5,793	7,525	30%
Inflation Adjustment	x1.00	x0.77	
Net Real Purchasing Power	5,793	5,795	0

Source: *The Tax Foundation*, July-August 1970.

There was a brief period of improvement in 1971, when the average worker's real wages increased with the economic recovery. But any surplus was dissipated in the escalation of food prices and employment taxes in 1972 and in the broad, general inflation of 1973–74. The impact of the rising cost of energy *alone* absorbed any wage gains for 1974, so it is altogether probable that the average American worker has been on a treadmill, going nowhere, for fifteen years. *Fifteen years.*

There are limits to this. If there was a "tax revolt" brewing in 1970, its power for 1976 should not be underestimated. While inflation is the popular villain, a close look at the Tax Foundation's figures shows quite clearly that taxes are a major factor in the static condition of the American worker's purchasing power. Where in 1960 they absorbed 23 per cent of total income, in 1970 taxes absorbed 32 per cent—all in spite of two rounds of "tax reform."

It might be argued here that this change, no matter how painful, is only the necessary response to the imbalance of public and private goods that existed in 1960. Harvard's John Kenneth Galbraith dramatized this disparity in a much quoted passage from *The Affluent Society:* "The family which takes its mauve and cerise, air-conditioned, power-steered, and power-braked automobile out for a tour, passes through cities that are badly paved, made hideous by litter, blighted buildings, billboards, and posts for wires that should long since have been put underground. They pass on into a countryside that has been rendered largely invisible by commercial art. . . . They picnic on exquisitely packaged food from a portable icebox by a polluted stream and go on to spend the night at a park which is a menace to public health and morals. Just before dozing off on an air mattress, beneath a nylon tent, amid the stench of decaying refuse, they may reflect vaguely on the curious unevenness of their blessings."[1]

Nor was Galbraith alone in citing this imbalance. He was joined by many others, and the sixties was filled with the now familiar arguments for new priorities, more public versus private goods, and so forth—all the tired stuff of disagreements between traditional conservatives and liberals. While the conservative defends initiative and the need to reward it, asserting that high taxation will slow economic growth and lead to general stagnation, the liberal argues that the individual accumulation of wealth is no longer a paramount goal; while much private need has been fulfilled, many public needs go unmet.

From the individual's direct point of view, however, it is difficult to see taxes as anything but subtractive. Priorities and moral impact are largely irrelevant. Those with ordinary incomes have no difficulty maintaining their initiative: The average man works to keep his head above water. He needs no other prod. While it may require gilded carrots to induce the well off to greater effort, only fear of the whip is required for the rest.

Quiet desperation does not preclude visions; the average man can still dream of "making it." Looking forward to the future, he is likely to imagine that someday—when outrageous affluence is finally and firmly his—he will be deterred from further effort because of the excise tax on diamonds, the high cost of airport usage for personal jets, or the removal of accelerated depreciation. Having passed the last step in the federal schedule so that he must give the major portion of his income to the Internal Revenue Service, he might think less fondly of work. At levels of income where taxation has finally managed to reduce incentive, it is possible to take long periods of time for indulging just such thoughts. The average man can only look forward to such a day, for it will be proof that his wildest dreams have at last come true: he can get off the treadmill.

Still, there is a basic problem with this line of reasoning. The individual who "sees" empirical proof that taxation has reduced his freedom of choice because it has reduced his real income— whatever the need for public goods—seldom stops to consider what his income would be if those taxes were not taken. This is the weakness of the conservative argument. It insists that taxes are subtractive, when all evidence indicates that government spending is responsible for maintaining a balance between employment and investment. If taxes and government spending were reduced, the level of economic activity would drop. So would incomes.

Those who complain about taxes must consider the alternative. In essence, we can have our incomes decreased either by taxes or by depression. The foolhardy, perhaps, will choose to risk the dangers of unemployment rather than accept the inevitability of taxation; the rest of us, whatever our misgivings, are bound to

take a more moderate course. Until the burden of taxes out-
weighs the general gains, we opt for more taxes. Thus government expenditures at all levels have been rising continuously
for more than three decades.

FIGURE 21

Total Government Expenditures, 1942–70
(in billions)

Year	Amount
1942	$ 46
1950	70
1955	111
1960	151
1965	206
1970	333

Source: Statistical Abstract of the United States, 1974.

Instead of blunting economic growth, taxation works to direct
it; rather than inhibiting the growth of capital, it works to funnel
it to areas where it can most effectively be used and prevents or
at least minimizes the development of periods in which there is
more investment than the economy can absorb. Without taxation, the private sector would have more money than it could
use. *The market economy, quite simply, needs taxation to maintain stability and promote orderly growth.*

The irony of this is that while liberals and conservatives still
argue the macroeconomic realities, another, larger truth has been
obscured. *Progressive taxation tends to depress specialization of
labor.* As the degree and amount of taxation increase, people
have ever more incentive to avoid forms of income subject to
taxes. This means that as taxation increases, there is an ever
greater temptation to avoid the marketplace, since it is the marketplace that generates taxable monetary transfers. The implication of this is that *the very force that stabilizes the market
economy also acts to encourage economic growth outside the
marketplace.*

We can see how this happens by examining the decisions of
individuals who choose between performing a service themselves
and hiring someone else to do it. If taxes did not exist, a person

who earned five dollars per hour would need to work only one hour to hire someone of equal skills and wages. If he hires someone for two-fifty an hour, he can command two hours of another person's time at the cost of one hour of his own. The greater the difference between the wages of the employee and the employer, the greater the amount of time and effort commanded by the employer. The lawyer who earns fifty dollars an hour will seldom consider cleaning his own office when he can hire someone to do it for two-fifty an hour. Similarly, the engineer who earns eight dollars an hour would willingly hire a housekeeper at three dollars an hour if not hiring one would prevent him from going to work. Yet, he might give careful thought to hiring an electrician for ten dollars an hour.

There is no magic to these decisions; they are the simple product of classical economic thought. This demands that each individual act to maximize his economic benefits and conserve his scarcest resources. The man who forgoes the $24-a-day housekeeper and his wage as a $64-a-day engineer loses forty dollars a day; obviously, such a decision does not represent the optimum economic use of the available resources.

Specialization results when individuals seek maximum economic advantage in an exchange economy. The person who is highly productive as an engineer may be highly unproductive as a short-order cook. And vice versa. The wages of short-order cooks are generally lower than those of engineers, because, among other things, there is a greater supply of the former than there is of the latter.

The more complex the economy, the greater the opportunities for specialization. Specialization also creates a wide distribution of wages. Some workers can hardly survive, finding fitful employment washing dishes or emptying boxcars from day to day. Others win more regular employment manning elevators in senescent buildings, opening doors at fashionable beauty parlors, or attending the sinks and toilets at bus stations. They also accept the very lowest wages. They are assured continued employment, because even the unemployed poor disdain these jobs. The average worker can buy two or three hours of such a menial's time for the price of one of his own.

At the other end of the spectrum, we can find the securities salesman who specializes in large institutions and reaps an an-

nual income of $250,000, more than some people earn in their
entire working life. The fruits of specialization for such individuals are enormous. Those with high incomes can command the
time of a small army of menials and a rather impressive collection of more-average people. The well-paid specialist can command ten or even twenty hours of average labor in exchange for
each hour of his own. He is at the top of the wage-and-time pyramid. Without that pyramid, French restaurants could not exist.
Nor could the Plaza Hotel, Cartier's gems, and Patek Philippe
watches. There would be no market for most of the goods and
services that generally define the boundaries of the Good Life.

Incomes, in actual fact, are based on more than labor; the
higher the income, the higher the probability that it is derived
in part (or in total) from capital. But, for most people, income
is a product of labor. The 95 per cent of the population earning
less than twenty-five thousand dollars a year—no matter how
bizarre their employment—trade minutes and hours for dollars.

FIGURE 22

Distribution of Family Income, 1970

Income Class	% of Families
$25,000 +	4.5
15,000 − 25,000	16.5
10,000 − 15,000	27.0 ⎰ 48.5
7,000 − 10,000	21.5 ⎱
5,000 − 7,000	11.5
3,000 − 5,000	10
Under $3,000	9

Median − $9,867

Source: *A Guide to Consumer Markets, 1971/1972*
(New York: Conference Board, Inc., 1971), p. 111.

Note in the table above that nearly half of all families had incomes between seven and fifteen thousand dollars a year, 60
per cent had incomes between five and fifteen thousand dollars,
and at least 70 per cent had incomes between five and twenty
thousand dollars a year. These figures are the main support for
the idea that America is a middle-class society. Generally speak-

ing, they are taken to represent a condition that is healthy and good. The middle-income, middle-class nation, we are told, is a healthy, happy, democratic nation.[2]

Moral attacks, over the past decade, have concentrated on the chasm that separates the top incomes from the bottom incomes. The press regales us with tales of how Jackie Onassis spends more on hairdressers than most executives earn, and how J. Paul Getty "earns" more in a single hour than most men earn in a decade. Similarly, newspaper accounts of Howard Hughes feature a record of his handsome hotel bills. And an occasional news piece will relate how John Hay Whitney is reputed to spend some $2.5 million a year on his personal staff.

Keeping to the spirit of incomprehensible wealth, Neiman-Marcus and a few other stores strive for creativity in marketing in order to exercise the whims of the ridiculously rich. So it is that rare wines are sold for ten thousand dollars a bottle and sterling-silver garbage cans are filled with caviar. All this we know and relish. While one section of the New York *Times* describes the one hundred neediest cases, another describes this year's record extravagances. Whether such tales fill our secret dreams or fuel revolutionary anger, their end effect is the same: *The narrow range of income within which most economic activity occurs is seldom examined.* Consequently, its implications are never considered.

Most of us in this middle range buy the time of others whose wages are very close to our own. As we noted before, six families in ten have incomes within 50 per cent of the median. The carpenter hires an electrician, the electrician hires a plumber, the plumber hires a mason; at the end of the year, each hires an accountant in spite of the fact that they all have nearly identical incomes and hourly wages. Why?

The answer is simple. And obvious. Because they are specialized; each worker is highly productive in one skill and unproductive in others. Just as we would never consider hiring a plumber to build our cabinets or rewire our house, the carpenter knows he is efficient as a carpenter but is uncertain of his abilities as a mason. In any case, he owns none of the equipment that the other trades use day in and day out.

None of this is a revelation. It is everyday common sense. We hire others because they can accomplish the same task far more "economically" than we could, meaning that a given amount of money finds its way to him who offers the largest amount of the desired product. The carpenter may earn nine dollars an hour, just as the plumber does, but he will hire the plumber to install the sink or clean the drain, because it would take him two hours, whereas the plumber can do it in one.

The decision we make on whether to provide a service for ourselves is based on more than a comparison of wages; it involves some estimate of the relative efficiency of the person we are hiring. Thus, we usually choose to *hire* someone to do a special task, assuming that someone else can do it for less than we could do it for ourselves. In the ideal free market we specialize to maximize our income and hire specialists to do that which we cannot. Everyone, presumably, is rewarded in accordance with his skills and productivity.

Taxation stands between the consumer and the clear working of this ideal market calculus. Taxes on income reduce the spending power of the worker. In effect, they penalize both exchange and productivity, the two main supports for a market economy. Even if taxes were not progressive, they would act as a deterrent to exchange; the man who repairs his own automobile instead of paying a mechanic is creating an economic good without the need to pay taxes on it. The same applies to all work done in the home, whether it is growing vegetables, completing tax forms instead of hiring H&R Block, or painting the living room. Just as Ralph Borsodi demonstrated that the cost of distribution is the institutional burden of the factory system, taxation is the institutional burden of a specialized, market society. *The taxation of earned income is an inducement to seek income in the household economy rather than in the marketplace.*

The higher the taxes on income, the greater the incentive to avoid the marketplace. If, for instance, state and federal taxes on income are 20 per cent (a not atypical rate), then the worker must commit one hour and fifteen minutes to the marketplace in order to hire someone who would receive the same wages for one hour.

EXAMPLE:
Wage rate
$1.00 less taxes of 20% =   .80   net effective wage
                          ×1¼ hours
                        ────────────
                         $1.00

We find ourselves in the rather peculiar position of having to work an hour and fifteen minutes to hire someone with equally valuable (but different) skills to work for an hour.

As the level of taxation rises, so do the impediments against marketplace activity. The table below indicates the effects of different tax rates.

FIGURE 23

The Specialization Penalty

Wage Rate = 100% = 1 hr.	Tax Rate	Effective Wage	Specialization Penalty %	Time
	20%	80%	125%	1:15
	25	75	133	1:20
	33	67	150	1:30
	40	60	167	1:40
	50	50	200	2:00
	70	30	333	3:20

(Amount needed to restore original earnings)

Taxes lower the effective wages received for marketplace labor. We always receive less money than we earned; every salary check notes for us the payments made for employment taxes, unemployment insurance, the state income tax, and the federal withholding tax. Recognizing the reduction, we complain, carp, and otherwise express displeasure. We seldom, however, consider the effect of taxes in terms of how much *more time* we must work to buy the labor of someone who earns, before taxes, exactly what we do. These figures are presented above, under the column "Specialization Penalty." Note that workers in the 50 per cent tax bracket must work two hours in order to hire someone in the same bracket for one hour.

The net effect of taxation is to penalize productivity achieved by specialization. If the worker in the 50 per cent tax bracket is only half as productive (or efficient) as the specialist he hires to do the same job, then who does it is a matter of economic indifference. He chooses between two hours of his own specialized work in the marketplace or two hours of relatively unfamiliar work in the household economy. Whatever he chooses, it will take the same amount of time. Only if the man hired is *more* than twice as productive would there be any advantage in hiring him. Otherwise, the decision is directed by subjective considerations rather than economic ones. The Roto-Rooter man will remain employed long after it has become economic folly to hire him.

Not everyone, of course, is in the 50 per cent tax bracket, so our case may seem overstated. As long as the general level of taxation remains at 20–25 per cent, a wholesale exodus from hiring specialists seems unlikely. After all, workers need be only one third more efficient at their specialty than their customers in order to offer an economic advantage.

It would be useful, here, to distinguish between progressive taxation of individual incomes and a rising level of general taxation. *Progressive taxation of individual incomes serves to deter individuals from becoming further specialized.* It creates a situation of diminishing returns. Some would call this the blunting of individual incentive, the death knell of initiative. A rising level of general taxation, such as that experienced by the United States and all the major Western industrial nations, has a similar effect on the entire population: Taxes penalize productivity achieved through specialization.

To economic liberals—those now called conservatives—these are damning facts, indications that government taxation is crushing the freedom of individuals and inhibiting economic growth. But there is a failure of vision here; if economic growth is inhibited in the marketplace, that does not mean it will not occur. *It means only that it will occur somewhere else.* Taxation inhibits marketplace growth but stimulates the household economy. Taxation, by penalizing productivity achieved through specialization, works to equalize the productivity of the marketplace and household economies. Initiative and incentive aren't lost, they are redirected. They reappear outside the marketplace in the efforts of individuals and families to create for themselves that for which they once paid.

Our theoretical arguments, so far, have understated the case for the growth of the household economy, because they assume that labor can be directly purchased. This is not the case. *Marketplace labor must not only bear the institutional burden of taxation, it must also carry the overhead costs of organization and the cost of distribution.* Even the most direct service organizations charge two and one-half times the cost of labor. The accountant who is paid ten dollars an hour is billed out to clients at twenty-five dollars an hour, a sum that makes it possible, without any consideration of taxes, for only the small minority of individuals who earn in excess of fifty thousand dollars a year to hire an accountant on an *equal-time* cost basis. *When both the general and the specific overhead burdens are considered, it becomes clear that any productivity that accrues to specialization is vitiated by the overhead burdens it must carry.*

Consider, for example, what happens when an eight-dollar-an-hour accountant hires an eight-dollar-an-hour service repairman, and vice versa. The repairman is billed out by his company at two and one-half times his hourly wage, or twenty dollars; to earn this money, the accountant must work three hours and twenty minutes, because 25 per cent of his wages are absorbed by taxes. Thus, to be truly economically efficient, the service repairman must be at least three and one-third times as efficient as the accountant at repairing things. The same applies should the repairman wish to hire the accountant to do his taxes. The accountant must be three and one-third times as efficient. Obviously, any task that is either simple or frequently repeated is likely to be something an individual may actively consider doing for himself.

If it is clear that taxation tends to favor the household economy over the marketplace, still, much in our current economy cannot be done "in your spare time at home." Few of us will attempt the home production of steel or aluminum, nor will we maintain gravel pits or granite quarries for our personal use; similarly, we are seldom inclined to produce automobiles at home, and the candle, for all its recent ubiquity, is not about to replace the incandescent bulb.

To list all the goods not likely to be produced at home would be an enormous undertaking. A session with the yellow pages should convince all doubters. The Sears catalog may be used to similar effect. As a last resort, a few hours spent contemplating the gears, washers, framitzes, extrusions, hinges, and truncated thingamajigs in Sweets or the latest General Motors parts catalog will shatter even the fondest dreams of self-sufficiency. The household economy, one might conclude, will be lost like the army of yore . . . for want of a nail.

Change, however, doesn't have to be absolute to be real. Steel, heavy industry, and all the paraphernalia of an industrial economy can coexist with home-baked bread. They are not mutually exclusive. For us, it is only necessary to note that the forces in motion favor the growth of the household economy and the relative stagnation of the industrial economy. Self-limiting factors are coming into play and will increasingly influence our economic decisions in the future.

What we are observing is a peculiar revolution. Perhaps that is why it has escaped wide notice. But it *is* causing a profound and self-perpetuating shift in the equilibrium that exists among the three sectors of economic activity. Day by day, it becomes more attractive for the consumer to consider providing services for himself and to acquire the capital equipment necessary to produce goods. *Only the household economy provides a haven from inflation and taxation.* As we have already noted, investment returns on household capital goods are often better than those obtained on marketplace investments. As the work week is progressively reduced, the full force of the bias toward removing labor and capital from the market economy will be felt. At the moment, it is constrained by our full devotion to the market economy. This devotion, however, is rapidly disintegrating.

Our observations raise one troubling question for our analysis. If the circumstances of economic growth favor the household economy, and if services are most amenable to transfer from market to household, then why is the market for services growing so quickly?

The answer is that the growth of marketplace services and the growth of household services are not mutually exclusive. *Both* are growing rapidly. Unfortunately, since no measure exists for the growth of work performed in the home, we cannot derive a growth rate for services in the household economy. We can only assume, having examined a small mountain of fragmented evidence, that it has been, and will continue to be, an area of rapid economic growth.

We should also note that it is the peculiar nature of some services that they require the participation of the consumer: Entertainment, leisure activities, and health care are examples. Although it is difficult to assign an economic value to the time spent participating as a consumer, the issue raised is real. The "product" of many services is a joint matter, highly dependent on the participation of the consumer. The oldest profession has known this for some time and charged accordingly.

If no specific short-term measures for the growth of the household economy exist, it remains that the longer-term trend is toward increase. Sebastian De Grazia, in a study of time and leisure for the Twentieth Century Fund,[3] concluded that although the typical work week had declined from sixty to less than forty hours since the beginning of the century, the typical American worker labored just as hard and long now as he had in the past. He did not work less; he worked at different things. Most of his new activities were outside of the orthodox definition of "job" and "work," because they were in the unpaid, or household, economy.

Thus, commutation has become a major time consumer for the modern worker, and the upper-middle-class household, which imported labor to wash, clean, and iron fifty years ago, now has incorporated all these activities into the household alone. Like the woman in the frontier household economy, the modern woman must fend for herself unless she is very wealthy. Most of these changes have received little note, because we measure only *time at the job* as work. All other time is usually considered "free," or "leisure," time, a fact hard to reconcile with the press of harried consumers at the local shopping center every Saturday. *The fact is that we are working as hard as ever, if not harder, but the organization of work time has changed.*

Taxes and inflation create a strong pressure to move work outside the market economy. But it is also clear that these pressures are resisted. Blind belief and force of habit play significant roles in this resistance, augmented and amplified by the high cost of information and the organization of our educational institutions.

Productivity, whether it comes through the capital equipment used in production or through the skills of those who work, is dependent upon knowledge; the acquisition of knowledge depends on the cost of information.

It takes time to train a carpenter or a computer programmer. Whatever the skill, it is generally admitted that people are not interchangeable and that providing someone with productive skills in any area requires an investment of both time and money. The question is: *how much* time and *how much* money? Usually, we conclude that it will require *too much:* We gamble that the rewards of our personal specialization will compensate for the costs incurred in hiring someone with another specialization.

Increasingly, this looks like a bad gamble, although the illusion is perpetuated by the propaganda of the educational establishment. Many who invested time and money to acquire esoteric knowledge in the early sixties now find themselves unemployed and unemployable. Some universities' employment counselors have recommended to recent graduates that they not tell prospective employers they have a doctorate. In less extreme cases, those who possess special knowledge find that it so limits their marketability and options that the extra money, if it exists at all, is not worth the risk. Labor Department studies indicate that we may have an oversupply of college graduates through the seventies and a shortage of skilled technicians at the same time.

The assumption that fueled the crush of students into our graduate schools—that specialization gave one special knowledge and a certain pre-emptive status when it came to employment—is less and less tenable. At best, the advanced degree that once promised a ticket to advancement now only guarantees admission to the job market. At worst, it closes doors.

As we shall see later, education and the concept of "human capital" is the equivalent of grace for the secular world; the poor and the dispossessed, not to mention those who are merely middle-class, correctly perceive that crass financial wealth can never be theirs. So they lunge for the educational Communion wafer. It does not matter that the lure has become tarnished, because there is no real alternative. In the accepted view of the world, one either believes in education or accepts a position of social despair. All this, however, assumes that the marketplace vision of society is unremittingly true. And since our educational institutions inflict this view on the young, it appears that the real bottleneck in social change is the educational apparatus, an apparatus that, ironically, makes ever greater demands on our money.

Once education is perceived as an investment for wholly personal, private use rather than as a means of achieving a competitive edge, the balance must swing in favor of the household economy. That change in view has already begun. Turmoil is inescapable. Funds and support are difficult to obtain for public and private institutions alike. Parents, aware that institutions must educate children for a society twenty years in the future, are increasingly prone to question the assumptions made by orthodox professional educators. Predictions of the imminent demise of all conventional educational institutions abound.

While small colleges close their doors in bankruptcy and large universities announce rising deficits and curtail, at long last, the exponential growth of obscure deanships, new, ad-hoc institutions appear daily. Adult education, once limited to opportunities for teachers to exhibit slides taken on summer tours, is now booming, and the bankruptcy of conventional credentials is ever more evident. Course offerings include all the arts and crafts, home repair, automotive mechanics, financial management, cabinetry—just about anything, in short, that relates to producing for oneself and one's family. The publication of *The Whole Earth Catalog* was more than an instrument for the counterculture; it was the signal that a radically different concept of the use of knowledge was taking root, for the book attempts to offer relevant knowledge not for the competitive advantage of the consumer but for his *personal* use. Whereas it was once beneficial to accumulate special knowledge, it is now best to accumulate general knowledge.

If this attitudinal shift is visible and growing, it is still necessary to note that attitudes alone are not sufficient. Implicit in *The Whole Earth Catalog,* the *Mother Earth News,* and all the other publications dedicated to dropping out of the marketplace is the assumption that the cost of information has declined dramatically.

At the moment, a small minority feel the need to make extravagant investments in acquiring general knowledge in order to fulfill their personal destiny, investments that a larger population will not make until the cost of information is much lower. For most of us, the horrors of the conventional world are not so terrible that it must be avoided at all costs. We participate in the market economy where it is to our advantage, and in the household economy as well. At best, participation is at the margins. Recognizing that marketplace activity is inflexible, we find more and more occasion to do work in the household economy. The burden of taxation gives us constant encouragement.

For most of us, change is anything but radical. It is, however, exceedingly real. Rather than violent revolution, we are experiencing a slow shift in equilibrium. Slowly, we move toward the household economy, still clinging tenaciously to the idea that special knowledge and special skill, exercised in the marketplace, is the only route to social and economic success, our only hope for personal fulfillment. We are wrong, of course, and the evidence of our mistaken belief mounts every day. Eventually, the reality of what we do and what we believe will collide. When that collision occurs, it will grow around the issue of taxation.

1. J. K. Galbraith, *The Affluent Society* (Boston: Houghton Mifflin, 1958).

2. At least one writer, Richard Parker (*The Myth of the Middle Class,* Liveright, 1972) would take issue with the idea of America as a middle-class nation. But it remains that the distribution of income in America is broader than elsewhere and that the distribution changes very little when capital income is removed. While it is true that we have ridiculous extremes of wealth and poverty, it remains that a large number of people, a majority, are middle-income. If that weren't the case, the 1972 election might have been quite different.

3. Sebastian De Grazia, *Of Time, Work and Leisure* (New York: Twentieth Century Fund, 1962).

14

The Scarcity of Time

TIME IS NEVER "FREE." It is always scarce and precious. It becomes more scarce year by year, and there is absolutely no indication that it will become less valuable in the future. When, for instance, was the last time you had an hour with nothing to do? Unless you are retired or otherwise excluded from most of the ongoing chores and needs of daily life, chances are that such occasions are rare. Uncommitted moments are to be struggled for and protected against unwanted invasions of busyness. To call such moments "free" is a travesty of the word.

We need time. We need time to work, to eat, to sleep, and to accomplish all the daily chores of living. We also need time to know and understand our mates, our children, and our friends. Most of our relationships, in fact, require more time than we have, and it is difficult to avoid the feeling that we could never have enough. Nor is the list of demands on our time complete. We have ignored the time we need to be alone, a necessary but invariably short-changed period. Why else do we find ourselves delighted at having a few moments to wait in a doctor's reception room or strangely contented while trapped in rush-hour traffic?

All these demands come before the proliferating hardware used in the consumption of still more time—before the possession, use, and maintenance of automobiles, small and large boats, tennis rackets, skis, and golf clubs, sewing machines and looms, bathing suits, hi-fi sets, tape decks, cameras, etc. All these things—the inevitable trappings of affluence—make still more demands on our ever-diminishing store of time. They are responsible for many of the sour notes sounded as affluence becomes more general and disappointing.

We might, at this juncture, spring into another discussion of the liabilities that accrue to materialist society. But to pit the crass materialist world against the world of finer, higher things is to miss a fundamental point: *Most of us are materialists.* While we may long for peace and quiet, there are few among us who have actively contemplated a life of silent thought and appreciation on the requisite Tibetan mountainside. We like our houses, our dishwashers, and our fiberglass sailboats; we relish our skis, our power mowers, ten-speed bikes, and four-speed automobiles. No realistic look at our economic life can discount this fact.

The conflict and disappointment many Americans feel is not one that involves a basic change in values but the belated discovery that affluence can never be as total as we had once dreamed. We joke about this, of course. A popular suburban lament is, "I've worked all these years to make this much money and now that I have it, I can't find anyone to mow the lawn. I *still* have to do it myself!"

For most of us, affluence is the privilege of waiting for help in a department store, of searching for a parking spot, of packing suitcases, and of waiting on silent telephones while reserving a hotel room, dinner table, or rental car. On rarer occasions, it also means being stranded in exotic places, being robbed by the less fortunate, or arousing the interest of the Internal Revenue Service. Our affluence is a slightly sour experience because it does less for us than we thought it would. Yet, few who have attained it are inclined to give it up. Whatever the liabilities that accrue to the crowded world of new affluence, the final balance does not favor the alternatives.

Now, where we once dreamed of so many *things,* we stand wistfully in our suburban surroundings, staring into the foreshortened environment, wishing for escape, for open spaces, fresh breezes, and clear, unchlorinated water. And for the time to enjoy them. The often-heralded age of leisure is a long way off; when leisure does abound, as among the unemployed, it is seldom welcome.

We often repeat the old adage "Time is money." But we seldom, if ever, give any real consideration to the exact relationship between the two. Time *is* money, because we exchange it for money via employment. But can we say the reverse? Can we say "Money is time"? The phrase is awkward, at best, and our experience disagrees. It is far easier to convert time to money than the reverse. Time can never be stored; nor can it be bought. It is our ultimate resource.

Time is our newest and final scarcity. This does not mean that money is in absolute surplus (most of us are pretty short on that, too); it means only that organizing time has become as pressing as managing money. The same industrial productivity that created our material affluence is also responsible for our temporal poverty. We simply haven't got enough time.

Material wealth and temporal wealth are mutually exclusive; as one increases, the other must diminish. This is the Catch-22 of industrial society. Productivity and leisure are mutually exclusive; the more we produce, the more we have to do.

Objects become precious because they are intrinsically scarce; productive time becomes scarce because we have made it so precious. No one has become more aware of this painful exclusion principle than the corporate manager and the professional. The demand for their time and services tends to increase constantly, as does their income, while they accumulate more and more unused toys and goodies.

Productivity is the true measure of time's value. When we say that we have increased productivity at an annual rate of 3 per cent, we are saying that we have decreased the amount of labor time required to produce an object. A typical factory worker may produce twice as much this year as he did twenty-five years ago. Theoretically, the worker can elect to take the fruits of productivity in the form of more goods (higher wages for the same amount of time) or more time (the same goods in less time). The historical record indicates that he has elected to compromise and take a little of both. We all enjoy a higher material standard of living and more "free time" in which to savor that abundance. The average work week, the Department of Labor tells us, has gone from sixty hours, at the end of the nineteenth century, to something under forty hours.

As a growing number of manufacturers experiment with the

four-day forty-hour week and an increasing number of unions bring labor time below thirty-five hours, we read ever more about the leisure boom. Leisure, the Sunday supplements would have us believe, is about to overwhelm us; its rate of expansion is absolutely cancerous and (oh, lament!) most of us are totally unprepared. These articles intimate we may be in for the biggest psychological crisis since the invention of the wheel or the discovery of venereal disease.

The only problem is that it is difficult to take the leisure boom seriously. I have been waiting for it for years. I keep a tennis racket at the front door. Not for one moment have I felt anxious about adjusting to leisure. But the boom, if it arrived, passed me by. It probably passed you as well.

The sad fact is that most people probably share the common fate of being trapped in isolated "pockets" of temporal poverty. Everyone else has time, while we have nothing but sodden money. Such is the fate of those with higher-than-average incomes.

We might question the reality of this apparent gain in time over the past half century and contemplate its import for the future. Sebastian De Grazia, in *Of Time, Work and Leisure*,[1] concludes: "We simply cannot accept as fact that the work week has gone down as much as claimed, and therefore that the worker has elected to accept part of his pay in free time. The time involved in activities off the plant premises but work-related nevertheless—activities like the journey to work, do-it-yourself chores, housework, geographical work, mobility, overtime, and moonlighting—this is not less than it was at the turn of the Twentieth Century. Such being the case, the American is actually working as hard as ever, and in his drive for shorter hours is, if anything, trying to keep his head above water to find time for shopping, repairs, family, . . . etc.—on all of which the job has made subtle inroads."

For commuters in the New York area, from New Jersey, Connecticut, or Long Island, the work day is long indeed. In many suburban areas, it is not uncommon for the working father to be out of the house by 7 A.M., not to return until 7 P.M., five days a week. That's sixty hours, right up to the nineteenth-century standard!

One might argue that the commuter commutes by choice. He

could live closer to work. But could he? While he may give lip
service to his sacrifice in providing the children with grass and
trees, his commutation, in fact, may be a rather bizarre form of
earnings.

The test is whether or not the average commuter would suffer
a decrease in his material standard of living if he moved into the
city. The answer, in most cases, is yes.

You don't pay a hundred and ten dollars a month to garage
your car in suburbia, as you do in New York. Nor do two-
bedroom apartments cost six hundred dollars a month, as they
do in Manhattan. Without even considering the costs of private
education in that city versus public education (via taxes) in the
suburbs, the upper-middle-income commuter may "earn" three
or four thousand dollars in effective standard of living by investing additional hours in commutation time. And commutation
earnings, unlike employment earnings, are non-market, non-cash
earnings and, therefore, tax-free. Thus, they are worth more. As
the commuters' cash income and tax liabilities increase, his incentive to exploit commutation income also increases, which explains
why men who earn forty thousand dollars a year often spend as
many as six hundred dull-witted hours a year on trains.

Although part-time employment is becoming increasingly acceptable, most employment is still inflexible. The company employee can seldom elect to work twenty or twenty-five hours; he
must work forty or not at all. Economic gains are to be taken in
the form of increased income rather than of less time at work.
Money is not time.

Some might argue that people choose more goods because they
want them more than they want time. In most cases, this would
be true. But the preference has never been put to the test, because work time is not flexible.

Now there are indications that the historic preference of goods
over time is ending. Recent *Wall Street Journal* articles, for instance, have noted that it is increasingly difficult to get factory
workers to accept overtime work, even at premium wages. Similarly, one of the prime recent negotiating points for the auto
workers was the right to refuse overtime work.* While some
sociologists believe that this reluctance is another sign of decline

---

* Oil prices solved *that* problem.

of the work ethic, it is also possible that workers are merely trying, as De Grazia suggests, to protect their equally necessary unpaid work time.

The housewife is probably the best and most frightening example of how productivity has made goods abundant and time scarce. Now, in spite of washers, dryers, dishwashers, vacuum cleaners, floor waxers, electronic air cleaners, central heat, electricity, burners with a brain, self-cleaning ovens, and frost-free refrigerators, the average housewife and mother still works fifty to sixty hours a week. All that has changed is the nature of the work. Where before she was a general laborer and drudge, now she is a general manager and drudge. Household work now requires a substantial capital investment in equipment, increasing the housewife's output of dishes, diapers, and clothing per hour.

The limit to all of this has been explored by economist Staffan Burenstam Linder.[2] If it requires time to produce things, it also requires time to maintain and consume them. While this may seem obvious to the harried, it is neglected in most economic literature. If we assume that each worker has a total of sixteen hours to "spend" and that each hour of productive work also requires a half hour of maintenance or personal work time (including eating, dressing, washing, etc.) and a half hour of consumption time, then we can expect an increasing pressure on our available time if we produce an increasing amount of goods in our hours of directly productive work. If a new machine doubles the output of goodies, we then will have twice as much product for the same amount of work. While this may be a delight, it also means that we have twice as much consuming and maintaining to do in our "non-work" hours. Thus we become ever more harried as our productivity increases.

If each hour of work in the marketplace produces more goods, thus requiring more of our time and attention *outside* of conventional work as well, then we must eventually run out of time. If eight hours of work commits us to four hours of personal work in the home (any activity from cooking and eating to repairing small motorcycles), then a doubling of productivity so that we have twice as much in the way of goods is also likely to double the personal work required. A doubling of productivity might require eight hours of factory labor followed by eight hours of personal work, leaving no time for actual consumption or enjoyment! While this may seem ridiculous, it is a close description of middle-class American affluence. Tripling productivity produces the absurd result that we must work eight hours in the factory and twelve hours in the home, thus losing four hours' sleep and still having no time for consumption! The table below shows the relationship between formal work time, personal work time, and consumption time, *if it is required that we maintain a reasonable ratio between the three demands on our available time.*[3]

FIGURE 24

A Model Productivity/Time Budget

			Productivity Index			
Present =	1	2	3	4	8	∞
Work Time (Hours)	8	5-1/3	4	3-1/5	1-7/9	0
Time in Personal Work	4	5-1/3	6	6-2/5	7-1/9	8
Sum of Time in Work Time and Personal Work	12	10-2/3	10	9-3/5	8-8/9	8
Consumption Time	4	5-1/3	6	6-2/5	7-1/9	8
Total Time	16	16	16	16	16	16
Number of Consumption Goods (Units)	8	10-2/3	12	12-4/5	14-2/9	16
Year	1975	2000		2025	2050	

Source: Burenstam Linder, *The Harried Leisure Class.*

Since the amount of goods produced per unit time increases with rising productivity, while the other functions are related to the quantity of goods, the worker finds that *the only way to maintain the proper balance between paid work time and personal work and consumption is to reduce paid work time. Ultimately, consumption in an affluent society is limited by the fixed quantity of time available.* Time is our scarcest and most limiting resource—not petroleum, uranium, or steel.

Let us suppose that these rather arbitrary relationships could be brought into the real world. What do they mean? Illustrated graphically, the figures presented above would indicate that we will, within seventy-five years, be within 10 per cent of the *ultimate* limit of our economic system. If productivity continues at 3 per cent, production per capita will double in twenty-five years, quadruple in fifty, and be eight times the present value in seventy-five years. Consumption per capita, however, will have less than doubled!

The likely shape of the next twenty-five years is of more immediate concern. If productivity advances at the rate of 3 per cent, output will double by the end of the century. Using Buren-stam Linder's model, *we might expect that paid work and unpaid work will then require equal amounts of time,* or about five and one-third hours each. The household economy, in other words, must grow with increasing productivity. As the market economy becomes more productive, it forces the growth of the household economy.

FIGURE 25

Projected Unpaid vs. Paid Work Time

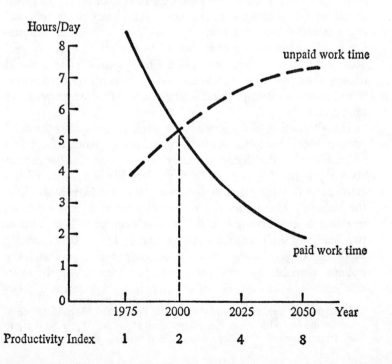

While the end result of this tendency will be a radical change in the structure and priorities of the industrial world, the immediate effect is to create tension in just about everyone as we all try to feed an ever-growing body of needs, demands, and desires with a fixed supply of hours. Worse, the inevitable shortage is aggravated by the conventions of employment. Although there are seven days in every week, most of us work on the same five and play on the same two. This means that we are always trying to do something when everyone else is trying to do it, a state of affairs that means our roads, garages, cities, parks, stadiums, theaters, etc., are either overcrowded or practically vacant. No happy medium is possible.†

The popularity of the four-day work week, "flex time," and other innovations in work scheduling is as much due to the demands on workers *outside* their jobs as it is to the improvements in productivity: The two go hand in hand. The most startling idea in this area is *the eight-day week,*[4] a system that would eliminate "peak loading" problems and redistribute the demands made on virtually all public facilities, thus making for more efficient operation of the entire economy. The heart of the proposal is the establishment of a four-day work week in a week comprising eight, rather than seven, days. The market economy would occupy four days of our time and the household economy would occupy the other four. While the idea may seem eccentric now, it will have increasing appeal as the scarcity of time grows more apparent.

The alternative to a shorter work week is to shorten the total years of work. Early retirement is increasingly popular for a few and achieved under duress for many. The illusion that the market economy is the dominant force in modern life is maintained because most workers retire to social and economic invisibility. Like the unhappy housewife, the retired worker does not exist; all meaning is concentrated in the market economy. This kind of psychological shell game can be played only in the early maturity of the goods-producing economy. As output increases and the options available to the average worker become nearly overwhelming, the maintenance of our current work patterns will be-

† This, by the way, creates some wonderful possibilities for countercyclical living for the few who can escape conventional schedules. It is a great joy to work Roman hours in American cities. It's also much cheaper.

come increasingly absurd, unpopular, and socially destructive. Only two factors can modify the future of our time limitation. The first is that Burenstam Linder's model (Figure 24) assumes that the worker uses most of his income to buy goods and little to buy services. Presumably, he *could* allocate his rising income so that a proportion would be automatically reserved to buy maintenance services for newly purchased products. A mountain of contrary evidence suggests that this is altogether unlikely.‡

Do-it-yourself is a national catchword. All manner of products arrive in varying states of disassembly, requiring the buyer to interpret obscure directions. Increasingly, services are prohibitively priced if they are available at all; gracious hotels and haute cuisine are the most commonly cited examples of rare and expensive luxuries. It is also a sign of the times that General Electric has now begun classes so that consumers may learn to service their own appliances.

What we are seeing in the growth of necessary unpaid work and the need for varied leisure is the inevitable collision between materialist dreams and finite human reality.

The growth of the market economy creates abundance. But it also creates a scarcity of time. Even the wealthy, who can afford services that are beyond the reach of the vast majority, are pressed for time. For all the special services available to the wealthy—dog and goldfish care, summer camp, and baby sitters —there is an ever-increasing number of chores that *must* be done personally, that cannot be done by someone else. Even the well-to-do care for their skis and boots, change light bulbs in their homes, gather their laundry, and on occasion affix a fresh roll of toilet paper in the holder. Inevitably, time becomes more and more precious, and work produces more goods than we can consume.

There is one final escape hatch for the market economy: We can consume more per unit time. We can balance our habits of consumption with our capacity to produce. This is what we have done in the recent past. Marketers and planners are quick to note that the last dollar of income is spent differently from the first. Food and beverage expenses level out as income rises, indicating that while absolute dollar expenditures may continue to increase,

‡ Burenstam Linder also shows, mathematically, that this is not a real possibility.

food absorbs an ever-diminishing proportion of total income. The same general pattern holds true for housing, clothing, and transportation expenses. The proportion of income spent on education and leisure, however, rises absolutely. Leisure alone is now a $105-billion market, indicating that we are spending a great deal of money to become harried.

One way to examine the dynamics of the relationship between time and income is to make some very broad assumptions: Let us assume, for sake of illustration, a family of four in which each member has free, or leisure, time amounting to about thirty hours a week, or fifteen hundred hours a year. Let us also assume that they enjoy a very rapidly rising income and devote an increasing percentage of that income to leisure activities. The average expenditure per hour·of leisure time might then work out to something like the table below:

FIGURE 26

The Rising Value of Leisure Time

Cash Income	% Leisure	$ Expenditure	Average/Hour (Based on 6000 hrs/yr)
$ 6,000	1 %	$ 60	$ .01
12,000	5	600	.10
18,000	10	1,800	.30
24,000	12½	3,000	.50
30,000	15	4,500	.75
40,000	20	8,000	1.33
50,000	25	12,500	2.04

Note: The relationship between income and leisure expenditures is an *arbitrary* one to illustrate. It is not based on empirical data.

The family tends to select a variety of leisure activities, so the *average* for all time and money expended equals the average hourly cost of their activities. The table below shows the average cost per hour for a variety of leisure activities.

TV, obviously, is the great, low-cost time absorber. It serves poor families as the least-cost method for absorbing enforced leisure. For more well-to-do families, television can be used to leverage more money for expensive activities; for example, the

Figure 27

The Cost of Leisure

Activity	Cost Per Hour
Radio	1¢
Television	2¢ to 4¢
Records	10¢ to 15¢
Newspapers	15¢ to 20¢
Magazines	20¢ to 25¢
Socializing	40¢
Hobbies	$1
Spectator sports & Concerts	$1 to $2
Hardcover books	$1 to $5
Movies	$1.25 to $5
Athletics (equipment, fees, etc.)	
Tennis	50¢
Bicycling	70¢
Boating	75¢ to $8 and up
Bowling	$1.50 to $2
Golf	$3 to $5
Travel	
Bus	80¢ to $4
Train	$1.50 to $10
Car	$3.60 to $9
Plane	$10 to $30

Including 610 hours of simultaneous activities.

Source: CBS Research, Gruntel & Co., Forbes Estimate. *Forbes,* January 1, 1974.

family that skis may watch TV but seldom see a movie or a play. TV is to leisure as soy beans are to hamburger; it extends a precious commodity. According to *The Opinion Research Quarterly,* the average adult watches television some two hours a day, thus consuming almost 50 per cent of his leisure time. Children watch even more.

Viewed in terms of investment, the popular derision evoked by the shanty with the TV antenna is unjustified. The indigent worker, for an investment of less than forty hours of labor, has literally thousands of hours of surplus leisure time absorbed. The rich man who indulged in the same investment would be suffocated in surplus income. For him, *inefficiency* in investment is necessary to bring his income and his time into an acceptable balance. Ultimately, he is forced to pursue leisure activities that provide displays of conspicuous depreciation. His leisure becomes "capital-intensive."

Just as a modern productive society employs more capital per worker than a less developed society, the modern leisure society must employ more capital per idler. *Unconsciously, we pursue an equilibrium between the amounts of time and of money at our disposal.*

Some will think this suggestion a bit cavalier. We could, after all, *save* the new surplus income. But there is absolutely no statistical evidence to support this rather handy idea. In spite of our rapidly increasing incomes, the national rate of saving has shown little tendency to change. Instead, consumer credit has mounted rapidly over the past twenty years, until it now amounts to more than 18 per cent of all disposable income; installment credit, moreover, has risen even faster, implying that consumers have rushed ahead to buy more and more large items as their incomes have risen.

It is precisely the capital-intensive pleasures that have exhibited the greatest growth. A few examples should suffice:

In 1960, individual swimming pools were rare. According to the National Swimming Pool Institute, the number of backyard pools has risen *fivefold* since then, to some 1.25 million. The Sunday home-and-garden section has become a clutter of ads from pool installers. A good pool is likely to cost in the neighborhood of five thousand dollars to buy; annual maintenance is not insignificant. Even if your children *live* in the pool, it's expensive.

Not long ago, the sauna was thought to be a Scandinavian perversion. Now you can buy one from Hammacher Schlemmer for six hundred dollars, ready to plug in. Thousands of saunas have been sold and most dealers see sales increasing at more than 20 per cent a year.

Skiing is a sport with wonderful capital-intensive possibilities. The basic equipment can cost as much as five hundred dollars (average is more like two hundred dollars). But these costs are only the start. You have to get there and then you need a place to stay: Not infrequently, the truly dedicated skier will own a five-thousand-dollar, four-wheel-drive vehicle for bad road conditions, a fifteen-hundred-dollar snowmobile (worthless in four years), and a forty-to-eighty-thousand-dollar ski lodge or condominium. With a minimum of effort, the enterprising skier can raise his skiing costs to upwards of thirty dollars an hour. With the sure knowledge that he can always increase the cost of skiing to outpace even the most outrageous increases in income, the beginning skier need have no anxiety about his new sport.

Tennis has enjoyed similar growth; the construction of private courts has boomed, in spite of the fact that a regulation court costs more than ten thousand dollars. According to the US Lawn Tennis Association, the number of courts is now 110,000 and the number of players is in excess of 13 million. *Fortune* calls it a growth industry.

The list of pleasures on which one can spend more money in less time is by no means complete. We have neglected golf (a $3-billion industry) and camping (a $415-million business)—not to mention water-skiing ($45 million), photography, mountain climbing, and bicycling. Most of these activities still qualify as *mass* activities, available, if not to all, then at least to a constantly growing small multitude.

We have neglected yachts and polo altogether. Polo requires the ownership of at least three suitable ponies, worth five to fifteen thousand dollars each. Since the useful lifetime of a pony is less than five years, the active player usually needs to devote more than ten thousand dollars a year to his chosen sport. Polo, obviously, could absorb the surplus of even the most outrageously productive society and would, no doubt, be far more widely enjoyed if it didn't require an extraordinary degree of physical fitness.

Yachting requires much less in physical prowess. Better yet, the pleasure boat is the most efficient instrument yet invented for bringing time and money into equilibrium.

Not long ago, *Fortune* magazine featured a portfolio of racing yachts commanded by executives who spend upwards of fifty thousand dollars a season to maintain and campaign their ocean racers. For the busy three hundred thousand dollars-a-year executive whose corporate amenities already include unlimited expense accounts, private dining rooms, company hideaways, chauffeur-driven cars, and private aircraft, the ocean racer may represent the only possible vehicle that would prevent him from saving money. Logically, the society that keeps producing more and deals with the problem by requiring its citizens to consume more must demand that its paragons of production—high-income executives—should also be paragons of consumption. The traditional rat race is very circular indeed.

One of the more peculiar side effects of increasing affluence may be that TV could begin to lose its appeal as an instrument for balancing money and time. The fact that it is "cheap but filling" will no longer be an asset as the amount of money available per leisure hour increases. TV may soon have to compete with intrinsically more expensive media such as movies and spectator events, not to mention such active pursuits as tennis, bicycling, and camping. It isn't difficult to imagine a long descent for network TV as prime time loses an ever-increasing portion of its present audience. Worse, the audience that remains will be centered on the poor, leaving the networks with an audience that can't buy the products its sponsors try to sell.

The trouble is that ever-increasing consumption gets a little silly after a while, not to mention its being ever more difficult to practice. While most of us are standing only at the very fringes of superconsumption, it is already clear that *everyone* can't do it, because the crowds are just too large. The world of things, the object of our earlier dreams, turns into a nightmare of clutter and inconvenience. The new yacht owner discovers that harbors are very crowded, that there is a waiting list for moorings, and that marinas are just about impossible. The yachtsman who cruises the East Coast in the month of August had best make his reservations for a berth (and dinner) at least a month in advance. Woe to him who falls behind schedule.

On Saturdays, Long Island Sound and San Francisco Bay are so full of boats you can't see the water for the sails; it is only a matter of time before we hear of the first chain collision, freeway style, between ten or more boats. Similarly, the National Parks are besieged with trailers and recreation vehicles, the beaches assaulted with dune buggies and ATVs, the mountains invaded by snowmobiles and trail bikes, the skies by gliders and private planes. Even the bottom of the sea isn't beyond reach, bombarded as it is by empty bottles and cans from above and cruised by tiny submarines and skindivers below. Affluent, goods-intensive America seeks out and molests the most distant and obscure corners of the world in order to maintain the precious equilibrium between time and money.

But this can't go on. We already know that the National Parks and camping grounds are morbidly overloaded, that the crush of boats defiles virtually every shore, and that every closet and garage in affluent America is bursting with the under-used, under-maintained goodies of leisure amusement, not to mention the all-too-necessary tools of home maintenance.

What you can do for some, you can't do for all. We may yet have mass leisure, but we have neither the time nor the space for mass affluence.

Where will it end? Given Burenstam Linder's theory, we know the limit of consumption will be reached within seventy-five years, as shown in Figure 24, earlier in this chapter. But, practically, we know it will be far sooner. We're running out of time, and the only place we can find it is in the market economy: the market economy will diminish while the household economy grows.

For some people, withdrawal from the market economy will be traumatic, but the changing nature of the market will ease the symptoms, because, as we shall soon see, the market economy of the future will be a very lonely place.

1. Sebastian De Grazia, *Of Time, Work and Leisure* (New York: Twentieth Century Fund, 1962).

2. Staffan Burenstam Linder, *The Harried Leisure Class* (New York: Columbia University Press, 1970).

3. While these assumptions are essentially arbitrary, they are not far from describing the present allocation of time, as a number of time-budget studies have indicated. As with Jay Forrester's world model in *World Dynamics*, the issue here is not its absolute correctness but whether or not the model defines the relevant relationships and thus illuminates the boundaries of our experience. As with most recent studies, we find ourselves heading rapidly toward a point of diminishing returns. We are surrounded by asymptotes.

The reader should also note that the amount of unpaid work hours (four) bears about the same relationship to paid work time as Sirageldin found in his study.

4. John Ward Pearson, *The 8-Day Week* (New York: Harper & Row, 1973).

15

The Very Lonely Crowd

THERE ARE CERTAIN VISUAL CONVENTIONS for presenting wealth. In the classic movie *Citizen Kane*, a series of incredible shots—the enormous entry hall of "Xanadu," Orson Welles standing dwarfed before a gargantuan fireplace, Welles and his estranged wife eating at a banquet table that could serve as a major section of the interstate highway system—convey the loneliness of wealth, the coldness of power, and the strange madness that grows in those vast spaces that are indicative of affluence.

Now, over three decades later, the world is a different place but the symbols haven't changed. Wealth is still symbolized by eerie expanses of depopulated space. Privacy, peace, and quiet are still fixtures in the conventional dream of wealth.

Our folklore serves to warn us of the bitter moment when precious privacy is transmuted into inescapable loneliness. Midas is a lonely man. In the conventional morality play, loneliness marks the Pyrrhic victory of those who have achieved moral corruption in the pursuit of wealth. Again and again our platitudes inform us that loneliness is the price of power and the inevitable accompaniment of wealth. Once he has set foot on the path of ambition, the seeker can never return.

But our images and adages do not represent the present, let alone the plausible future. For *in the world that is coming, the poor will be lonely, not the rich.* Poverty, once measured by a scarcity of goods, will then be measured by a scarcity of people; the poor will at last have achieved the goods so desperately sought, only to learn that the measure has changed. The reason for the change is no sublime redistribution of moral deserts, but crass, dogged productivity, our capacity to do more per unit time.

In manufacturing, the index of productivity is the amount of goods created per unit of labor; our goal is to invest less time in the production of more goods. Given that the index has both a numerator and a divisor, goods and time, we can elect to make *more* goods in the same amount of time or make the same amount of goods in less time. The tendency is to accept goods over time and to move toward a condition of ever-increasing clutter.

Productivity in services is a bit more complicated. Theoretically, government productivity does not exist at all, let alone increase. And some services, such as education, exhibit a tendency to have *losses* rather than gains. But while many may argue and carp over productivity in the service sector, there are a few things we can clearly anticipate.

Productivity, whether it is in services or manufacturing, makes *time* more valuable. Precious commodities are economized more rigorously than cheap commodities, and thus we can expect to have less and less contact with other human beings as the service sector becomes more productive. Nor is this pressure for less time one-sided. If we produce more goods in less time, then we must also deal with the problem of distributing those goods to a consumer who has more money. Implicitly, the consumer needs to increase the number of transactions and decrease the amount of time per transaction. The unhappy consumer is burdened with the "need" to spend ever more time in transactions that offer little intrinsic pleasure. Few Americans, for instance, enjoy shopping for food, even though we eat far better than we did a half century ago.

Some might argue that increasing the number of transactions or interactions will mean a constant enrichment of human life. Caroline Byrd did so in *The Crowding Syndrome*.[1] But it is obvious that increasing the number of interactions necessarily decreases their *quality*.

Most often, the effect is manifest in the depersonalization of commerce. No one wants it that way; it's just that the circumstances of our transactions make it inevitable. The surly souls at

the supermarket whose lives seem to be consecrated to destroy-
ing our eggs, bruising our produce, and thawing our ice cream;
whose only recognition of our existence is an incoherent but bel-
ligerent grunt, probably wake up every morning vowing to be
pleasant, not because they are supposed to (as per employer
rules) but because they also share our basic friendliness.

Sadly, most of us have a limit to the number of rejections we
can absorb in a day. If half the people we meet pretend that we
are a piece of peripheral equipment attached to an NCR or Bur-
roughs cash register or, if we are customers, a vinyl pocket on a
conveyor line, then eventually we won't bother to distinguish
between those who attempt to make human contact and those
who don't.

Telephone operators are probably the best example (and most
regular victim) of depersonalized interactions; people pretend
they are recordings. If you say "good-by" after getting "information," the response is likely to be incredulous shock; personal
warmth, gratitude, and love will flood the receiver.

Since the number of rejections we can respond to remains constant while the number of interactions must increase, we tend to
withdraw psychically and to specialize on interactions of high
value. Those who work at supermarkets and department stores
are seldom accorded a high priority. Inevitably, our commercial
interactions are depersonalized, cold, and machine-like. Some of
us forget what it is like to be human; we accept instead the machine metaphor and turn on and off, forsaking entirely the risk
of acceptance or rejection.

The depersonalization that now abounds is the simple result of
our drive for abundance. Achieving abundance requires productivity, productivity requires increasing specialization, and specialization changes the basic nature of relationships, usually by
encapsulating the service to be rendered and offering it through
a third, impersonal (often corporate) party. There is a difference
between a full-time maid and an Arthur Treacher employee; but
both clean your house. There is a difference between a governess
and a day-care center; but both accept responsibility for your
children.

Those who are compulsively liberal would quickly point out
that the specialization which has removed many personal relationships from the realm of human intercourse is also the logical

consequence of having an economy that can fully employ its human resources, an economy that expands at such a rate that it can offer increasing opportunities to all its members.

Industrial progress has liberated millions from relationships of unbearable dependence and servitude at the small cost of inconveniencing a very few. While there have been losses in personal contact and relationships, the encapsulation of human services in a non-personal form has also allowed many of us to escape the rough edges of constant personal conflict, perhaps the second-most-important goal for American culture, after the achievement of abundance.

Whatever the intrinsic merit of liberal beliefs, they are more acceptable than their conservative counterparts, which are in favor of opportunity until it diminishes the supply of people who will clean toilets. Alas! It is one of the sad facts of life in an industrial society that as abundance increases, the supply of people who aspire to cleaning toilets must decrease. Perhaps someday this relationship will be accorded the title Burns's 1st Law of Productivity.

It would be very easy to discount a trend because we examine the behavior only of the wealthy and affluent. The woman who complains too loudly of the difficulty she has experienced in finding "household help" finds little sympathy beyond her immediate peers. Worse, she may be held up to ridicule as being socially obtuse, insensitive to the fact that such problems are the mark of privilege. Similarly, we feel little compassion for the Rolls-Royce owner who laments the national shortage of service facilities or for the yachtsman who decries the decline of age-old crafts. The affluent are supposed to know and recognize that their hardships and inconveniences are the best of all possible hardships and inconveniences. They must accept the burden of their position with grace, lest they wake the slumbering ghost of Scarcity.

It is, however, one thing to *depersonalize* services—as was necessary to create a mass, consumer society—and yet another to *depopulate* them. The difference for the consumer is parallel to the difference between mechanization and automation for the producer. Mechanization increases output at the expense of personal involvement; automation augurs for the nearly total removal of human labor. Now, after fifty years of ever-increasing depersonalization in both manufacturing and the services, we are standing at the threshold of a new era, one in which the services, like manufacturing, will be automated . . . and depopulated. As a rather peculiar case in point, consider the fact that the burlesque house of yore has been supplanted by porno-film houses and dirty-book stores.

Sociologists have devoted much attention to the problems that will accompany automation. Some project a world of Roman circuses, driven by the continuing displacement of low-ability workers and the ever higher demands of technology. On one hand we hear predictions of a glorious flood of leisure, with its attendant boom in jockstrap sales, while on the other we are asked to think deep thoughts about the real implications of leisure.

As we have already seen, the era of leisure may never exist, but the age of loneliness may be next to inevitable. Since productivity makes people dear and machines cheap, people will become more and more scarce. They may virtually disappear from most aspects of commercial life. While the reader may find this notion a bit difficult to accept, the fact is that it is happening now, very quickly, and began with the disappearance of the household maid.

One of the better contemporary examples is the task of washing one's car. Those who have their cars washed (to do it by yourself at home is one of middle America's most rapidly declining rituals) can no longer find a service station that will perform the work and must choose from among three kinds of specialized, automated service.

For $2.50 you can have your car washed on an assembly line: Two men will pass vacuum-cleaner wands in the general vicinity of your car, another will spray the car with a steam gun, and later, after the car has passed through a series of machine operations, others will dry the exterior and clean the windows. For $2.50 you get to see at least five men make gestures toward performing *actual work* on your car.

For a mere dollar, you can have your car washed in three minutes in a totally automated building by a single, multi-hosed robot. While you will save $1.50, you will be totally deprived of all human contact, because the installation will be completely untended: Even your change will come from a machine.

Obviously, the mere proximity of human beings is expensive. It is also clear that the first people to forgo the presence of other human beings will be those with relatively low incomes. If the need to economize will result in displacing human beings from services and replacing them with robots, we might also consider displacing the robot, for there is still another type of carwash available to the indigent consumer.

For a trifling thirty-five cents, you can rent a covered bay and five minutes' use of a small steam gun. Converted to hourly wage rates and costs, the least-expensive facility costs $4.20 per hour ($.35 × 12), while the robot facility costs twenty dollars per hour ($1.00 × 20). By imputation, the robot is getting paid at the rate of $15.80 per hour, a wage that would put it among the top income earners in the United States! The implicit wage for the self-service washer, however, is a mere $7.80 [($1.00 − .35) × 12], less than half of the robot's wage but still a respectable sum, since it is about double that received by the average factory worker.

While our example may be a bit eccentric, it clearly illustrates the economic forces that will lead to the eventual displacement of human beings from most services. Indeed, the clear trend is for producers to work *less* and consumers to work *more*. *The consumer, ultimately, will have to choose between hiring a robot and hiring himself.*

Retail trade is a prime example of this trend. While it now accounts for about 35 per cent of all service employment—50 per cent if you exclude government—the revolution that began with the discount store is about to be carried a step further, with the growth of catalog stores.

The focus for the change is the two measures of productivity for retail operations: sales per employee and sales per square foot. Increases in either or both can be used to (a) increase the profitability of the store or (b) decrease the total cost of doing business. In actual practice, the long-run profitability is increased by lowering prices (decreasing gross margin for profit) to attract customers, thus increasing sales volume and inventory turnover. The drive of these two factors is responsible for the transformation of food retailing over the past thirty years. Where once food marketing was fragmented and dominated by a multitude of small "Ma and Pa" stores, in which the proprietor was likely to personally assemble your groceries, now more than 50 per cent of all food is sold in gigantic outlets with annual volumes in excess of one million dollars. "Self-service" began at the nation's food stores.

The consumer realizes these rather abstract ideas in the reality of lower prices at the discount store. Naturally, he tends to buy more at such stores, although they provide fewer customer services. In effect, the discount store is devoting itself to providing what economists call a "utility of time and place" rather than a complete service; the consumer *employs himself* to provide the service in exchange for a price break. Now even expensive household furnishings are discounted.

One of the peculiarities of this trend is that it tends to distort the common measures of our cost of living. The Department of Labor, for instance, does not distinguish between a widget purchased at a department store and a widget purchased at a discount store. If discount stores capture a rising portion of all widget sales, the consumer price index for widgets does not accurately reflect the consumer's purchasing experience.[2]

EXAMPLE

	1960 Price	1970 Price	Actual Index: $\dfrac{1970\ Price}{1960\ Price}$
Department store widget	1.00	1.50	150
Discount widget	.80	1.20	150

Suppose, however, that discount stores sold no widgets in 1960 but sold 80 per cent of all widgets sold in 1970. Then the consumer price index for widgets would be made like this:

Department store
  widgets $20 \times 150 = 3000$
Discount widgets $80 \times 120 = \underline{9600}$
                   $12600 \div 100 = 126 =$ consumer price index

In other words, unless you as an individual consumer change your personal buying habits in step with the average consumer, your experience of price increases will be far more painful than what is indicated by the index.

While business school professors may debate whether the discount store is intrinsically more efficient than the orthodox store or is merely reducing the service it provides, it remains that discount operations account for a constantly increasing portion of all retail sales. Consumers have gained access to more goods at lower prices at the cost of human service: The only people you are likely to see at a discount store are other shoppers and the face of a check-out clerk that will probably reveal cosmic boredom.

Worse, the environment seems to make such afflictions infectious. Those who find it difficult to imagine a more depersonalized shopping experience than that of the discount store are suffering from a lack of imagination. It is already here, among us, and growing. The catalog showroom, the newest entry in retailing, may yet achieve the ideal of depopulation. According to a *Wall Street Journal* article,[3] there are some eighteen hundred catalog sales showrooms in the United States, and business is expected to exceed $2 billion a year. Sales may increase, but the number of people required to run such stores can be cut by a full two thirds, virtually eliminating contact between buyer and seller. The transaction magically *occurs*.

The operation that may be a source of isolation for the consumer has substantial benefits for the retailer: Losses through theft are only 0.5 per cent of sales, compared to 6.5 per cent of sales in discount operations, and sales per square foot (the other measure of productivity) are about double, or two hundred dollars per square foot per year. Not to mention that all delivery is done by the consumer.

If the lonely consumer thinks that he can find solace at the friendly local bank, he is due for a rude disappointment. The nation's banks are moving into high gear for depopulation. There are some seven hundred electronic tellers and cash dispensers in current operation. The American Bankers Association has estimated that by 1980 there will be *thirty-four thousand* of them, enabling the consumer to deposit or withdraw money without seeing another human being.

The customer obtains the advantage of being able to get money locally at any time; the banker benefits because his new, robot employee has absolutely no predisposition to take protracted vacations in South America. Better yet, the bankers have noticed that some people are *embarrassed* about borrowing money from *people* but borrow from machines with abandon.

On a more practical level, the suburbanization of America has produced the phenomenon of branch banking: While competition for depositor dollars is fierce, branch banks are expensive, can be basically disastrous if ill-placed, and have opened grand new vistas of opportunity for the budding bank robber. The all-electronic branch bank is less vulnerable and costs a mere fifty-five thousand dollars—one fifth the cost of an average bank with human tellers. And you never have to buy it a gold watch, let alone provide it with a pension.

If the desire to achieve multibranch profitability is driving the banks to automation, they are also being lured by the machine mystique. In Ohio, one bank purchased and installed automated equipment because its competitors had. "We suspected," the banker commented, "that we were . . . losing image because we didn't have the machines."[4]

Losing *image?* Somehow the juxtaposition of the disappearance of people and the thought of "losing image" strikes a chord of hysteria. To be mechanized, robotized, and depopulated is to be at the leading edge . . . to have *Image!* The nation's sixteen thousand banks will no doubt be followed by its five thousand savings and loan associations into the depopulated void.

It takes little imagination to contemplate the joyous spread of robots to the local brokerage office. While there has been no discussion of robot brokers in the public press, we should consider that there are some sixty-five-hundred brokerage offices providing erratic employment for almost two hundred thousand people. Since the broker receives about thirty-three cents on every commission dollar, and the market for securities is in sad shape anyway, it is a reasonable speculation that we may soon see the advent of automated, discount brokerage houses.* The broker with his Dunhill suits and monogrammed shirts may soon find himself in head-to-head competition with a little black box installed at the local laundromat.

If banking and retailing are at the forefront of the move to depopulate the services, a multitude of other transactions also deprive the consumer of human contact.

Oral Roberts University is cited by Audio-Visual Freaks as the new model for education. The new school is completely computerized and "televised," so the student may spend virtually four

---

* A few already exist, and more and more people are wondering why it costs sixty dollars to transfer one hundred shares of stock from one party to another when banks do very much the same thing, with personal checks, for fifteen cents.

years without the need to leave his dormitory room. Other schools now offer similar, if somewhat less total, degrees of automation. Almost 5 per cent of the nation's gasoline is now sold through self-service pumps. Although several states have legislation forbidding self-service, for safety reasons, the growth of such stations has been nothing less than amazing. The savings offered usually ranges from two to four cents per gallon, providing the average driver with a savings of about forty-five cents per fill-up and an imputed hourly wage for the transaction of about $6.75 ($.45 per filling times 15 fillings per hour). Atlantic Richfield now has an experimental pump that accepts credit cards, checks them by computer inquiry, and issues the customer a bill after he has finished pumping his own gas.[5]

Vending machines sell some $6.5 billion yearly in goods ranging from hot lunches to pornographic books. The population of vending machines has risen at an alarming rate; almost a half million new machines are installed each year.[6] We may soon be fighting with the vending machines for space.

Restaurants have tended to specialize and shift work from the kitchen and waitress to the customer. The open salad table and limited menu are inescapable examples. Both reduce the labor content per meal sold (that measure of productivity again). Joseph Baum, former president of Restaurant Associates Industries, was quoted in a *Playboy* magazine article as believing that within ten years we will have two kinds of restaurants—the large, precooked, mass-prepared, volume establishments such as Howard Johnson and McDonald's, which will serve the hoi polloi, and a small number of incredibly expensive restaurants that will preserve the traditions of fine food and service.[7]

Natural gas and electricity continue to displace oil as a home heating fuel—just as oil once replaced coal—largely because oil must be delivered by truck and requires direct human labor.

Virtually no area of commerce escapes the depopulation drive. A recent article in *U.S. News & World Report* described the automated hotel of the future:

When an arriving guest asks for a room, the clerk will push a button that shows what types are available. The guest is issued a credit card for the room he selects. He may be escorted to his room by a bellboy, or in cost-cutting establishments, he may have to carry his own luggage on a hand cart.

Instead of using a key, the guest will insert his credit card in a slot to open the door. If he wants a beverage of any sort he will insert the card in a device in the room and the beverage will be dispensed automatically and the charge recorded on a central computer. All purchases of food and other items in the hotel will be made by card and centrally computed.

At check-out time, the bill will be transmitted to the room automatically and the guest will simply pay the cashier on the way out.

In the same article, a hotel man comments: "We have got to cut costs for most of our guests. What it boils down to is offering additional services only to those guests who are willing to pay the price for luxury."[8]

The presence of other human beings, in other words, is fast becoming the most extravagant luxury, and luxuries, whatever the condition of general affluence, will be something only the very rich can afford.

The depopulation of commerce does not end with our regular transactions; it is now beginning to appear in a curious reversal of our housing habits. In urban areas throughout the country, lofts, industrial buildings, and other old, low-rise structures are being renovated for the affluent and wealthy; the poor and middle-income families, by contrast, are being housed in the fantastic high-rise buildings that once marked success. *The difference is access to community and people. Only the rich can afford such amenities;* the rest must rely on triple-bolted doors so that they may at least achieve loneliness with safety.

We will, no doubt, adjust to all this. Perhaps we will develop a fondness for certain vending machines, perhaps we will become more sensitive to the emotional nuances in the way automatic change makers accept our currency and convert it to silver. Perhaps we will become partial to certain voltages. Perhaps. But we may also miss much we can ill afford to lose.

Then again, perhaps the loss of human contact from the service industries would improve them. There is no end to complaints about quality of service. Cab drivers are rude, waitresses are incompetent, gas-station attendants are a menace to public health, and appliance repairmen are unreliable. Those who do offer personal service are often fraudulent, e.g. the concerned aluminum siding salesman, the thoughtful encyclopedia vendor, the tanned purveyor of arid southwestern "ranchos." We may gain as much from this trend as we lose.

But consider these events as an eerie *totality* rather than as changing fragments of our familiar experience. Consider the ubiquitous silence of the future in which one shops by television or catalog store, banks by robot depository, travels in an air-conditioned vehicle between automated filling and service stations, and in which the only crowd one ever sees is composed of other consumers. Horn and Hardart were far ahead of their time. *Inevitably, the bulk of an ever-increasing amount of invested capital stands between consumer and producer in both the services and manufacturing.*

A few, of course, will still have the pleasure of regular contact with real human beings. Just as Joseph Baum suggested, we are likely to see the clear development of two classes of service: the mass, automated service that can be afforded by everyone, and a tiny, almost vestigial, grouping of small enterprises that serve the fortunate few and remind them, on very special occasions, of what affluence and wealth once were.

Personal service as we know it—or wish for it—is rapidly becoming subject matter for the world's museums. It isn't too far-fetched to consider that one automated day there may be a special wing in the Museum of Natural History in which dioramas will illustrate long-passed forms of human service and contact.

Imagine the Disney World of the future, where people will go to watch clever robots perform feats of human proximity! And children will thrill to the display of an interpersonal department-store sale, just as those of the present are excited by a mechanized rhinoceros. Where human replicas now depict men of importance and a 110-volt Abraham Lincoln is condemned to repeat the Gettysburg Address, future robots are likely to depict the man-in-the-street as compensation for his peculiar absence. Art, for the future artist, may be serving the patron breakfast in bed or washing an automobile by hand in public. And we will pay dearly to watch.

Such is the nature of the future offered by the marketplace. If we consider it an unpleasant likelihood, we should bear in mind

that the marketplace itself has no intentions. It is neither benign
nor malignant. It has no identity; it simply *functions* in accord
with the conditions necessary to support its continued existence
and growth. Labor and land do not accumulate. But capital does.
As it accumulates, it must displace labor. Some of this labor is
displaced absolutely; i.e., it is done by machines. Other labor is
displaced by moving it outside the boundaries of the marketplace
and into the household or collective economy.

As the complexity of the service and manufacturing infrastructure increases, we are likely to see a growing introspection among
consumers. We may begin to doubt the value of what we receive.
Many do already. We may silently begin to weigh other economic
possibilities, because our commitment to the marketplace holds
enormous liabilities. At the moment, a small mistake by a bank
or a credit-card company can absorb hours and sometimes days
of our time. As the number and complexity of these distant relationships grow, the cost of any single error will grow as well.
Now we view such costs and difficulties as inevitable, part of the
price we pay to participate in the most productive economic
system yet devised. But, in the future, we may no longer accept
these inconveniences, because the basic *form* of our lives will
have changed. While paid work time is decreasing, unpaid work
time is increasing. That the two will one day be equal, and that
unpaid work time will eventually absorb more hours than paid
work time, is the inevitable result of productivity. *Once this has
occurred, we will be much less likely to tolerate mistakes in the
operation of the marketplace, because it will no longer dominate
our economic life.* Once we have reached the crossover point, we
will be just as determined to be efficient managers of our *unpaid*
work time as we are now of our *paid* work time.

We may, in fact, see a complete reversal of attitudes toward
unpaid and paid work time. The cart will have become the horse.

One further factor is likely to accelerate this shift: As the marketplace grows more complex and our access to the people within
it diminishes, our perception of the relative cost of information
may change radically. At the moment, we use the marketplace
because the cost of acquiring information and the difficulty of
managing our limited unpaid work time makes it "diseconomic"
to do otherwise.

We still assume, by virtue of our conditioning, that hired experts are more efficient than our own, untrained hands; we expect that specialization will continue to bring us rewards as both producers and consumers. But the odds are shifting very quickly to favor the consumer. While the producer has, in effect, specialized himself into a corner, economic opportunity has expanded for the consumer. Greatness—at least the economic variety—is being thrust on the consumer by the inevitable maturation of the market economy. And it is reinforced as the market economy becomes ever more incapable of providing meaningful human contact and a sense of community.

1. New York: David McKay, 1972.
2. Victor Fuchs pointed this out in *The Service Economy* (New York: Columbia University Press, 1968).
3. "Buying by the Book," *The Wall Street Journal,* July 5, 1972.
4. "Click, Whir, Thack," *The Wall Street Journal,* September 6, 1972.
5. *This Week,* May 6, 1973.
6. *National Automatic Merchandising Review,* 1972.
7. Roy Andri DeGroot, "Service Without a Smile," *Playboy,* April 1973.
8. "What's Being Done to Keep Your Service Bills Down," *U.S. News & World Report,* April 10, 1972.

16

The Age of Externality

THE RISKS UNDERTAKEN by businessmen serve to benefit the entire society. This is a sacred article of belief, synonymous with support for free enterprise. The idea has much support in the history of investors and businessmen. We are told throughout our educational experience that modern society is beholden to the few individuals who persevered in the face of great odds and hardship. One of the corollaries of this belief is that the large rewards demanded and received by those who succeed are a small price to pay for the benefits received. We don't pay for all the failures.

But we *do* pay, of course, because the experience of failure is a burden to the society as well as to the individual. Worse, we pay once more by having invested the power to change and direct society in organizations that are self-serving.

The most common price of entrepreneurial self-preservation is the social burden of spillover effects: the price of items not included in the cost of production. This cost is inflicted randomly on society as a whole in the form of pollution, unhealthy work environments, unsafe products, etc.

We are now conscious of these spillover effects. Our awareness has grown in proportion to our affluence and the size of the market economy. *Increasingly, our economic life is seen as less wholly positive, as a nearly zero-sum-game, in which each gain for one party requires a corresponding loss for another party.* This is a

remarkable change in consciousness, one that severely undermines the continued dominance of the market economy.

As producers, as people bent on overcoming the scarcity of
goods, we have been intent on the *primary* effect of our actions.
We want more food, more cars, more houses, more water, and
more electricity. We want more of everything. We have organized to obtain those goods and ignored the side effects.

The action was remarkably effective. Now our consciousness
has been changed by the very success of our previous single-
mindedness. No event has illustrated this new consciousness more
clearly than the Russian wheat sale of 1972. To those concerned
with primary effects, the deal was simple: The United States
Government sold Russia $1.2 billion worth of wheat. Russians
would have bread, farmers would have money, and the United
States would have a sorely needed plus in the balance of international trade.

Even if we dismiss the immediate flurry of accusations about
windfall profits to wheat dealers and a few insiders, a regular
flow of news stories have been pointing out the side effects of
the wheat deal. The sale, for a variety of reasons, caused delays
in the delivery of flour to school lunch programs. Bread manufacturers united to complain that they were being forced out of
business by the unexpected rise in the price of grain and predicted smaller bakers would be bankrupt within weeks. The huge
shipments also caused a shortage of railroad cars, delaying all
kinds of badly needed goods and equipment. Slow deliveries of
the wheat itself resulted in having a dozen U.S. freighters tied up
for weeks in Houston while U.S. taxpayers subsidized their
idleness. Feed lots paid more for feed grains and increased the
price of beef. The price of poultry, pork, dairy products, and
cereals also rose.

Now we are facing a national shortage of grain, and bakers are
threatening that bread may become scarce or unavailable. There
is discussion of imposing strict export controls now, or of facing
the need to import grain later. Perhaps from the Russians.

No one, at this writing, has totaled all the spillover costs of the
Russian wheat deal. Perhaps no one will. But everyone is pain-
fully aware of them and pays for them daily. Sadly, there is no
end to the costly ramifications. The skeptical reader should con-

sider the fact that a one-cent rise in the average price of beef increases the national beef bill by something like $220 million. Obviously, a few small changes have dramatic effects.[1] It is altogether likely that the Russian wheat sale cost the American consumer far more than the Russians paid.

We are slow learners when it comes to externalities and to accounting for the true costs of production. We had to invent the institution of real property in order to "internalize" the cost of materials, and it has taken nearly two millenniums to internalize the cost of labor by abolishing human slavery. Only in the past century did we finally internalize the cost of raising and educating a labor force by creating public education, or the cost of industrial accidents by creating workmen's compensation and other benefits. We are still internalizing the costs of industrial diseases and have hardly made the first steps toward internalizing the cost of cleaning up pollution and preventing future environmental travesties.[2]

As we become more conscious of side effects, we become increasingly aware that the market organization is uniquely constituted to benefit from ignoring them. Frequently it can create externalities with impunity, because its goals are highly concentrated and definable, while the goals of the social whole are more elusive. While ardent environmentalists see a kind of diabolism in this, a more realistic view sees pollution and all our other ills as the inevitable product of the market system itself.[3]

All this is changing, a fact witnessed by the content of virtually every newspaper and magazine in the United States and by an outpouring of books dedicated to raising public consciousness. I will not attempt to do that here; I think it has already been done, at least for those who have survived the preceding seventy thousand words.

What is worthy of note, however, is that the decline of faith in the market economy, combined with our rising ecological consciousness, augurs well for the household and its economy. Having seen the consummate failure of traditional big business and big government to create a just and livable world, we are likely to reduce the horizon of our plans and deeds. Like it or not, the household is the only institution that still retains any semblance of public faith.

It is also the only institution capable of long-term coexistence with the natural world. Inevitably it will grow.

1. Derived from figures provided in the Statistical Abstract of the United States, 1972.
2. I am indebted to Garrett Hardin for these observations as seen in *Exploring the New Ethics of Survival* (New York: Viking Press, 1972), pp. 77–87.
3. No one should try to blame all pollution on private industry. Consider the AEC, the Department of Defense, etc. Monolithic governmental institutions are just as prone to ecological abuses.

17

Technology Comes Home

THE SPACE PROGRAM of the sixties is one of the favorite examples of modern technology and its massive requirements for men, capital, and organization. In the course of the interminable discussion that preceded, accompanied, and followed every rocket launching, we were informed that the complex project of getting a rocket to the moon required a literal army of technicians, managers, and scientists as well as an incredible array of equipment. The immutable truth that these facts were supposed to burn into public consciousness was that technological progress—and therefore economic progress—was the product of ever larger projects and investments. The age of the lone inventor and clever improver of mousetraps was loudly proclaimed to be closed.

It has become a public truth that big science, big investment, and big progress are absolutely dependent on one another and that we would all suffer if such projects did not exist. While it is a verifiable and authentic fact that sending people to the moon is a complicated project, it is too seldom remarked that the economic benefits of this variety of progress are small. With the obvious exception of warfare, we would be hard-pressed to find any technological activity that offered smaller economic benefits than the space program. So perhaps we might question the reality of this public truth: Perhaps big technology and investment are not the cornerstones of economic progress, and perhaps the centripetal force that seems to drive the modern, industrial economy is not the single force at work.

That this centripetal tendency exists cannot be denied: We are surrounded by feats of big technology, by large, centralized production plants in which one single facility can produce all that is needed of a given product. Thus we are informed that the one-time model for technical and economic efficiency, the automobile industry, has been superseded by a newer and yet-more-efficient model: the continuous-process industries typified by chemicals, plastics, and oil in which the production process can no longer be identified by the completion of discrete tasks but by an endless, efficient, plastic flow of goods, almost entirely automated, in which the only intrusion of the human worker is the monitoring of the process.

There are, however, limits to centralized production efficiency, and we are already bumping against them. The problem is best illustrated by the logistics of big cities. Cities are convenient, convivial mechanisms for an exchange of goods, ideas, and labor. They offer a greater general economic efficiency than random locations. Hence their growth. Yet we are now facing the fact that continued growth of our cities is largely unproductive. The cost of operating them regularly outstrips their capacity to create economic goods, and the productive work day of the city worker has been shrinking for years. The momentary response to this reality is the creation of yet more suburban sprawl. Worse, we must witness regular displays of absurdity as architects and planners continue to assume that it is technologically (and humanly) possible to introduce an infinite number of people into a finite space, an event that occurs twice daily beneath the Pan Am Building in New York.

The problem is that *economic efficiency is not the product of centralized production alone* but of a complicated balance of the entire process, from conception to consumption. Goods and services must not only be produced; the materials and labor must also be gathered and organized before production can begin; later, the final product must be distributed. The economic problem is one of balancing and optimizing, not of mere technological power. A point arrives at which larger automobile factories are "counterproductive" and not only fail to generate further production savings but actually create delivery and distribution problems that serve to increase the economic costs of the product. Similar problems exist in the production and distribution of oil and chemical products, fabrics, clothing, books, beer, and housing. (The discipline of operations research was created to solve these complex problems.) Moreover, as we devote more and more of our economy to services, we must be ever more concerned that the productive organization not overreach the capacity of the market. It is not wise, in other words, to build a big whorehouse in a small village.

There is also, then, a centrifugal tendency—a decentralist impulse—as well as the more commonly cited centralist tendency. This idea achieved some notoriety with the "global village" of Marshall McLuhan. But its true extent and import are seldom recognized, because of the obvious importance and drama of the centralist impulse and the fey quality associated with most of McLuhan's disciples. The decentralist impulse is real and powerful. We can see some of it in the accumulation of household machinery (as shown in Chapter 3), but we can see even more for the future, in the accelerating disintegration of mass markets. Here we find another paradox of the market: *Efficiency in meeting an economic need ultimately leads to the disintegration of the product's market.*

The origins of the market economy lie in the scarcity of goods and the perceived need to achieve production economies by specializing on a single item. The Model-T Ford typifies specialized production for the sake of general consumption. By definition, such concentration is beyond the ken of the household economy. The affluent consumer, having grown accustomed to the product, now expects more than the Model T. Alfred P. Sloan built the General Motors Corporation on this perception and received obvious benefits until very recently.[1] Increasingly, product markets are fractionated; product choices proliferate with affluence. This effect has been noted many times before. One writer calls it "boutiqueism" and assumes that the market economy will take it in stride, failing to note that its logical extension is the growth of the household economy.

Certainly disaster awaits those who *don't* accommodate to the trend. Of all the mass-circulation magazines, only the *Reader's Digest* survives; *Life, Look,* the *Post,* and *Collier's* have all passed on, yet the magazine rack at the local drugstore was never more crowded with material to read. What happened? The mass audience disintegrated. The ability to read is no longer a compelling common denominator.

Similarly, computer manufacturers who concentrated on large and superlarge machines in the sixties found themselves investing money they could never recover. A decade of scrambling for buyers and intense competition ended in a wave of corporate deaths and consolidations climaxed by the departure of RCA. Bigger wasn't better.

The concentrated power and speed of the large computers was so enormous that it outstripped the capacity of any and all output devices. Users found that medium and small computers were more practical and convenient.

The RCA Videocomp, an inspired creation that needed three computers to drive it, had such a capacity for work that *seven* of them could have set the type for every word printed in the entire United States. Dramatic as the machines were, investors in the few companies that bought them soon saw their investment fade into the oblivion of the bankruptcy courts. Meanwhile, William Garth, the founder of Photon, started Compugraphic and made himself and investors millions. Both companies produce small photocomposition machines designed to meet the needs of small newspapers and that fit handily in small spaces.

Newspapers, significantly, are following the same trend as magazines. As large newspapers in the major cities shut down their presses year after year, suburban weeklies are proliferating; while the enormous printing presses of the big-city papers are sold for scrap, Goss and Dexter are enjoying a miniboom in the smaller presses required by the weeklies.

The import of these events is a curious reversal of the capital-goods sector and the consumer-goods sector. In the past, equipment for manufacturing (capital goods) tended to be large and specialized. The machine that *made* the millions of widgets was a one-of-a-kind, a unique and often virtually hand-made item. Now the pattern is reversing: *Mass markets for small pieces of manufacturing equipment are developing, while the mass markets for consumer goods (the finished product) are disappearing.* Xerography is the paradigm for this process.

This is not a ho-hum occurrence. It raises a very basic question about the future role of the market economy. The marketplace as we know it is organized for the centralized, mass production of standardized consumer goods, not for local, custom production. Some would protest here that the prophets of automation have decreed that the automated society will be ultimately flexible, capable of producing an infinite variety of things with total ease in a single facility. Perhaps so. But they have never dealt with the problem that logically follows: If you produce centrally, you must *store* the goods somewhere. Flexibility in a centralized production system becomes an inventory problem for the store that must sell this marvelous diversity. The answer, obviously, is to move production closer to consumption and eliminate the inventory problem. Strangely, the very success of the traditional marketplace now threatens its existence.

Nowhere is this dilemma of central production more apparent than in conventional retailing. The variations in style, color, and pattern in men's shirts have grown so rapidly that department managers can no longer control inventories or know what to reorder. Only fifteen years ago, the typical men's store would have 90 per cent of its stock in white, yellow, and blue shirts, all with button-down collars. Now the man who appears at work in a white shirt is an oddity liable to be given free tickets to the next MacDonald Carey revival.

The increased diversity in choice is reflected in the price of shirts. Where a shirt might have cost four to six dollars ten years ago, it now costs three times that. Custom-made shirts were at least twice as expensive as ready-made shirts in those bygone days; now they cost about the same as some of the more fashionable brands of ready-mades.

The same thing has occurred in women's dresses. Where ten years ago a custom-made dress was relatively expensive, now it will very likely cost *less* than a comparable dress at one of the larger department stores. Small dressmaking shops abound, where only a few years ago they were a dying institution.

While many observers would credit this development to affluence, the hard-nosed economic truth is that the small shops are price competitive and make purchasing decisions easier for the shopper than the overwhelming choice that confronts one in the department store.

Obviously, we cannot generalize about the entire economy from changes in the cost of shirts and dresses; the pattern we are seeking has many ways of manifesting itself. In the end, it always comes to the same thing: *The act of production is moving constantly closer to the consumer and the household economy. The market economy is becoming, in effect, a subcontractor to the producing household.* Rather than establish mass production at remote points, it is becoming more efficient to consider limited production at the local level. The reason for this change was theorized more than four decades ago by Ralph Borsodi.

An enemy of what he called "the factory system," Borsodi postulated a simple rule: *Decreases in the cost of production are offset by increases in the cost of distribution.* He identified the costs of distribution as the "institutional burden" of the factory, noted that these costs were artifacts of factory production that did not exist for home production, and concluded, ". . . the factory system ceases to be economic unless it is efficient enough to absorb the institutional burden which is its inescapable concomitant."

Product markets were artificially enlarged, Borsodi held, by the use of national advertising to convince consumers that a particular product was superior to another product; its effectiveness was such that national manufacturers were capable of selling their product for more than the virtually identical product produced by local manufacturers. Good economics for the producer, he found, has not always resulted in good economics for the consumer.

Borsodi cited the economics of soap as an example. The growth of Procter and Gamble illustrates how advertising overpowered the direct economic decision and caused the decline of small, local producers. Significantly, Procter and Gamble is one of the nation's largest advertisers and spends more than $275 million a year to convince consumers to buy P&G products.[2]

The same process is occurring today in the beer industry. Traditionally a highly fractured industry with numerous regional brands whose markets were limited by the economics of batch production and the high cost of transporting the final product, the beer industry has undergone an enormous consolidation over the past three decades. National brands have been able to command a price premium of 20 per cent through advertising, invest in enormous continuous-process plants to reduce production costs, and then underprice the local brands, region by region, until they

FIGURE 28

The Institutional Burden of the Factory

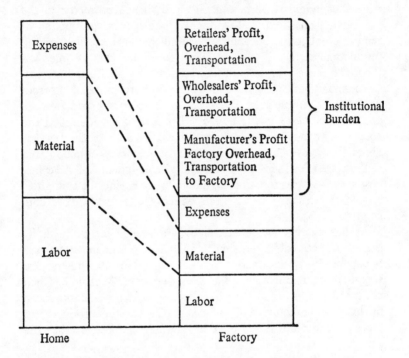

Source: Ralph Borsodi, *This Ugly Civilization*, p. 36.

are driven out of business. The pattern of consolidation and control is the familiar stuff of talk about big business.

The question is, What *follows* the consolidation? If the economic and intangible virtues of the product are the creation of advertising, it is reasonable to assume that brand loyalties are short-lived; hence the need to constantly introduce new products. Breakfast cereals and household soaps are excellent examples of this effect. So, in a sense, are automobiles.

Ultimately, the institutional burden becomes manifest in higher prices and opens the way for local competition to underprice the products of large manufacturers. One example of this trend is that small shops are thriving while waves of bankruptcies are overtaking the once thriving discount sales business. Local can mean limited-production organizations or the household itself.

Aside from the examples of household-equipment sales growth used in earlier chapters, we might also consider that one M.I.T. researcher, Barry Stein, found that the minimum size for an efficient productive unit has been declining for more than a decade and that new plants tended to be smaller than old plants. While there is still much worship of Big and Central, it is interesting to note that the 3M Company now prides itself on the extent of its decentralization and the small size of its manufacturing plants.

As we noted earlier, the credibility of big business has diminished significantly in the past decade; in the past, a low level of consumer confidence would have meant little, because "big business" was the only game in town; now there are a growing number of alternatives and a willingness to try them.

We see this effect most clearly in products that require little capital—in clothing of all kinds and a wide variety of services. In other areas, where the product is more specialized and requires some capital, the attrition of the mass market is not so clear, because only labor costs are passed on to the retailer or consumer. This is usually forced by price competition and is another example of externality, as discussed in the preceding chapter. Few of the eight or nine million bicycles sold annually, for example, are sold assembled; at best, the decision belongs to the retailer. Toys of all kinds arrive in various states of disassembly for the consumer to complete.

The increasing cost of distribution provides a larger and larger "umbrella" under which smaller and "less efficient" operations can compete; ultimately, that competition finds its way to the home.

When people see that the cost of manufacturing a product is a quarter or a third of its purchase price, they are tempted to produce it for themselves, whether the item be clothing, food, or home services. Just as IBM, by dominating the market and controlling prices, has created a "price umbrella" for small competing manufacturers, the centralized system of manufacturing, with its "institutional burden" of distributive costs, acts to offer a constantly expanding opportunity as new equipment makes smaller-scale production competitive. Thus the household economy grows.

The subtle and indirect cause of this change is the slow movement of technology toward more local production and away from massive fixed plants. This trend is a product of both the economic optimizing problem mentioned earlier and the subjective problem of meeting personal needs and demands.

The net effect of all these factors is to move the act of production ever closer to the household economy and create an environment in which the market firm is ever more suspect. All this is visible today. It will be absolutely obvious tomorrow.

We have seen, so far, that there is something called the household economy, that it is large and growing, and that even now its importance rivals that of the market economy. We have also seen that a variety of forces, most of them integral parts of the market economy, augur for an enormous growth of the household economy in the next two decades and the relative decline of the market economy.*

Yet none of this is part of the orthodox and commonly accepted view of the present or future. We might benefit from examining that orthodox view and seeing where and how it goes astray.

This is the subject of Part Four.

* In his recent book *Earthwalk*, sociologist Philip Slater outlines a process of social "eversion," which he believes will change the nature of Western culture. The process described here might be considered *economic eversion:* The market economy developed so far that it created the circumstances for its *opposite* to thrive.

1. That GM's notion of efficiency is passing is best discussed in Emma Rothschild's *Paradise Lost: The Decline of the Auto-Industrial Age* (New York: Random House, 1973).

2. *Advertising Age*, December 11, 1972, p. 92.

Part Four

An Expedition
in the Current Mythology

A close look at the unreality of the new industrial state

18

The Narcissistic Vision

WITHOUT IDEAS TO SHAPE IT, our experience would be sadly amorphous. So we are grateful to those who offer ideas. Few, after all, are capable of doing so. Worse, the market for thought is notoriously thin and ridicule often awaits ideas with large dimensions.

For these reasons, we owe a considerable debt to John Kenneth Galbraith; he has consistently rejected the addiction most economists have for regression analysis, demand curves, mathematical models, and all the elegant and esoteric tools economists have used to insure the isolation of their profession. Instead he has chosen to be master of the pathless woods that separate most economists from popular thought and consciousness. While the bulk of the profession devotes its attention to studies of the bark, roots, leaves, and fruit of the tree we clearly observe, Galbraith offers a vision of the forest. With the publication of *The Affluent Society* (1958), he provided a map of the social and economic forest for a society that was only dimly aware of how incredibly rich it was and largely ignorant of the implications of that wealth. *The New Industrial State* (1967) extended that map and served to change further the public perception of the realities of economic life; it served notice that our true concern was *political economy* and that the pure economics so carefully cultivated by

An Expedition in the Current Mythology

the noncommittal was largely irrelevant to questions that needed immediate answers.

The book was broad enough to enjoy attacks from both left and right and served to consolidate the work of many others whose thoughts were similar but who were doomed to relative or total obscurity because they lacked the wit and style Professor Galbraith has in abundance. Recognition of this fact leads us to a larger truth: The real measure of Professor Galbraith is literary, not economic. His achievement is to have been the eloquent voice of what Charles Reich later identified as Consciousness II, the liberal state of mind and belief dominated by the idea that it is the fate of modern man to live within, and by means of, increasingly large and complex organizations.

Whether or not Galbraith is recognized as its author, the idea of the new industrial state was impressive. Its tenacity still is. It works its influence, directly or subliminally, on the decisions of men with power and informs the social vision of many who are not the least bit interested in the stuff of economics. It does this in spite of its incapacity to explain the true shape and content of economic affairs.

The fact that it has been attacked from both left and right is another positive sign. Any idea so constituted can't be *all* bad. Yet it is in error, because it is based on the past and summarizes what has been, rather than giving us insight into what *will* be.

The new industrial state rested on three main arguments. The first of these was that the era of the individual entrepreneur was dead and that business ownership and management are now divorced, where before they had been inseparable. More than a few people are still unwilling to accept this idea. By definition, they are pre-Galbraith in their views, the stuff of what Charles Reich called Consciousness I.

For these people, nostalgia and wish fulfillment have overcome reason. As worldly, realistic people, we have to face the fact that Horatio Alger's heroes would be hard-pressed to seek their fortunes in the labyrinths of Procter and Gamble, the enormity of General Electric, or the elaborate network of American Telephone and Telegraph. Charlotte Ford's first husband was not a poor boy; and after the marriage, he was never employed, in any capacity, by the Ford Motor Company.

We speak with deft realism of the death of individual initiative

and consign the entrepreneur to the management of Dairy
Queens, obscure Howard Johnson franchises, and an assortment
of untrustworthy car dealerships. The Industrial Magnate has
been cruelly shrunk into the small businessman. His public image
is very small indeed. His destiny falls far short of the omnipotence
enjoyed by the Planning Committee of General Motors. The Alger
hero presides over the nooks and crannies of the economy, the
leftovers. He is the man who follows the beautiful horse with pan
and broom.

Realists all, we agree with Mr. Galbraith in his anticipatory
rejoinder to those who disagree: "It will be urged, of course,
that the industrial system is not the whole economy. Apart from
the world of General Motors, Standard Oil, Ford, General Electric, U. S. Steel, Chrysler, Texaco, Gulf, Western Electric, and
DuPont is that of the independent retailer, the farmer, the shoe
repairman, the bookmaker, narcotics peddler, pizza merchant,
and that of the dog and car laundry. Here prices are not controlled. Here the consumer is sovereign. Here pecuniary motivation is unimpaired. Here technology is simple and there is no
research and development to make it otherwise. Here there are
no government contracts; independence from the state is a
reality. None of these entrepreneurs patrol the precincts of the
Massachusetts Institute of Technology in search of talent. The
existence of all this I concede."[1] The concession is made easily,
because all that is conceded is taken to be insignificant. The fact
is that it is not insignificant, as we shall soon see.

We have some measure of the durability of an idea when we
consider that the age of wild capital creation and individual
initiative reached its true zenith more than seventy years ago,
with the formation of the United States Steel Corporation. In
1860, total investment in manufacturing was slightly over a billion
dollars; only a million and a half industrial workers were employed in the United States. In less than fifty years, manufacturing employment tripled and the total value of all manufactured
goods increased almost fifteenfold.[2] Nothing in the world, before
or since, has matched this amazing change and growth. Most of
this expansion came from the direction and initiative of individual men who sought to exploit opportunities that were readily
available. Many would call this period "The Good Old Days."

By 1890, the combination and affiliation of formerly separate enterprises had become popular; by 1900, 75 per cent of all our manufacturing facilities were owned by associations of stockholders rather than by single proprietors or partnerships. In 1901, some fifty-three hundred separate manufacturing plants were combined in some 318 trusts with a total capital in excess of $7 billion, to form the United States Steel Corporation.[3] The die was cast for the slow separation of ownership and management. Ownership, thereafter, would increasingly mean no more than the possession of a few engraved certificates entitling their possessor to the regular receipt of dividend checks. Ownership became increasingly abstract and passive, while management, although it lacked any property rights, assumed most of the power associated with the possession of assets.

In the years since then, the fashion of combination and consolidation has continued to flourish, albeit with minor ups and downs and the occasional intervention of the Antitrust Division of the Justice Department. The control a single man or family may have exercised over a particular enterprise has been steadily reduced. The caution of lawyers has also helped, no doubt. And so has the tendency of the founding fathers to do more than merely perpetuate themselves.

It was the thesis of Adolf Berle and Gardner Means, as early as 1934,[4] that ownership and management were separate, and that the modern corporation, as a result, was a very different creature from its predecessors. Individually owned corporations were thought to be opportunistic, exploitative, short-sighted, and generally malignant in comparison with corporations in which ownership and management were separated.

Company owners were the fierce stuff from which Consciousness I was fashioned. They were assumed to favor a world in which dogs resorted to cannibalism. They believed in laissez-faire and were enthusiastic over the ideas of social Darwinists. All in all, their domination of social values made for a very hard-nosed society.

Somehow the diffused identity of ownership had a socializing and rounding influence on corporate behavior, perhaps because the profit motive was moderated. "Corporate executives as individuals," Berle notes in *Power Without Property*, "are not capitalists seeking profit. They are men seeking careers, in a structure offering rewards of power and position rather than profit or great wealth."[5]

More than a few observers are less than content with this formulation.[6] It forgets, for one thing, that wealth is still very concentrated and that irrespective of whether it is reposed in the securities of one or of ten corporations, its absolute possession alone gives its holder power. Moreover, the corporate executives who are merely seeking careers rather than profit would confidently agree that corporate profitability and their careers are very closely related; the higher one is in the corporate power structure, the more directly can progress and profits be related.

The change in modern corporations is more subtle than mere profit moderation and, more likely, lies in the diffusion of decision power throughout the organization so that it no longer bears the clear imprint of a single owner but, rather, has the softened appearance of a committee. Perhaps the most troublesome assumption in all this is that individuals are believed to have tendencies to evil while communities tend to good—or at least moderated—behavior. The active malevolence of some communities in lynchings and, more typically, the passive malevolence of others (the murder of Kitty Genovese, for instance) leads one to wonder if such generalizations are not a bit naïve.

While the relative malice of both individuals and committees is likely to remain a moot point for some time, we can conclude with some safety that *there has been a change* in the modern corporation, and it is most likely associated with large size, increasing capitalization, and generally diffused and indirect ownership. Certainly for all except those at the very top, the modern corporation is a very different social structure from the family firm.

C. Wright Mills offered a workable synthesis of diverse views in *The Power Elite.* "Sixty glittering, clannish families," he wrote, "do not run the American economy, nor has there occurred any silent revolution of managers who have expropriated the powers and privileges of such families. The truth that is in both these characterizations is less adequately expressed as 'America's Sixty Families' or 'The Managerial Revolution,' than as the managerial reorganization of the propertied classes into the more or less unified stratum of the corporate rich. As families and as individuals, the very rich are still very much a part of the higher economic life of America; so are the chief executives of the major corporations. What has happened, I believe, is the reorganization of the propertied class, along with those of higher salary, into a new corporate world of privilege and prerogative. What is significant about this managerial reorganization of the propertied class is that by means of it the narrow industrial and profit interests of specific firms and industries and families have been translated into the broader economic and political interests of a more genuinely class type. Now the corporate seats of the rich contain all the powers and privileges inherent in the institutions of private property."[7]

Some sociologists were content to take the managerial-revolution thesis and swallow it whole. The literature of the fifties was engulfed by the spirit of anomie, overwhelmed by the impact of large organizations on our social life.[8] It has even been suggested that corporate America is a new kind of feudalism which has transcended the usual geographic boundaries, and that the lives of most people are bound and measured not by the values and aspirations of the local community but by the values encouraged and rewarded by their corporate employer. William H. Whyte's *The Organization Man* suggests that the corporate employee on the make is a kind of courtier and should conduct himself accordingly. The struggle is for power, for the ear and favor of the king. Mere money is only a partial measure of our access to that power. A more recent popular book, *Management and Machiavelli*, suggests much the same.

In spite of inflation and economic growth, incomes above twenty-five thousand dollars a year are still relatively rare (less than one family in twenty), and the issue of owner power vs. managerial power is largely irrelevant to most workers; the worker's *experience* is of an enormous labyrinth, a system of alliances and loyalties in which the aspirant to income and power must be constantly aware, devoted, adroit, clever, and completely attuned to the expectations and needs of those above him. The self-help books that abound concentrate their advice on the *behavior* the rising executive must exhibit; little, if anything, is said about the financial maneuvers that might be used to take power directly. The multitude at the bottom and middle of General Electric's twenty-odd levels of management have little use for information on financial maneuvers; they have an existential need to believe that their *behavior* alone might influence their future. Success accrues to those who have taken Dale Carnegie courses.[9] Significantly, the most popular treatise on rising to corporate power (Vance Packard's *The Pyramid Climbers*) is virtually devoid of any discussion of power through ownership. Corporations are assumed to be large and publicly owned; the aspirant manager is advised to be wary of those few that are not. The pyramid is climbed because . . . it is there.

If the audience for the economic arguments was relatively small, the audience for the sociologists was enormous. In the fifties and early sixties, the human side of corporate America appeared as a dramatic panorama of inadequately anesthetized pain. The price of affluence, we learned, was a banal existence; the social landscape was haunted by the specter of mass conformity. Inner-directed, frontier America was being supplanted by other-directed, corporate man. Bland, cautious, and deferential to his superiors as well as willing to move on a moment's notice, the ideal American was to be conspicuous for his interchangeability with others. Popular magazines regularly warned the housewife that she must grow with her husband or risk being cast aside, discarded in favor of a new wife that might "fit" better. The last act of the machine age was to be the standardization of its people as well as its mechanical parts.

The second major argument that supported the new industrial state was that *the economic power of the nation is increasingly concentrated in the activities of a small number of enormous companies.* General Motors, the largest of the *Fortune* 500 industrial companies, had assets in 1973 of some $20 billion and annual sales of $36 billion. The annual sales of General Motors, to provide broad relative measures, amount to slightly less than the gross national product of Sweden and substantially more than that of Belgium, Austria, Denmark, Norway, Portugal, or Switzerland. It also employs more than three times as many workers as the state of Alaska has residents and would, if ranked in population size, be larger than ten of our fifty states. Its annual sales, as Ralph Nader is fond of pointing out, amount to about $3 million a *minute,* and the company spent some $40 million when it changed its signs across the country to include "Mark of Excellence."

When we look for still broader measures, we find that the hundred largest manufacturing firms now employ some 9 million people and have managed to enlarge their share of corporate assets held from just under 40 per cent of the total in 1950 to almost 50 per cent in 1970. Taken as a group, the five hundred largest industrial companies employ almost fifteen million people, or 75 per cent of all those employed in manufacturing.[10] The rest of the work force, not quite five million, are distributed over some two hundred thousand smaller corporations. Not surprisingly, the majority are employed in "the second five hundred." Similar patterns of giantism appear in the retailing, banking, and life-insurance industries. The age of the Leviathan seems inescapable.

While sociologists bemoaned the passing of the individual, economists took note of another striking fact: The corporation was responsible for some 70–80 per cent of "gross capital formation"—meaning that the very organizations that had so recently shed themselves of owner control had also largely rid themselves of the need to raise capital from individuals and were directly responsible for most of the nation's economic growth. They controlled investment in new plants and equipment. They had become self-contained, self-sustaining units free from any direct outside control. Where they decided to invest that capital was a controlling factor in the shape and size of economic growth.

It is difficult, at this juncture, not to be reminded of the Frankenstein myth. Many observers had the feeling that the corporate creature was not only something of a monster but that he was no longer responding to the commands of any master. Indeed, the corporate creature seemed to be in control and was issuing commands to *us*.*

His first command was, "Consume!" Without consumption there would be no demand, and without demand there could be no profitable production. Without profitable production there could be no continued generation of new capital for investment. Individuals who hoarded money, who lived within or under their incomes, became suspect. Slowly they lost status, for the measure of success, logically, was the standard of consumption upheld; the higher the standard, the greater the assurance of individual loyalty to the corporation and, naturally, the higher the probabil-

---

* While sociologists still discuss the modern corporation as independent, the economic facts have changed entirely in the last ten years. Very few corporations are self-financing.

ity of advancement to a higher standard of consumption. For most, it requires no whip to encourage us to consume. The carrot will suffice. If we balk at all, it is in the occasional realization that, as our incomes have increased, so has our employers' control over its disposition: the higher the income, the more rigid the standards applied to its expenditure. In some instances this control is overt—as in the height and color of IBM employees' socks and ties, and the length of their shirt sleeves—but in most it is covert, dictated by the large penetration of the corporation into all dimensions of the employees' social life. The forty-thousand-dollar-a-year executive who considers remaining in his old, forty-thousand-dollar house is likely to consider the desire to remain a liability to his future security and advancement, because it does not reflect his position.

Thus, the savings function is largely removed from the individual and resides now with the corporation and a few large financial institutions. The growth of company pension and profit-sharing plans is another way of taking the responsibility for savings from the consumer. Similarly, the enforced savings of the federal employment tax have become increasingly important; the steady increase in the percentage of income taken and the rapid rise in the maximum income covered has insured that Social Security deductions now limit the ability of most families to save independently; the employment tax has become an erratically used tool for the regulation of consumer demand. The figures below understate the institutionalization of savings, because the end of the decade witnessed a rate of personal savings that provoked extreme anxiety on the part of government policy makers and interfered with bringing an end to the 1970–71 recession. People were saving "too much." The fact is that individual discretionary savings is being surpassed by huge corporate and public programs.

The final argument in support of the new industrial state was that *the guiding principle in its operation (now that the owners have been disposed of and it has achieved control of its sources of capital) is technology.* The increasing maturity of the economy requires the use of ever more sophisticated technology for the efficient production of the necessary (and many unnecessary) goods. Technology requires planning and large investments of people and money over increasingly long periods of time; this requires in turn that companies have effective control of their

FIGURE 29

Personal Savings, Employment-tax Receipts, and
Private Pension Contributions (in billions)

Year	Personal Savings	Employment Tax	Private Pensions
1960	17.0	11.2	4.7
1965	28.4	17.4	7.4
1966	32.5	20.7	7.7
1967	40.4	27.8	9.0
1968	39.8	29.2	9.9
1969	37.9	34.2	11.5
1970	54.1	39.1	12.6

Source: Statistical Abstract of the United States.

markets if the company is to avoid catastrophic risks. Few companies, after all, are large enough to absorb a $500-million write-off, as RCA did in deciding to get out of the computer business.

The working result of these three factors was an increasing sense among most people that all but the smallest decisions in life are beyond their control, and the familiar litany of nerve-deadening conformity and psychic oppression in corporate America is being intoned.

If we were to paint a portrait of life in corporate America it would not be a tall, visionary spire but an enormous, labyrinthine machine, without top or bottom, front or back, covered with knobs, dials, valves, and handles, tended by faceless minions, all of whom are expectantly waiting. Something will emerge from one of the machine's many orifices. No one knows exactly what it is, but it is assumed to be good. Each white-coated functionary is well versed in just what his valve, handle, or dial means. But nothing else. The rows of TV consoles at Cape Kennedy are not a poet's metaphor; they are a reality, an expression of the peculiar, one-eyed voyeurism implicit in the industrial state.

Human economic affairs, obviously, were marching to a different and largely invisible drummer, a stranger to the free individual of yore. What, after all, is "the technostructure"? Does it really make decisions?

This is not a casual concern. If the large corporation has abrogated the power of the marketplace, it has risen above the power of individuals; only government collective power stands between the individual and the coercive power of corporations. It is easy to see why the relationship of government and business has attracted concern and more than a little hysteria. In this relationship alone, according to most economic views, lies the deployment of human and physical capital and the future quality of human life. It is an intersection that must pass much traffic in anxiety.

Few rational observers of either the government or business could clearly state that they have spotted the unalterable source of all decisions. No one can locate the true seat of power, a fact that provokes much anxiety in those who prefer to conceive of the world as controlled by a diabolical and monolithic source.

Instead, we witness a highly developed symbiosis in which government increasingly influences the behavior of business in exchange for allowing the individual firm (or firms within an industry) to avoid the risk of the marketplace. Government expenditures and projects tirelessly underwrite new technology; in an ever-widening circle of involvements, the state provides a structure that underwrites a minimum return on investment. The demand for toothpaste and soap, uncomplicated by high technology in either production or distribution, can be left to the vagaries of the marketplace and the individual; new aircraft cannot. Directly or indirectly, we are told, government resources are now used to underwrite technology and research and development. Thus, we went to the moon to develop fabrics that would not burn and fought in Vietnam to improve the artificial limb and the helicopter. The threat of nerve gas in future wars inspired the atropine auto-injector, which has since been adapted for use by potential coronary victims.[11] We are also advised that someday the fuel cell will mean a great deal to us and we owe it all to the spirit of man as interpreted by the Congress and made manifest by NASA and its assorted subcontractors. Thus big government and big business support big investment to maintain and perpetuate a highly organized, centralized, and steeply hierarchic society.

Our role as citizens is rather confusing. Our lives are functionally simpler, because so much has been removed from them and entrusted to the marketplace and government. At the same time, they are more complicated, because nothing is as it appears. We can't say, for instance, that money has been taken from us and given to businesses. In national economies, such subtraction sometimes means a larger economic product. Nor is it possible, in the conventional imagination, to consider any alternatives to the powerful intertwining of business and government.

In answer to this dilemma, economists and sociologists of both the moderate left and the moderate right have found an ambivalent corollary of the industrial state, an argument that might be called the Theory of Ultimate Convergence. This theory declares that there are more similarities between socialism and capitalism than there are differences. *Technology and industrial development, in this view, have become a kind of philosophical sink in which all ideology must ultimately disappear.* Socialism is really state capitalism, representing the formal centralization of planning and the control of consumer demand; the differences between this and the less formal planning and control that occurs in the new industrial state are subtle indeed, particularly if your judgment is made within the ambit of consumer experience.

Returning to our theme of deposed ownership: If the owners of capital are removed and powerless and an ever-increasing portion of the nation's capital is beneficially owned by its less substantial citizens through pensions, trusts, mutual funds, and other institutions in which all property rights (except the right to receive dividends) are no longer in effect, and if we perceive that our progress to power is not to be made through the crass accumulation of capital but by exhibiting appropriate behavior within large and centrally controlled organizations dominated by an even larger centrally controlled organization, then maybe the two systems *do* have more in common than we admit on July Fourth. Yes? The dominant influence of our time is not the import of our political organization; it is our *productive* organization that counts. Everywhere, it is the same: industry. Dominated, of course, by technology.

The popularity of this view with intellectuals is almost absolute. Harvard sociologist Daniel Bell offered *The End of Ideology* in 1960, subtitled *On the Exhaustion of Political Ideas in the Fifties;* Herman Kahn, who is more inclined to "be" than to "mean," holds forthrightly that bald economic growth, not ideas, will dominate the future. Socialism and capitalism, once adversaries, thesis and antithesis, have found a strange synthesis in the new industrial state.[12]

These are the conceptual glasses through which we view much of our economic experience today. The lenses, granted, may be smudged by our daily confusion or we may choose not to use them at all, thus liberating ourselves for blurry flights of fantasy with Horatio Alger, but in the end it is this conception of the world that dictates the deeds of men in power, particularly in government. This is Galbraith's economic achievement: He has been responsible for replacing an outdated conception of economic life and public decision making with one that is obsolescent. This is not a small achievement. Ideas are tenacious and durable, even when irrelevant, a sad fact that Galbraith's own ideas are now in the process of confirming.

The problem with the new industrial state is that it is basically retrospective and backward-looking. It serves to describe (and explain) the forties, fifties, and sixties with great accuracy and will apply to the seventies with some veracity. But *it cannot be taken as a guide to the influences that will* change *our future experience and constitute its foundation.* Alas, the most compelling ideas describe declining experiences, and *The New Industrial State* represents the final, broad, and perfected popular expression describing conditions that no longer exist. At long last, the past is clear.

The new industrial state and all its corollaries, however, do not survive a closer look at the facts. The first thing we shall consider is, "Where did it come from?" What are its sources of strength and support?

The answer is in the academic community, whose position, on examination, seems less than objective.

Few things are more pleasing than discovering that you possess something whose worth has just been drastically revalued upward. The academic community had such an experience when the new industrial state was posited: Suddenly the value of expertise leaped upward, and all those with some vaguely measurable special ability found that what had long been regarded as a respectable but rather quaint vocation was now commanding a premium. Not surprisingly, academic salaries have soared in the past decade,[13] while opportunities for secondary income through consulting (in some fields) have grown even faster. At some of our more prestigious institutions, faculty members regularly make more money consulting than they do teaching.

The role of our educational institutions in helping business and government make decisions has expanded rapidly. Not only are they responsible for providing the regular supply of necessary trained manpower—their traditional function—but they are needed to serve as intermediaries, technicians to the vast and complicated machinery of BusGov and GovBus, filling the gap between both and providing a needed stopover for those in transit between the two. Education has become "the knowledge industry."

Another corollary of the new industrial state and an extension of the industrial analogy is *the growing importance of "human capital."* If the entrepreneur is dead, so is the pre-emptive power of his money capital; now the enterprise is lost not for want of a dollar but for want of a physicist or a marketing MBA. This shift has been attributed to the growing importance of technology and the need for a longer planning scope; both require highly educated and sophisticated workers to manage the entire process and to use the equipment required for the product.

Those who are reluctant to accept the idea of human capital have never worked as management consultants, a service industry in which highly educated individuals are likely to be installed in rows of identical offices on long corridors and their time sold, like the use of motel beds, by the day or the hour. A doctorate in, say, agribusiness, combined with a degree in international law, is more valuable (is a greater capital asset) than an MBA degree, and that, in turn, is more valuable than a bachelor's degree with a major in Tunisian history. Hence, the time of one costs more than the time of another.

The popularity of "human capital" is difficult to overestimate. It solves a number of problems. First, it serves to stimulate and vastly increase the market for education, thereby insuring the employment of the teacher. This is a multifold blessing, because education not only employs people but, by definition, removes even larger numbers from the labor market altogether by turning them into students. Second, it provides hope, for those with no significant conventional capital, that they may yet achieve some power and prestige. Since the vast bulk of the population has no significant capital, they are existentially predisposed to believe in *human* capital, and education thus acquires a kind of infallibility. It is not surprising that education is regarded as a safe bet. When in doubt, stick it out. Education is the means by which upper-middle-class youth maintain a "holding pattern." All human problems will ultimately be resolved by massive applications of sublime expertise. Finally, education also means that the academics will at last have their day of power.

This last item is no small consideration. It marks the culmination of a very long struggle. More than two millenniums have passed since Plato first declared that the rulers of the republic should be philosopher-kings. Now, at last, their time has come. Patience paid off. One oligarchy will be replaced by another.

Yes. *One oligarchy will be replaced by another.* That is the limit of the academic imagination; concentrated financial power will be replaced by concentrated knowledge power. Where once the society was controlled by those with money, it will now be controlled by those with knowledge. Since sublime knowledge is intrinsically superior to crass money, we will be a better society for it. We learned that in school, remember?

There should be no mistake about this. The vision of the academic community of its role and the importance of human capital is, at its very root, self-serving and narcissistic. It is also almost morbidly unimaginative, for it offers a future that is no more than a sequel to the past.

The intellectual community can see itself reflected in the power of the state and admire. "See," it might say, "I am beautiful, I am good."

Any tyranny of power that might develop, we are assured, will be of the benevolent variety; it will be thoughtful, careful, and considerate. But we must never question its primacy. The new industrial state is merely a checkpoint for the passing of the baton of power from the moneyed establishment to the intellectual establishment.

We can be sure that the transition will be smooth, for the two institutions have remarkably similar structures. Using the same measure that Berle, Galbraith, et al. use in their arguments for the managerial revolution, we find that student enrollment is nearly as concentrated in a few large universities as worker em-

FIGURE 30

Relative Concentration in Industry
by Education and Income

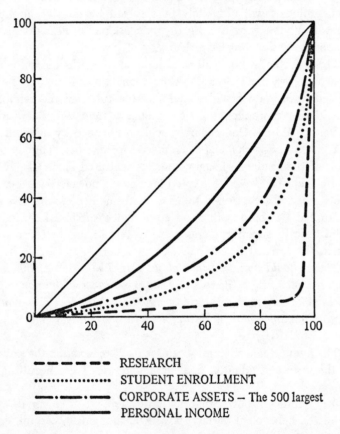

——————— RESEARCH
·················· STUDENT ENROLLMENT
—·——·—— CORPORATE ASSETS — The 500 largest
——————— PERSONAL INCOME

ployment is concentrated in large corporations! The diagram above is called a Lorenz curve, commonly used to compare distribution. If all things (e.g. dollars, cars, degrees, employees, assets, sales, etc.) are distributed equally among all involved parties, the distribution will be a straight line at a 45° angle from left to right, e.g. 1 per cent of the goodies will go to 1 per cent of the recipients. If distribution were totally unequal and one man or institution had everything, there would be no line. The bending line is a means for comparing concentration; the deeper the bend, the more unequal the distribution. Note that student enrollment is less concentrated than research but slightly more concentrated than corporate assets and personal income. *Slightly.* Research and development is most highly concentrated. A bare handful of institutions—one hundred in all—do 93 per cent of all the research.[14] If such concentration existed in any other industry, it would no doubt bring down the full wrath of the antitrust laws.

No such event occurs, because dangerous concentrations of power are still associated with concentrations of physical or money capital, not human capital, by the governmental institutions that might redress the balance. A clear dual standard is operating when we witness the frequent academic criticism and comment on the dangers of corporate bigness and concentration. It belies a desire to replace one power structure with another.

We can, however, carry the argument for human capital two steps further. We know and grant that the universities and public schools are responsible for shaping this "capital equipment" (just as the machine-tool industry is responsible for much of the capital equipment of manufacturing industries), but we also know that the true owners of that capital, once formed, are the individuals who use their degrees as assets. Anyone who doubts this, need only examine the increasing rigidity of the corporate ladder and the higher degrees that serve as rungs.

In a way, this circumstance is expected, because the individual operator is exposed to the greatest risk in conventional business operations; similarly, no capital is more easily squandered than the human variety. It depreciates with frightening speed, often faster than it can be recouped. One of the annual rituals at M.I.T. is to inform new undergraduates that much of what they learn in the following four years will be out of date within three years of graduation. In such manner are the young now welcomed to life's treadmill.

Since this human capital is so vital to the existence of the new industrial state in particular and technological society in general, we should ask if it has been included in discussions of capital formation. We find, in fact, that Professor Galbraith asserts the importance of human capital but *neglects to include it in his measures of capital formation.* Thus, the capital formation of the

new technological society is measured by the conventions of the
old, early-industrial society.

The vital autonomy of the new industrial state, as we noted
earlier, is guaranteed by the observation that the modern corporation is not dependent on the individual saver for its capital. Evidence supporting this fact is that the vast bulk of what is defined
as "gross private domestic investment" is made by businesses, not
people. In 1965, corporations made investments of $84 billion in
a total of $108 billion. In 1969, corporations contributed $98 billion of the $140-billion total.[15] *In the same year, however, $30
billion was invested in primary and secondary education, and
another $30 billion has been estimated as the "output" of the na-
tion's institutions of higher learning.*[16] Adding the components
of gross private domestic investment again, we find that individuals controlled slightly more than half of the total—$102 billion
—when human capital is included. Moreover, we have entirely
neglected the $84 billion spent in the same year on "consumer
durables," a form of capital investment made by households. Instead of accounting for only 30 per cent of gross capital formation, individuals account for at least 50 per cent. When consumer
durables are included, individuals and the household economy
are responsible for *two thirds* of gross private domestic investment. Household investment, in other words, is *twice* as large as
corporate investment.

FIGURE 31

Gross Private Domestic Investment, 1969

1. Conventional Addition		*2. Including Education*			*3. Including Education and Consumer Durables*		
Corporations	$ 98	Corporations	$ 98		Corporations	$ 98	
Individuals	42	Individuals	42	} 102	Individual	42	
	$140 billion	Education	60		Education	60	} 186
			$200 billion		Consumer		
					Durables	84	
						$284	

Sources: Statistical Abstract of the United States, 1970;
           New England Economic Review, March, April, 1971.

The implication of these figures is that the modern corporation
isn't nearly as powerful or autonomous as it is portrayed; more
than half its real capital resources are supplied by individuals,

and the corporation itself is a relatively minor part of *total* capital formation. Nor does it control the direction of economic growth. Radicals, with their usual diabolism, would likely assert that most of these assets in human capital are put to the service of corporations and that the universities, in effect, are the lackeys of their corporate masters. This is doubtful. No workers have been more transient than those who are highly educated; their lack of loyalty is well known, making corporations highly vulnerable to a loss of human capital if, for instance, management installs policies that are unattractive or fails to offer the necessary financial inducements to stay. The plight of the nation's urban telephone companies has been attributed to their massive losses of human capital over the past three decades.[17] *Total* rejection of the corporation is most prevalent among those who have the most human capital, a fact that caused at least one commentator to suggest that the "greening" of America by middle-class youth would lead to the "blueing" of America as working-class Americans rose to positions of conventional power.

The real issue in human capital is how those who possess it will choose to employ it. In the service of a centralized business economy, it will allow the hierarchic social structure that now exists to perpetuate itself; employed differently, in diverse activities such as communes, co-operatives, associations, and in the orthodox home, it can work a social revolution. This certainly is the direction of both the counterculture and the environmental movement. And as we shall soon see, even the structure of the conventional economy is bound to become less centralized and hierarchic.

Concentrated, specialized knowledge is not always an asset, as many Boeing and Lockheed employees discovered in 1969 and 1970. If it can be shown that knowledge may have a higher and more secure return while suffering less depreciation if differently organized, then the existing patterns of specialized education are unlikely to survive, and the small minority that presently constitute the counterculture may suddenly bloom into a new majority.

In this light it is not surprising that the problem of the university is that it can no longer meet the needs of its students. They are asking for education with a different structure and end. The entire drive of the counterculture and all the "alternative institutions" is toward decentralization and despecialization, a drive that is supported by all the forces we have already discussed, as well as the growing concern for personal freedom and the evasive "quality of life."

If the singular importance and autonomy of the modern corporation are questionable, so is its domination of the economy as a whole. In *The Service Economy*, published in 1968, Victor Fuchs wrote: "The first major finding, plainly in evidence but not sufficiently appreciated, is that the balance of employment in the United States has shifted dramatically (and probably irrevocably) in favor of the service industries. The service sector's share of total employment has grown from approximately 40% in 1929 to over 55% in 1967. Between 1947 and 1965 alone, there was an increase of 13 million jobs in the service sector, compared with an increase of only 4 million in industry and a decrease of 3 million in Agriculture."[18] Later he notes that even these impressive figures *understate* the true growth of service employment, because goods-producing industries often take on activities that would be classified as services if they were not conducted within a producing firm.

To express concern about the increasing concentration of industrial assets in the hands of a few ever larger corporations is akin to expressing alarm about the consolidation of the buggy-whip industry; the proper subject of concern is the automobile, not the buggy whip. Yet, just as we still focus on scarcity rather than on abundance, we still concentrate our attention on the production of goods rather than on services. We erroneously view the future through the bias of the past.

For most of us, employment is an important concern. We don't encourage our children to develop an interest in the tanning and leather hides industry, nor do we express great enthusiasm for textiles. The reason for this is simple: We all have a pragmatic interest in continuing employment. Jobs are most available where there is growth. If the services are growing, then the services are where our attention should be. Everyone seems to have recognized this but the economic community; they are still worried about the production of steel.

The changing distribution of United States employment is illustrated below. Obviously, manufacturing is not the most vibrant

FIGURE 32

The Distribution of Employment by Sector 1948–80

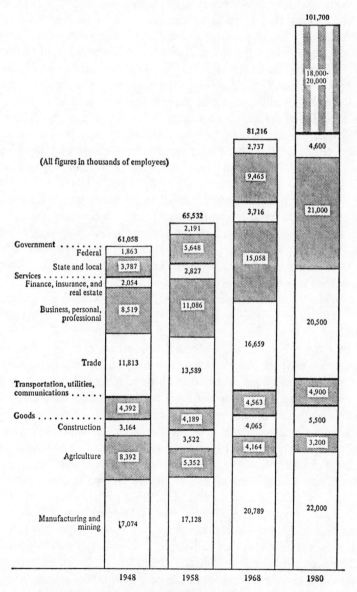

(All figures in thousands of employees)

	1948	1958	1968	1980
Total	61,058	65,532	81,216	101,700
Government				18,000–20,000
Federal	1,863	2,191	2,737	4,600
State and local	3,787	5,648	9,465	21,000
Services				
Finance, insurance, and real estate	2,054	2,827	3,716	
Business, personal, professional	8,519	11,086	15,058	20,500
Trade	11,813	13,589	16,659	
Transportation, utilities, communications	4,392	4,189	4,563	4,900
Goods				5,500
Construction	3,164	3,522	4,065	
Agriculture	8,392	5,352	4,164	3,200
Manufacturing and mining	17,074	17,128	20,789	22,000

Source: *Fortune*, "There'll Be Less Leisure than you think," March 1970.

sector of the economy. The future of American society will not
be written there.

But what about all those men in gray flannel suits? What about
corporations that have more employees than most cities have
residents? What about huge government bureaucracies filled with
pale people who think Franz Kafka was a historian? What about
International Harvester, Ford, Bell Telephone, and Xerox? What
about all those enormous companies with offices everywhere and
glossy, hundred-page annual reports that are sent to a million
shareholders? What about companies with sales of $n billion?
With minor divisions that control markets in industries of which
two thirds of the board of directors have never heard? What
about all that? Surely they are more important than dog and car
laundries.

No amount of incantation will change *Fortune* 500; we have a
right to suspect those who project Arcadian futures, because it is
unlikely that anything short of thermonuclear war will cause
General Motors to disappear. The state is more likely to "wither
away" than American Telephone and Telegraph, and the state
has shown a robust health and growth.

Power and importance, however, are matters of proportion.
A millionaire is usually accorded special treatment and respect
unless he is in the company of multimillionaires. Then he is
likely to feel neglected. No one, for instance, can deny the importance of food. We eat it every day; the need for nourishment
is our common bond. Yet there is little evidence that agriculture
—or even the entire locus of food production and distribution—
commands our lasting attention and respect. True, we worry
about the price of hamburger and prime ribs, lament (and sometimes protest) the cost and taste of tomatoes, and understand
that the high price of iceberg lettuce, like its namesake, represents the 90 per cent of the vegetable we never see. And we
regularly complain about the high price of farm subsidies, the
declining quality of service in fine restaurants, and other vital
matters. But, in the end, agriculture is not very important to us:
It employs few now and will employ even fewer in the future.
The production and distribution of food in all its forms requires
the effort of only one eighth of the employed labor force, or about
10 million workers. Almost 2.5 million of those are employed in

"eating and drinking places." We do not, in spite of all this, consider ourselves an agricultural nation.

Similarly, we must soon stop considering ourselves an industrial nation or a manufacturing nation. Our decline in these areas is common knowledge, but the import of this situation is remarkably unassimilated. The phrase "post-industrial" comes to mind. Unfortunately, like the word "non-fiction," it informs us negatively rather than positively. We know what it isn't, but we don't know what it *is*.

We can benefit by taking a closer look at patterns of growth and employment. More clearly than anything else, these figures show the future decline of corporate America. Below, the employment figures for various sectors of the economy are ranked by rate of growth. Note that manufacturing, the center of the industrial economy, experienced relatively slow growth, while the service sectors experienced substantial gains.

FIGURE 33

Employment Growth 1960–69

Sector	1960	1969	% Gain
Services	7,423	11,103	50%
State and local government	5,570	8,160	46
Finance, insurance and real estate	2,669	3,559	37
Wholesale and retail	11,391	14,644	28
Federal government	2,430	3,006	26
Manufacturing	16,796	20,121	19
Construction	2,885	3,411	18
Transportation, utilities and communications	4,004	4,448	11

Source: *County Business Patterns*, 1970, Statistical Abstract of the United States, 1972

This pattern of relative growth is expected to continue. It indicates that the industrial behemoths that constitute "the technostructure" will occupy a diminished position. Nor are people, as some might suggest, merely exchanging large manufacturing firms for large retailing companies or large government bureaucracies. They are increasingly finding employment in small organizations.

There is no justification for continuing to support notions of mass conformity, corporate coercion, and the other complaints

usually associated with the dominance of corporate America, because *our work experience is going to be dominated by the
growth of relatively small, local organizations.* The figures below show the percentage of all workers employed in organizations with fewer than fifty employees.

To some extent, these figures understate the case for the
growth of small organizations, because service and manufacturing
are intrinsically different. A manufacturing company can be quite
large, complex, and integrated; it might actually *require* five
thousand employees to sustain its profitable operation. But where
a rather complex creature might be the biological analogue for
the modern manufacturing company, the *tapeworm* serves very
well for the service industries. These tend to have a large number
of independent, virtually identical, and rather simple operating
units. Often the only connection between the various operations
is the creation of an accountant, an artifact of financial operation
rather than of functional operation.

What, one might ask, are the boundaries of work experience
for the man who sweeps the floor at McDonald's, the manager of
the local Singer Shop, or the hostess at Ho-Jo's? No doubt their
horizons are substantially closer than that of corporate head-
quarters or even of the hopeful shareholder. While franchising
clearly illustrates the principle, the larger fact is that service industries, by their nature, are local, small-scale operations, whose
size may be brought to illusory greatness by virtue of a corporate
balance sheet. It is only someone in New York who wants to make
Gino's or Kentucky Fried Chicken more than the sum of its parts.
Unlike the General Electric employee who moves when the plant
closes down, the retail employee, stockbroker, or insurance salesman just looks for another store, because they are all basically
the same. Nor is this effect necessarily isolated to service companies; manufacturing firms are finding increasing resistance to
corporate transfers. The willing mobility of those employed in
corporate America is coming to an end.

While we tend to think of government as one large, monolithic,
intractable glob, it is, in fact, usually based on rather small units
of organization. Of the more than eight million people employed
by state and local governments, *more than half* were employed
as teachers in the public schools. The typical school, particularly
at the primary level, is locally oriented and relatively small. A

FIGURE 34

Percentage of All Employees in Firms
with Fewer than Fifty Workers

Sector	% Under 50	% Growth 1960-69	% Over 500
Services	56.6	50	—
State and local government	n.a.	46	n.a.
Fire	36.7	37	24.0
Wholesale and retail	59.6	28	13.6
Federal government	n.a.	26	n.a.
Manufacturing	14.3	19	44.3
Construction	58.5	18	6.4
Transportation, utilities and communications	25.7	11	41.8

Source: *County Business Patterns*, 1970;

total staff of fifty represents a fair-sized school. Secondary schools, though larger than primary schools to accommodate a degree of specialization, are still rather small organizations, in which all the employees can be accommodated in the school lunchroom. Community and junior colleges, the fastest area of growth in higher education, are known for their small size.

The second-largest category of state and local employment is the public hospital; some eight hundred thousand are employed here in state institutions (which tend to be large) and local hospitals (which tend to be quite small). Other governmental functions, such as police, fire, sanitation, and highway departments are organized in small, relatively autonomous units that serve a given area or population. Much federal employment is similarly organized; the recent trend is to increase local control and operation rather than decrease it.

Clearly, economic growth favors finding future employment in small, rather than large, organizations. This fact is not accounted for in the popular vision of indenture to Ford Motor Company. Manufacturing, instead of employing one worker in three, will provide work for just over one worker in five by the end of this decade. The impact of this shift has yet to be fully explored—but it is inescapable that the anonymity and powerlessness that describe the experience of workers at the endlessly chronicled GM plant in Lordstown, Ohio, will be increasingly atypical as the economy matures. Years ago, a statement such as "What's good for General Motors is good for the United States" was met with a rather threatened indignation. Indignation because it seemed outrageous that the goals of one corporation could be equated with the goals of an entire nation; threatened because almost everyone knew that if something *wasn't* good for GM, it probably wouldn't do the nation much good either; replacing GM, were it to disappear, would be something of a task. Like it or not, GM was a vital mainstay in our economy. This will not be the case in the future.

Corporate America is a has-been. Its dominance of the American economy ended in the late fifties, and its power in culture and politics was badly injured in the sixties. There is every indication in our present economic crisis that it will diminish enormously in the seventies. Victor Fuchs concluded that "in the first half of this century, the corporation's role grew steadily but its relative importance apparently reached a peak about 1956 when corporations accounted for over 57% of total national income. Since then there has been a tendency for this fraction to remain stable, or even to show some decline despite tax laws which encourage incorporation."[19] As we have already shown, business capital formation was surpassed at about the same time by that of households.[20] Now, corporate America neither controls investment nor represents the most significant areas of growth in capital or employment. The destiny of the new industrial state is akin to that of the old soldier: It never dies, it just fades, fades away.

1. John K. Galbraith, *The New Industrial State* (Boston: Houghton Mifflin, 1967), p. 395.

2. Charles and Mary Beard, *The Rise of American Civilization*, Part 2 (New York: Macmillan, 1933), p. 176.

3. James Truslow Adams, *The Epic of America* (Boston: Little, Brown, 1931), p. 343.

4. Adolf A. Berle, Jr., and Gardner C. Means, *The Modern Corporation and Private Property* (New York: Macmillan, 1934).

5. Adolf A. Berle, Jr., *Power Without Property* (New York: Harcourt, Brace & World, 1958), p. 68.

6. The most voluminous articulate observer in this area is probably Ferdinand Lundberg, whose *The Rich and the Super Rich* (New York: Lyle Stuart, 1968) is a milestone work in documenting the intricate, subtle linkages of power and property in the United States.

7. C. Wright Mills, *The Power Elite* (Toronto: Oxford University Press, 1956), p. 147.

8. The same spirit *still* informs much of "the new journalism," for it assumes that corporate man is a diabolical enemy and bends many data to prove a social point. The abuses of corporate power are such that one is inclined not to voice protest against all means used against it—except that the diabolist view is simplistic at best. Perhaps the most interesting fact is that perspective and the complication of modern economic life are beautifully suited to provide the socially concerned writer with dramatic content. The sad reality is that most conclusions so generated are largely artifacts, by-products of the means of examination, so the exercise, ultimately, is one of sensibility rather than content.

9. This entire phenomenon is akin to a kind of feminization of business. Masculine prerogatives, decisive action, etc., are no longer crucial; like the woman of yore, the business executive must charm and seduce his way to betterment.

10. Statistical Abstract of the United States, 1970.

11. The atropine auto-injector, a device for automatically injecting the antidote to nerve gas in field combat conditions, is manufactured by the Survival Technology Company, an enterprise whose lugubrious name, unlike a multitude of other hot stocks, reflects its product lines. The auto-injector, of which more than 6 million were produced for the Defense Supply Agency has since seen service by astronauts (for other drugs) and has been introduced in a, yes, "six Pak" to be used by potential heart-attack victims.

12. The literature of the Freudian Left—Marcuse, N. O. Brown, Roszak, and others—is an example of the formation of a new antithesis to replace the "thesis" that arrives at the merging of capitalism and communism. If you feel, as this writer does, that there is no comfortable (or credible) intellectual middle ground between the arid world of expertise and technology and the lubric liberation of the Freudian Left, then by all means read William Irwin Thompson's *At the Edge of History* (New York: Harper & Row, 1971).

13. From *Statistics of Higher Education; U. S. News & World Report.*

14. Daniel Bell, "Knowledge & Technology," in *Indicators of Social Change: Concepts and Measurements*, ed. by Eleanor B. Sheldon and Willbert E. Moore (New York: Russell Sage Foundation, 1968).

15. Statistical Abstract of the United States, 1970.

16. J. Philip Hinson, "Higher Education—How to Pay," *New England Economic Review*, March–April 1971.

17. Ironically, this is one area of "social accounting" where corporate America, in spite of its many laggards, is at least on a par with academia and government. "Social accounting" now appears prominently in business publications, and a number of large corporations, particularly the Telephone Company, have made significant efforts to account for the "value" of their employees in their operations.

18. Victor R. Fuchs, *The Service Economy* (New York: National Bureau of Economic Research/Columbia University Press, 1968), p. 2.

19. Ibid., p. 192.

20. Harry T. Oshima, "Consumer Asset Formation and the Future of Capitalism," *Economic Journal*, March 1961.

Epilogue

Un-Money, or The Making
of a Non-Economic Society

"THE CONNECTION between money making and rational thinking is so deeply engrained in our practical lives that it seems impossible to question it."

N. O. BROWN

THE INTRODUCTION to a book on lawns and lawn care notes that lawn care would be the single most important economic activity in the vicinity of Denver, Colorado, if those who indulged in it were paid the minimum wage. No doubt, lawn care is equally important in other areas as well. Applying similar reasoning to the 1965 "Survey of Outdoor Recreation Activities,"[1] we find that Americans expended 2 million *man-years* employed as picnickers, as sightseers, and as bicyclers. That's 2 million man-years in *each* category. We also expended more than 4 million man-years each in swimming, driving for pleasure (!), walking for pleasure, and playing outdoor games and sports. Not to mention our lesser pursuits, in which several more million man-years are frittered away: fishing, spectating, and boating. Nor should we forget the millions of man-days invested in such obscure interests as bird watching, camping, horseback riding, and hiking. No less important are those spent water-skiing, canoeing, and sailing.

All in all, these activities represent an investment of just under 30 *million* man-years, a sum 50 per cent larger than the total effort employed in all the manufacturing industries in the United States and comfortably ahead of the sum of manufacturing and farm employment. Strikes and work stoppages annually consume an amount of time larger than that devoted to wildlife and bird photography, but smaller than that consumed by water-skiing. Similarly, we devote about as much time to picnicking (456 million man-days) as we do to being ill (412 million). If the all-consuming importance of work and the economic imperative does not seem somewhat diminished by the foregoing, we have yet to consider the hours devoted to eating and sleeping, to the pursuit of conjugal bliss, or any number of mundane activities generally thought vital to the preservation of the species.

In spite of these realities, it remains that economics has become the most pressing concern of our time. The volume of economic commentary, angst, and worry that has risen to the early pages of the daily newspapers and commanded the covers of the nation's weekly magazines is nothing short of amazing. Economic thought is the language of the time. It is our metaphor; it is the logical calculus upon which the metaphysics of industrial society must rest. We are in love with the law of supply and demand, the idea of economies of scale, and the rule of diminishing returns. We are fascinated with the power implied in the process of compounding. We look forward to ever more.

We seek out those few who can subject themselves to the discipline and magic of numbers and charge them with the task of finding and enlarging that which is written on the bottom line. So it is that the nation supported the efforts of some seven hundred thousand accountants and auditors in 1970; whatever color the ink, there is always much to be writ. "Accountability" strides forth and becomes the rule of the day. It will prevail everywhere. Even in education. Nay, even in government, we have promises of accountability (but *only* promises). We shall find a bottom line in everything, and it—the notion that somewhere, some entity such as the bottom line exists—will yet come to be known as the Rosetta Stone for the twentieth century.

Economic thought is profoundly seductive. Once begun, it is hard to escape. I do not mean to include in the realm of economic thought our day-to-day worry about money and bills. There is little doubt that most of us would soon replace financial worries with other problems if money were no longer a concern. Most people suffer from a constitutional need to worry at least a few minutes every day. Economics lends itself handily to this need. There is probably no other area of human endeavor that so easily allows anxiety to be disguised as sustained intellectual effort. But alas! The language of economizing is inescapable and relentless far beyond the daily grind.

Those who want to escape economic thought usually find that it is impossible. Just as Consciousness I disallows the validity of Consciousness III (and vice versa), economic thought declares other modes impossible, improbable, or intrinsically foolish. One is either economic or diseconomic. And we all know that it is a sin and impractical to be diseconomic. It violates the principle of the bottom line.

No system of thought is complete without its opposition and denouncers. We have, already, a counterculture—an undercurrent that has declared the spiritual bankruptcy of economic man and called for a revolution of love. Norman Brown, writing in *Life Against Death,* notes that "the alienated consciousness is correlative with a money economy. Its root is the compulsion to work. This compulsion to work subordinates man to things, producing at the same time confusion in the valuation of things and devaluation of the human body. It reduces the drives of the human being to greed and competition (aggression and possessiveness, as in the anal character). The desire for money takes the place of all genuinely human needs. Thus the apparent accumulation of wealth is really the impoverishment of human nature, and its appropriate morality is the renunciation of human nature and desires: asceticism. The effort is to substitute an abstraction, *Homo economicus,* for the concrete totality of human nature, and thus to dehumanize human nature."[2]

Perhaps I am being a bit obtuse when I wonder how it is that Neiman-Marcus, Tiffany's, and an assortment of other purveyors of fine goods, have managed to survive so long in a system that supports "asceticism." Yet we must also admit that there is a terrible, bone-chilling coldness in economic thought and that most of us have wished, in moments of self-flagellation, to embrace the Transcendental Spirit.

But, alas, this writer cannot. I am earthbound and glad of it.

Even if I could find some way to rid myself of economic thought, I would still be left with mortgages and a family to support. I suspect many readers are in the same position—because it must be admitted that for all the "alternative life styles" available, marriage, childbearing, and householding is the one that prevails. And it provides, when it works, the most fulfilling satisfactions and pleasures. *Few fundamental facts receive less attention than this one.*

So we are back again at the household economy. Sadly, it lacks the glamour of the marketplace. Nor is it preoccupied with the transcendental. But it *can* lead us to something beyond economics, to a way of life that is beyond our present surrender to considerations of price and cost, wage and profit. It can lead us, first, to the decline of money and its tyranny and then to the making of a non-economic society.

The mechanisms and forces for accomplishing this change have already been described. Taken one at a time, any of the forces we have described might be accommodated by a modified version of the present system. But, taken together, they require nothing less than a transformation of economic life. They require, in fact, the abolition of economic life as we currently experience it.

Taxation and inflation—the need to provide for "social overheads" in a complex society—induce people to seek means for employing both labor and capital outside the marketplace.

Technology, under the pressures of market competition, forces the movement of the means of production ever closer to the individual or the collective, abandoning the marketplace.

Productivity, the very life blood and vitality of the marketplace, increases the value of time and decreases the value of goods, leading to a new allocation of time between marketplace and household.

The need to sustain the failing basic industries in spite of their lack of appeal to both marketplace investors and those who labor within them will lead to their effective nationalization. Sometime later, it will evolve into some form of contractual service which may eventually become the basis of the subsistence economy.

The leveling of population, in addition to encouraging people to think in terms of capital stocks rather than income, will release many women from motherhood earlier and reduce the number of dependent people. The net effect will be to distribute less work to more people.

The combination of these events means that the market economy, at the very most, will account for no more than 50 per cent of our economic activity by the end of the century. Most probably, it will account for much less, perhaps as low as 25 per cent, depending upon the growth of the collective sector.

When a discipline is no longer adequate to describe most of its subject area, we are likely to question its relevance. Contemporary economics is such a discipline, heading rapidly toward the world of un-money, non-markets, and invisible exchange. We are moving toward a post-economic society, yet the fact is little recognized.

Those who are moved by great passion to either preserve or destroy the marketplace will, no doubt, be disappointed by what is coming. It is neither here nor transcendentally there. It conforms to no ideology, no idea, no dream. It fits no preconception, economic or otherwise, about what life should be like. It only reflects what *is* and what, very likely, will be. Sometimes that's called reality. It'll be good for all of us.

1. Statistical Abstract of the United States, 1972.
2. Norman O. Brown, *Life Against Death* (New York: Vintage Books, 1959), p. 237.

Selected Bibliography

Adams, Henry. *The Education of Henry Adams.* New York: Modern Library, 1931.

Adams, James Truslow. *The Epic of America.* New York: Little, Brown, 1931.

Baker, O. E.; Borsodi, Ralph; and Wilson, M. L. *Agriculture in Modern Life.* New York: Harper & Brothers, 1939.

Baran, Paul A.; and Sweezy, Paul M. *Monopoly Capital.* MR Press, 1968.

Bauer, Raymond A., ed. *Social Indicators.* Cambridge, Mass.: M.I.T. Press, 1966.

Beard, Charles; and Beard, Mary. *The Rise of American Civilization.* New York: Macmillan, 1933.

Bell, Daniel. *The End of Ideology.* New York: Free Press, 1960.

——. *Work and Its Discontents.* New York: Free Press, 1960.

Berle, Adolf A., Jr. *Power Without Property.* New York: Harcourt, Brace & World, 1958.

——; and Means, Gardner C. *The Modern Corporation and Private Property.* New York: Macmillan, 1934.

Bernstein, Peter L. *The Price of Prosperity.* New York: Vintage Books, 1966.

Bookchin, Murray. *Post-Scarcity Anarchism.* San Francisco, Calif.: Ramparts Press, 1971.

Boorstin, Daniel J. *The Image: A Guide to Pseudo Events in America.* New York: Harper & Row, 1964.

Borsodi, Ralph. *National Advertising vs. Prosperity.* New York: Arcadia Press, 1923.

———. *The Distribution Age.* New York: D. Appleton, 1927.

———. *This Ugly Civilization.* New York: Simon & Schuster, 1929.

———. *Flight from the City.* New York: Harper & Brothers, 1933.

———. *Prosperity and Security.* New York: Harper & Brothers, 1938.

Brown, Norman O. *Life Against Death.* New York: Vintage Books, 1959.

Burenstam Linder, Staffan. *The Harried Leisure Class.* New York: Columbia University Press, 1970.

Byrd, Caroline. *The Crowding Syndrome.* New York: David McKay, 1972.

Chase, Stuart. *The Most Probable World.* New York: Harper & Row, 1968.

———. *The Economy of Abundance.* New York: Macmillan, 1934.

Cornuelle, Richard C. *Reclaiming the American Dream.* New York: Random House, 1965.

De Grazia, Sebastian. *Of Time, Work and Leisure.* New York: Twentieth Century Fund, 1962.

Desmonde, William. *Magic, Myth and Money.* New York: Free Press of Glencoe, 1962.

Forrester, Jay W. *World Dynamics.* Cambridge, Mass.: Wright-Allen Press, 1971.

Fuchs, V. R. *The Service Economy.* New York: National Bureau of Economic Research/Columbia University Press, 1968.

Galbraith, John Kenneth. *The Affluent Society.* Boston: Houghton Mifflin, 1958.

———. *The New Industrial State.* Boston: Houghton Mifflin, 1967.

———. *Economics and the Public Purpose.* Boston: Houghton Mifflin, 1973.

Gauger, William H. *The Potential Contribution to the GNP of Valuing Household Work.* Paper presented at the June 26, 1973 conference of the American Home Economics Association, Atlantic City, N.J.

Ginsberg, Eli; Hiestand, Dale; and Reubens, Beatrice. *The Pluralistic Economy.* New York: McGraw-Hill, 1965.

Goodman, Paul & Percival. *Communitas,* New York, Vintage Books, 1960.

Hall, Bolton. *A Little Land and a Living.* New York: Arcadia Press, 1908.

———. *Three Acres and Liberty.* New York: Macmillan, 1907.

Herrnstein, Richard J. *I.Q. in the Meritocracy.* Boston: Atlantic Monthly Press, 1973.

Hardin, Garrett J. *Exploring the New Ethics of Survival.* New York: Viking Press, 1972.

Juster, F. Thomas. *Household Capital Formation and Financing, 1897–1962*. New York: National Bureau of Economic Research, No. 83, Gen. Series; dist. by Columbia University Press, 1966.

Kahn, Herman; and Bruce-Briggs, B. *Things to Come*. New York: Macmillan, 1972.

Kahn, Herman; and Wiener, A. J. *The Year 2000*. New York: Macmillan, 1967.

Kapp, K. William. *The Social Costs of Business Enterprise*. Bombay Asia Publishing House, 1963.

Katona, George. *The Mass Consumption Society*. New York: McGraw-Hill, 1964.

———. *The Powerful Consumer*. New York: McGraw-Hill, 1960.

Kelso, Louis O.; and Hetter, Patricia. *How to Turn Eighty Million Workers into Capitalists on Borrowed Money*. New York: Random House, 1967.

Kerr, Walter. *The Decline of Pleasure*. New York: Simon and Schuster, 1962.

Larrabee, Eric; and Ralph Meyersohn. *Mass Leisure*. New York: Free Press of Glencoe, 1958.

Lundberg, Ferdinand. *The Rich and the Super Rich*. New York: Lyle Stuart, 1968.

Lydall, Harold. *The Structure of Earnings*. Oxford, England: Oxford University Press, 1968.

Margolius, Sidney. *The Great American Food Hoax*. New York: Walker, 1971.

McGregor, Douglas. *The Human Side of Enterprise*. New York: McGraw-Hill, 1960.

Meade, J. E. *The Stationary Economy*. Chicago: Aldine, 1965.

Meadows, Donella H.; and others. *The Limits to Growth*. New York: Universe Books, 1972.

Mill, J. S. *Principles of Political Economy*. New York: D. Appleton, 1890.

Mills, C. Wright. *The Power Elite*. Toronto: Oxford University Press, 1956.

Morgan, J. N.; and others. *Productive Americans*. Ann Arbor, Mich.: Survey Research Center, University of Michigan, 1966.

Nearing, Helen; and Nearing, Scott. *Living the Good Life*. New York: Schocken Books, 1970.

Odum, Howard T. *Environment, Power, and Society*. New York: Wiley-Interscience, 1971.

Packard, Vance. *The Waste Makers*. New York: David McKay, 1960.

———. *The Pyramid Climbers*. New York: McGraw-Hill, 1962.

Parker, Richard. *The Myth of the Middle Class*. New York: Liveright, 1972.

Passell, Peter; and Ross, Leonard. *Retreat from Riches*. New York: Viking Press, 1973.

Pearson, John Ward. *The 8-Day Week*. New York: Harper & Row, 1973.

Perry, George L. *Unemployment, Money Wage Rates, and Inflation*. Cambridge, Mass.: M.I.T. Press, 1966.

Polanyi, Karl. *The Great Transformation*. Boston: Beacon Press, 1957.

——. *Primitive Archaics and Modern Economics. Essays of Karl Polanyi*. Boston: Beacon Press, 1971.

Rostow, W. W. *The Stages of Economic Growth*. London: Cambridge University Press, 1960.

Roszak, Theodore. *The Making of a Counter Culture*. Garden City, N.Y.: Doubleday-Anchor, 1969.

Schmitt, Peter J. *Back to Nature: The Arcadian Myth in Urban America*. New York: Oxford University Press, 1969.

Schwartz, Eugene S. *Overskill*. New York: Quadrangle Books, 1971.

Sirageldin, I. *Non Market Components of National Income*. Ann Arbor, Mich.: Survey Research Center, University of Michigan, 1969.

Slater, Philip. *The Pursuit of Loneliness*. Boston: Beacon Press, 1970.

——. *Earthwalk*. Garden City, N.Y.: Doubleday, 1974.

Spengler, Joseph John. *Declining Population Growth Revisited*. Chapel Hill Carolina Population Center, 1971.

Stent, Gunther S. *The Coming of the Golden Age*. Garden City, N.Y.: Natural History Press, 1969.

Tawney, R. H. *The Acquisitive Society*. New York: Harcourt, Brace & World, 1920.

Teilhard de Chardin, Pierre. *The Phenomenon of Man*. New York: Harper & Row, 1959.

Theobald, Robert. *Free Men and Free Markets*. New York: Doubleday-Anchor, 1965.

——. *The Economics of Abundance: A Non-Inflationary Future*. New York: Pitman, 1970.

Thompson, William Irwin. *At the Edge of History*. New York: Harper & Row, 1971.

Thurow, Lester C. *The Impact of Taxes on the American Economy*. New York: Praeger, 1971.

Toffler, Alvin. *Future Shock*. New York: Random House, 1970.

Walker, Kathryn E. *Effect of Family Characteristics on Time Contributed for Household Work by Various Members*. Paper presented at the June 26, 1973, conference of the American Home Economics Association, Atlantic City, N.J.

——; and Gauger, William H. *The Dollar Value of Household Work*. Information Bulletin 60 from New York State College of Human Ecology.

ARTICLES

Bain, Joe S. "Economics of Scale, Concentration, and Conditions of Entry in 20 Manufacturing Industries," *The American Economic Review*, March 1954.

Becker, Gary S. "A Theory of the Allocation of Time," *Economic Journal*, September 1965.

Bell, Daniel. "Knowledge and Technology," *Indicators of Social Change: Concepts and Measurements*. New York: Russell Sage Foundation, 1968, ed. Eleanor B. Sheldon.

——. "Notes on the Post Industrial Society," *Public Interest*, winter and spring 1967.

Boulding, Kenneth. "The Household as Achilles Heel," *The Journal of Consumer Affairs*, winter 1972.

Burch, Gilbert. "Hard Going for the Game Plan," *Fortune*, May 1970.

Byners, Gwen J.; and Galwson, Marjorie. "Time Horizons in Family Spending," *Journal of Home Economics*, Vol. 60, No. 9, November 1968.

Carlson, James E. "Economy—Ecology—and Zero Population Growth," *Architectural Record*, August 1970.

Charnes, A. "Theory of Search; Optimizing Distribution of Search Effort," W. W. Cooper, *Management Science*, Vol. 5, No. 9, October 1958.

Frejka, Thomas. "Reflections on the Demographic Conditions Needed to Establish a U.S. Stationary Population Growth," *Population Studies 22*, November 1968.

Glass, Bentley. "Science: Endless Horizons on Golden Age," *Science*, January 8, 1971.

Hall, F. T.; and Schnader, P. "The Effects of Family and Housing Characteristics on Time Spent on Household Tasks," *Journal of Home Economics*, Vol. 62, No. 1, January 1970.

Hanson, J. Philip. "Higher Education—How to Pay," *New England Economic Review*, March–April 1971.

Herrnstein, Richard. "I.Q.," *Atlantic Monthly*, September 1971.

Juster, F. Thomas; and Lipsey, Robert E. "Consumer Asset Formation in the United States," *Economic Journal*, December 1967.

Juster and Shay. "Consumer Sensitivity to Finance Rates," *N.B.E.R. Occasional Pages #88*, 1964.

Loomis, Carol J. "An Annual Report for the Federal Government," *Fortune*, May 1973.

Meyer, Lawrence A. "U.S. Population Growth: Would Slower Be Better?" *Fortune*, June 1970.

——. "New Questions About the U.S. Population," *Fortune*, February 1971.

———. "The Clouded Prospect for Corporate Profits," *Fortune*, May 1973.

Miller, George A. "The Magical Number Service," *Psychological Review*, Vol. 63, No. 2.

Oshima, Harry T. "Consumer Asset Formation and the Future of Capitalism," *Economic Journal*, March 1961.

Poopst and Waters. "Rates of Return on Consumer Durables," *Journal of Finance*, December 1964.

Sametz, Arnold W. "Production of Goods and Services: The Measurement of Economic Growth," *Indicators of Social Change: Concepts and Measurements*. New York: Russell Sage Foundation, 1968.

Scott, Maynes E. "The Payoff for Intelligent Consumer Decision Making," *Journal of Home Economics*, Vol. 60, No. 9, November 1968.

Stigler, George. "The Economics of Information," *Journal of Political Economy*, June 1961.

Wellemeyer, Marilyn, ed. "The Return of the 500," *Fortune*, May 1973.

UNSIGNED REFERENCE

Finance Facts Year Book, National Consumer Finance Association, 1970, 1971, 1973.

Toward Balanced Growth: Quantity with Quality, National Goals Research Staff, July 1970, Washington, D.C. Superintendent of Documents.

Toward a Social Report, U. S. Dept. of Health, Education, and Welfare, January 1969, Washington, D.C. Superintendent of Documents.

Population and the American Future, Commission on Population Growth and the American Future, U.S. Government Printing Office, Washington, D.C., 1972.

Statistical Abstract of the United States, U.S. Government Printing Office, Washington, D.C., 1970, 1972, 1974.

The U.S. Economy in 1990, Conference Board, Inc., prepared for the White House Conference on the Industrial World Ahead, New York, 1972.

Grocery Industry Barometer, prepared by Conference Board. Inc., 1970.

Energy to Millennium Three, Technology Review (entire issue), December 1972.

"What's Being Done to Keep Your Service Bills Down," *U.S. News & World Report*, April 10, 1972.